Function in
English

Jon Blundell
Jonathan Higgens
Nigel Middlemiss

Oxford University Press

Oxford University Press, Walton Street, Oxford OX2 6DP

Oxford New York Toronto
Delhi Bombay Calcutta Madras Karachi
Petaling Jaya Singapore Hong Kong Tokyo
Nairobi Dar es Salaam Cape Town
Melbourne Auckland

and associated companies in
Berlin Ibadan

Oxford and *Oxford English* are trade marks
of Oxford University Press.

ISBN 0 19 431168 6

© Oxford University Press 1982

First published 1982
Eighth impression 1990

The contribution made by Michael Macfarlane to the development of the work is
gratefully acknowledged.

Illustrated by:

Frank Dickens
Colin Hawkins
Michael Heath
Edward McLachlan

Cover illustration by:

Ken Cox

Set in Plantin and Univers by Santype Ltd, Salisbury, UK

Printed in Hong Kong

Contents

What is the book about?

This book helps you to say the right thing, at the right time, in English. It does this by giving you common expressions in English that we use for certain purposes (or 'language functions'), such as *agreeing*, *apologizing* and *thanking*. The book can be used for reference, but there is also practice material that will help you learn how to use these expressions.

How is the book divided up?

Introduction

Here you will find an explanation of what language functions are. Here also you can find advice on how to choose the right expression for a certain occasion.

Using the book

This explains the contents of a typical functional section, and shows you how to make the best use of the book.

List of functions

Apart from the list itself, you will discover here how the functions are grouped together.

The functions

Each functional section gives you a number of expressions, and the chance to practise them in exercises.

Extra practice material

This section gives you a further chance to practise the functional expressions. Different functions are here grouped together in the various exercises. If you are working with a partner, this section will be especially useful.

Structural code list

This shows you how to use the expressions to produce sentences that are grammatically correct.

Key word index

This alphabetical list of words and phrases enables you to find all the functional expressions that are connected with the particular word or phrase you are referring to.

Introduction

What are language functions?

Language functions are the *purposes* for which people speak or write. You can say that everything we do, including using language, has a purpose. When we switch the radio or television on, for example, our purpose is to be amused or entertained, or to find something out. In the same way, we only speak or write with a purpose in mind: to help someone to see our point of view, perhaps, or to ask their advice, or to reach agreement with them. We call these purposes the functions of language.

Every language, including your own, has such functions. But, of course, different languages express these functions in different ways. In this book you will find some of the ways English people use to express various functions. So under the function *Greeting people*, for example, you will see expressions like 'Good morning', 'Good afternoon', 'Hello!', 'Hi!', and under *Saying goodbye* you will find 'Bye', 'Bye-bye', 'See you' and so on. Altogether, over 3000 such expressions have been collected together, under 140 functional headings.

Which expression shall I use?

In your own language, as well as in English, there are some expressions, within one function, that you can use at any time. It doesn't matter who you are talking to, or when, or where. These are called *neutral* expressions. 'Thank you', for example, is one of many neutral expressions in English. It can be used whenever you want to thank anyone.

The *first* group of expressions in each functional section contains all the *neutral* expressions you need.

But are some expressions specially suitable at certain times, and rather unsuitable at others?

Yes. In your own language, you probably don't, for example, greet your employer in the same way that you greet your best friend. You are most likely to use formal language to greet someone in authority, and informal language to greet someone you know well. It is the same in English. We are more likely to say a formal 'Good morning' to an employer, but an informal 'Hello' to a friend.

The *second* group of expressions in each functional section contains all the *informal* expressions you need. They are marked by an **I** in the margin.

The *third* group of expressions in each functional section contains all the *formal* expressions you need. They are marked by an **F** in the margin.

How do I decide whether to use formal or informal language?

You decide according to what situation you are in. That determines what kind of language you use. Like this:

Situation	Language
formal	formal
informal	informal
neither very formal nor very informal	neutral

Four main things help you to decide how formal or informal a situation is:

Where you are and when (THE SETTING)

For example:

What you are talking about (THE TOPIC)

For example:

Who you are talking to (YOUR SOCIAL RELATIONSHIP)

For example:

What you feel about the topic or the other person (YOUR PSYCHOLOGICAL ATTITUDE)

For example:

All four factors combine to influence the way you speak. The table below shows some typical aspects of *neutral*, *formal* and *informal* situations:

with this SETTING	pub	bus stop; shop	boardroom; ceremonial reception
	+	+	+
and this TOPIC	the latest football match; a TV comedy programme	weather; travel	important business deal
	+	+	+
and this SOCIAL RELATIONSHIP	friend; child; close colleague	stranger in street; taxi-driver; customs officer	senior colleague
	+	+	+
and this PSYCHOLOGICAL ATTITUDE	relaxed; light-hearted	no strong feelings either way	very serious
	↓	↓	↓
you will probably choose	**INFORMAL LANGUAGE**	**NEUTRAL LANGUAGE**	**FORMAL LANGUAGE**

Do all four factors influence the way I speak, every time?

Yes. It would not be right to take just one factor into account, and think, for example that

INFORMAL SETTING   =   INFORMAL LANGUAGE
(e g hotel bar)

because, in fact,

INFORMAL SETTING
(e g hotel bar)

+

FORMAL TOPIC
(e g important
business deal)

+ **FORMAL SOCIAL
RELATIONSHIP**
(director of
overseas company)

+ **FORMAL PSYCHOLOGICAL
ATTITUDE** (e g extremely)
serious)

= **FORMAL LANGUAGE**

So all four factors count.

Why is it important to say the right thing at the right time?

Because it helps people to communicate effectively. Using language appropriately helps to improve communication. But using it inappropriately can have the opposite effect:

Here, Mr Jones's very informal reply, in a formal situation, will probably cause the chairman not to think well of him. But:

Mr Jenkins uses the right formal language for the situation, and has no problems.
In the same way:

Debbie's over-formal reply in an informal situation seems perhaps a little ridiculous, certainly unfriendly. But:

Here Jill answers informally in an informal situation, and, despite the accident, good relations are maintained.

So how can I get a 'feel' for saying the right thing at the right time?

Study the situations given in the functional sections in this book. Listen carefully to the way English-speaking people use formal and informal language. If you are talking to an English-speaking person, try to follow his or her lead. If he or she uses formal language, for instance, try to use formal language too. You will soon develop a 'feel' for saying the right thing at the right time.

Using the book

What does a typical entry look like and how does it work?

There are 140 sections. Each section deals with one function. This shows you what all the different parts of a section mean (it contains material from several sections):

The number of the function   The title of the function   The cartoon

13 | **Asking if someone is sure about something**

1 *Are you sure about...?*   4–6 9

---

1   *Are you sure about...?*   4–6 9

The number of the expression

1   *Are you sure about...?*   4–6 9

The words in this first expression are as simple as possible. The expression itself is *neutral.* All the expressions down to the *informal* section are *neutral.* This means they can be used in both *formal* and *informal* situations or in situations that are neither particularly *formal* nor particularly *informal.* (Because use of language is personal, the division of the expressions into *neutral, formal* and *informal* types cannot be final or absolute.)

1   *Are you sure about...?*   4–6 9

These dots mean you have to complete the sentence with some words of your own. (But you may not have to, if 0 is one of the structural code numbers. See p 262 for a further explanation.)

1   *Are you sure about...?*   4–6 9

These are the structural code numbers for this expression. They refer you to the Code List on p 262. There you will discover which structures to use with the expression. The hyphen (–) in 4–6 means you can use all the codes between, and including, the two numbers, that is 4, 5, 6.

A friend puts his head round your door at lunchtime.

Let me buy you a pint and a sandwich down the 'Blue Lion'.

2 *You're on!*
3 *Ra`ther!*   4 *All right (then)!*

A friend puts his head round your door. . . .

This sentence 'sets the scene'. It puts you in an imaginary situation, telling you who you are talking to, what about, when and where.

Let me stand you a pint and a sandwich down 'The Blue Lion'.

What the other person says to you.

2 *You're on!*

What you say to the other person.

3 *Ra`ther!*
4 *All right (then)!*

Other things you could also say in that situation, i e *alternatives*.

The presentation dialogue shows how the expressions work. The situations in these dialogues are drawn from social, travel and business/professional contexts. There is a spread of these three types across the three levels of formality (*neutral*, *informal* and *formal*). One type of situation cannot be automatically equated with one level of formality.

in other situations

5 *I'd love to.*
6 *With the greatest of pleasure.*
7 *Thanks very much/a lot.*
8 *I'd like ... very much, (please).*
9 *That's really very nice/kind etc of you.*

in other situations

5 *I'd love to.*
6 *With the greatest of pleasure.*

Other things you could say in situations that are the same in terms of function and formality, but different because they do not fit what has just been said. (Here, 'I'd love to' is not a possible response to the invitation 'Let me buy you a pint'; and 'With the greatest of pleasure' is much too strong for such a small matter.)

7 *Thanks very much / a lot.*

The slant mark / means *alternative* words. You can use any one of the words/phrases that are divided from one another by slant marks, e g 'Thanks very much' *or* 'Thanks a lot'.

8 *I'd like ... very much, (please).*

Brackets ( ) mean *optional* words. Words that are bracketed may be left out or kept in.

9 *That's really very nice/kind etc of you*

'Etc' here means 'and similar words'. In this case, you can use any *one* of the words that are divided from one another by slant marks, *or any similar word you know* e g 'That's really very kind of you' *or* 'That's really very good of you' *or* 'That's really very generous of you' (and so on).

10 *Like ... ?*   **11** *Why don't you have ... ?*   **12** *Have ....*   6
13 *What's it to be?* }
14 *What's yours.* } [usually for drinks]
15 [Nod and smile]
16 *Really?*
17 *Thank* ⟍*you.*

 Dear Sir

18  *... speaking.*

I

You should only use the expressions under this symbol in *informal situations*.

10 *Like ... ?*   **11** *Why don't you have ... ?*   **12** *Have ....*

Expressions on the same line have the same code numbers

13 *What's it to be?* }
14 *What's yours?* } [usually for drinks]

Helpful extra information about an expression/expressions.

15 [Nod and smile]

You don't need to *say* anything. You just *do* what the instruction says.

16 *Really.*
17 *Thank* ⟍*you.*

Pitch markers. They show the main syllables you should stress, and which way your voice should go (*up* or *down*), when you stress them. Pitch markers are shown to help you avoid expressing something quite different and unintended by using a wrong pitch. For example, ⤳*Really* expresses surprise. But if you used different intonation, (e g ⤴*Really*) it can express boredom.

F

You should only use expressions under this symbol in *formal situations*.

18   *.... speaking?*

You can only use this expression over the telephone.

Practice

Practice

In this section there are exercises practising material explained *in this function only*.

This shows what someone is saying.

This shows what someone is thinking.

Key a 1, 7, 9, 11 **b** 8–11 **c** 1–6 most appropriate, 8–12 also possible **d** 4–6 (11–13 equally possible) **e** i and iii

---

Key

Answers to the exercises. (If your English is very advanced, or if you are working with an English person, you may find that different answers to those given in the key are possible. This is because feeling for formality and informality is to some extent personal.)

a 1, 7, 9, 11

The answers. They are given as numbers of the expressions in the presentation section. Sometimes, the expression alone will be a correct answer. At other times, to form a correct answer, you will need to add words to the expression according to the structural code number(s) given.

b 8–11

This means all the numbers between and including the two shown are correct answers (here, 8, 9, 10, 11).

c 1–6 most appropriate, 8–12 also possible

1–6 are the best answers.

c 1–6 most appropriate, 8–12 also possible

8–12 are acceptable answers, but not as good as the best.

d 4–6 (11–13 equally possible)

Just as good as the first answers (here 4–6), but for a different level of formality.

e i and iii

The correct answers from a choice of several given in the exercise itself.

How do I make the best use of the book if I'm working alone?

There are two ways of using it. Either you can work through it from beginning to end, or you can dip into it. If you want to work through it from beginning to end, you might do it like this:

- Read as much of the Introduction as you can.

- Do as much of Section A of the Extra Practice Material as you can to accustom yourself to choosing the right function or to deciding whether a situation is formal or informal before starting the main part of the book. If you prefer, leave work on Section A until you have completed part or all of the main text.

- Start at Function 1.

- Look at the picture and read through the text.

If you are a near-beginner or not very advanced, you need not use the Informal or Formal sections. If you are at intermediate level or quite advanced in English, you can use all the sections.

- Look at the Practice section.

If you are a near-beginner or not very advanced, you should be able to answer at least question **a**. If you are at intermediate or advanced level, you should be able to answer all the questions.

- Use the Structural Code List to check that the sentences you make are grammatically correct.

Check your answers in the Key.

- Refer to Section B of the Extra Practice Material either when you have completed the rest of the book, or when you have completed the specific group of functions that a particular part of the material deals with. If you are working with a partner who is also learning English, you can use both the Pairwork and Self-study sections. But you might want to 'dip into' the book from time to time. In that case, you can refer to a particular function you are interested in, and either use it for reference material only (for example, to check that you are using language appropriate to your purposes), or as reference *and* practice material by working through the relevant Practice Section.

- You can use Section A of the Extra Practice Material at any time. Section B will be most useful if your 'dipping in' covers the functions that are practised together in the various parts of Section B.

- Remember you can use the Key Word Index to help you find a particular section and set of expressions.

What if I want to use the book as teaching material?

You may use it:

- As an adjunct to a coursebook at levels varying from near-beginner to very advanced.

- As a composite element in a course, selected elements or the complete book being used, according to the appropriate level.

- As a source of reference for the teacher who is preparing his own materials.

- In class, for work with the whole class in groups or pairs.

- For homework by the student alone or with a partner.

List of functions

Functional areas occurring in the book

Section 1: About information, attitudes and action

There are three types of function in this section: *Informational*, *Attitudinal* and *Active*. Before you can have an *attitude* towards something (a feeling, an opinion, a judgement), you need *information* to base your *attitude* on. Similarly, before you can establish a course of *action*, you need to have formed an *attitude*. Look at the table below:

Informational	Attitudinal	Active
You won't forget to write to Jonathan, will you?	**I can't make up my mind whether** to write to him this evening or not.	**I'd** do it this evening **if I were you,** otherwise you'll never do it.
Function: Reminding	**Function:** Saying you are not sure	**Function:** Advising someone to do something

Section 2: Social formulas

Sometimes our purpose in saying something may be to conform to what we think society expects us to say. In this case words are expressed as *social formulas* which often, although not always, have the purpose of confirming social relationships rather than expressing strong feelings. Saying 'Hello!' to someone could be an example of this. Because of this difference in emphasis, functions of this type are grouped together.

Section 3: Making communication work

Another purpose we may have in speaking is to *help communication* rather than to communicate actual ideas, feelings, etc themselves. That is to say we may keep a conversation going ('Really! ... Oh! ... I see! ... Mmm ... Aha! ...'), check we have understood something, repeat something, say something another way, give examples of what we mean, change the subject and so on. The purpose of the speaker here is to make communication possible rather than to communicate something for its own sake. Because of this difference in emphasis, functions of this type are also grouped together.

Section 4: Finding out about language

The final section of the book is written specifically to help the student *ask questions about language*. Such questions are functions in the sense that they have a purpose behind them as outlined in section 1 above. They are collected together, however, because the student may find it useful to refer to such questions on language as a group, rather than haphazardly throughout the book. Note that there are no exercises for this section, as it is intended for information and guidance only.

Section 1: Main functions

About information

About attitudes

About action

Section 2: Social formulas

Section 3: Making communication work

Section 4: Finding out about language

I Asking for information

1 *Could you tell me . . . , (please)?* 6 8–10

You are at an airport information desk. You want to ask about an arrival.

2 *(Excuse me,) d'you know if flight BH 106 is on time?* 6 8–10
No, I'm afraid it's going to be ten minutes late.
3 *Can you tell me . . . , (please)?* 6 8–10
**4 *(Sorry to trouble you, but) is flight BH 106 on time?/is
flight BH 106 on schedule?/will flight BH 106 arrive as
scheduled?*** [or any other suitable question] 28
5 *(Can you help me?) D'you happen to know . . . ?* 6 8–10

---

in other situations

6 *Could anyone tell me . . . ?* [when you are talking to several
people, and you are not sure who has the information] 0 6 8–11
7 *I'd like to know, (please,) . . . .* 0 6 8–11

I You've been chatting to a friendly fellow-passenger on a plane.

8 *Can we get duty-free cigarettes on this flight, d'you know?* 34
9 *(Happen to) know . . . ?* 8–10
10 *(Got) any idea . . . ?* 0 8–10
11 *Any clue . . . ?* 8 9

F You are visiting a company in Britain for the first time. You have an appointment
with Mr Brown. You have just arrived at the reception desk.

12 *I wonder if you could tell me where Mr Brown's office is.* 0 6 8–10
Yes, if you'll come with me, I'll show you.
13 *I hope you don't mind my asking, but . . . ?* 34

---

in other situations

14 *I wonder if someone could tell me . . . .* [when you are addressing 0 6 8–10
several people, and you are not sure who has the information]
15 *I should be interested to know . . . .* 0 6 8–10

Practice

a ▶ What do you say in these situations?

  i You stop someone in the street. You want to know the time.

  ii You are planning a trip to Paris. You are at the travel agent's, and you want to find out the cost of an economy return ticket.

  iii You are in an important meeting. The discussion is about a new project. You must find out how much the project will cost. But you do not want to offend anyone.

b You have decided to go to the cinema with a friend.

  ▶ Do you say: *I wonder if you could tell me what time the film starts?*

  ▶ If not, what do you say?

c ▶ Who would you say this to?

  I wonder if you could tell me Mr Brown's home number?

  i to one of Mr Brown's colleagues, whom you have never met

  ii to an old friend and colleague

  iii to the switchboard operator at Mr Brown's company

d You are speaking to a senior official in your company:

  I hope you don't mind my asking, but have you read my report on the ADO project yet?

  ▶ What will the official think?

  i *At least he's being polite.*

  ii *That's no way to talk to me.*

Key a i 1–5, 11 also possible ii 1–3 iii 12–15 most appropriate, 1–3, 5, also possible **b** No 9–11 most appropriate, 1–3, 5 also possible **c** i and iii **d** i

2 Asking if someone knows about something

| 1 | *(Can you help me?) D'you know about . . . ?* | 4–6 |

You are travelling to the U.S.A. You do not know about customs regulations there. You ask a fellow-passenger about them.

| 2 | *(Excuse me,) d'you know anything about customs regulations in the U.S.A.?* | 4–6 8 |

3	*(Can you help me?) D'you happen to know anything about . . . ?*		4–6	8	
4	*(Excuse me,/Sorry to bother you, but) d'you know . . . ?*		7–11		

in other situations

5	*Did you know . . . ?*	0	6	7	
6	*Did you know about . . . ?*		4–6		
7	*Do you realize . . . ?*		6	7	
8	*Has John/Mr Jones etc told you . . . ?*	0	6–10		
9	*Did John/Mr Jones etc tell you . . . ?*	0	6–10		
10	*Have you heard . . . ?*	0	6–10		
11	*Has John/Mr Jones etc told you about . . . ?*	4–6	8	10	
12	*Did John/Mr Jones etc tell you about . . . ?*	4–6	8	10	
13	*Have you heard about . . . ?*	4–6	8	10	
14	*You know about . . . , don't you?*		16		

I Your car won't start. You think the battery is the cause of the problem, but you're not sure. You ring your friend, Ted, who knows about cars.

15	*Have you got any idea about batteries?*	4	6	8–10
	A bit. Got trouble, have you? I'll come round.			
16	*Know anything about . . . ?*		4–6	8–10
17	*Have you got any idea . . . ?*	0	6	8–10
18	*Know . . . ?*		6	8–10

in other situations

19	*Heard about . . . ?*		4–6

F You are writing a business report. You need some information. You go to a colleague you do not know well in another department to ask for it.

20	*Could you give me any information about sales for 1978–79, please?*	4–6	8
	Er, yes, I think I've got the file. Could you wait a moment, please?		
21	*Can you give me any information about . . . ?*	4–6	8
22	*Can/Could you give me any information on . . . ?*	4–6	8
23	*I wonder if you could let me know . . . ?*	0 6	8–10

in other situations

24	*Are you aware . . . ?*		7–9
25	*Are you aware of . . . ?*	4–6	8 9

Practice

a ▶ What do you say in these situations?
  i You want to find out the way from London to Cambridge by car. You ask a policeman.
  ii You are visiting a city in Britain for the first time. You want some information on good places to eat. You ask someone at the tourist information bureau.
  iii Something has been stolen from your hotel room. You have reported it to the receptionist. Now you are talking to the manager. You want to find out if he has been told about it.

3

b You are a salesman visiting Coles Ltd, Leeds. You want to find somewhere to play golf in your spare time. You ask different people, as follows:

who	*where*
i managing director of Coles Ltd	in his office
ii an old friend	in his house
iii a salesman who you don't know very well	in the bar at Coles Ltd

▶ What do you say to each one?

c ▶ Who would you say this to?
Didn't you know that I'm going to South America next Wednesday?
   i to your managing director, who would like to talk to you next Wednesday afternoon
   ii to a friend who has asked you to a party next Wednesday evening

Key a i 4 ii 4, 20–22 iii 24, 25 most appropriate, 1–14 also possible **b** i 20–22 most appropriate, 4, also possible **b** ii 16–18 most appropriate, 4, 14 also possible **b** iii 4, 16–18 **c** ii

3 Saying you know about something

1 *(Yes,) I know . . . , (thanks).*   0 6–9

A helpful stranger is explaining how to use a public telephone in Britain.

And remember, you put your money in when the other person answers—not before.

2 *(Yes, in fact,) I did know about that, (thanks).*   4–6
Fine, well, I hope that's all clear now.

3 *(Yes,) I do know about . . . .* 4 *(Yes,) I know about . . . .*	4–6
5 *(Yes,) I heard/have heard about . . . .*	4–6 8
6 *(Yes,) I do know . . . .*	0 6–8
7 *(Yes,) I heard/have heard . . . .*	0 6–8 14
8 *I've been told . . . .*	0 7 10 14
9 *I've been told about . . . .*	4–6

in other situations

10 *I gather . . . .*	7
11 *Someone told/has told me . . . .*	0 7–9

12	**Someone has told me about . . . .**		4–6
13	**So I hear.**		0
14	**I hear . . . .**		7
15	**Did you know . . . ?**	[a modest way of saying	0 6 7
16	**Did you know about . . . ?**	*you* know something]	4–6

I You are going on a long drive tomorrow. Your friend, Jane, warns you about the weather conditions, but you already know about them.

	They said it's going to be really foggy tomorrow.	
17	**That's what I heard.**	0
	Well, mind how you go.	
18	**So John/Mr Jones** etc **said/was saying.**	0

---

in other situations

19	**Guess what: . . . .**		33
20	**They say . . . .**	7	14
21	**. . . , you know.**		33

F A potential client rings up to tell you that a meeting has been postponed. In fact, you already know this.

	I'm just ringing to inform you that the meeting is now scheduled for tomorrow, at the same time.		
22	**So I gather.** But thank you for ringing.		0
23	**So I've been told.** 24 **So I'm told.** 25 **So I understand.**		0
26	**(Yes,) I do/did appreciate . . . .**		6–8
27	**(Yes,) I do/did realize . . . .**		0 6–8

---

in other situations

28	**I am quite/fully aware . . . .**	[could sound impatient]		7 8
29	**I am quite/fully aware of . . . .**		4–6	8 9
30	**It appears . . . .** 31 **It would appear . . . .** 32 **I'm told . . . .**		7	14
33	**My information/understanding is . . . .**			7
34	**I have it on good authority . . . .** [very formal]		0	7

Practice

That costs £58·50.

a ▶ What does he say?

b You are talking to a friend, John.

John: *You can bet petrol prices'll rocket next year.*

You: ....

John: *Yeah? At least 15p a gallon, I reckon.*

▶ What do you say?

c ▶ Who is saying something inappropriate?

Key a 1–6 **b** 1, 5, 7, 11, 17, 18 **c** Mr Stevens (too informal)

4 Saying you do not know

1 *(I'm sorry,) I don't know.* 6 8–11

You are in a bookshop and have been talking to another customer. She shows you two books about garden flowers.

> Which of these two books is better, do you think?

2 *(I'm afraid) I don't know anything about* gardening.   4–6 8
  Oh, I see. Never mind. I'll ask an assistant.
3 *(I'm afraid) I don't know much about* 4–6 8
4 *(I'm afraid) I don't know* 0 6 8–11
5 *(I'm sorry,) I really don't know* 0 6 8–11
6 *(I'm sorry,) I can't help you there.*   0
7 *(I'm afraid) I couldn't say* 0 7 8 10

6

in other situations

8 *(I'm afraid) I've no idea . . . .*   0 8–11

I At a party a friend, Dave, asks you the name of a pretty girl on the other side of the room.

Who's that girl over there?
9 *(Sorry, I) don't know.*   0 6 8–11
Oh, pity. She's really something.
10 *(Sorry,) no idea . . . .*   0   8–11
11 *I couldn't tell you . . . .*   12 *I wish I knew . . . .*   0 6 8–11
13 *Don't ask me . . . .*   0 6 8–11
14 *Search me.*   } [could sound rude]   0
15 *(I) haven't (got) a clue . . . .* }   0   8–11

---

in other situations

16 *I don't know the first thing about . . . .*   4–6 8
17 *I haven't got a clue about . . . .* }   4–6 8
18 *I haven't got the faintest idea about . . . .* } [could sound rude] 4–6 8
19 *I haven't got the faintest idea . . . .* }   0   8–11

F You have just met a new business client for the first time. He expects you to be able to tell him about your company's sales figures.

Do you know your sales figures for the XO range last year, by
any chance?
20 *(I'm afraid) I haven't got that information (with me).* But
I'll get it to you by the end of the day.   0

---

in other situations

21 *I am not able to help you with your enquiry/request* etc.   0
22 *(I'm afraid) I have to say I know very little about . . . .*   4–6 8–10
23 *I have to admit I don't know a great deal about . . . .*   4–6 8–10
24 *I'm sorry to say that . . . is not something I know very*
much about.   16

Practice

a ▶ What does she say?

b You meet an important person at a reception. He starts talking about his travels.
Of course, Spain is marvellous, isn't it?
▶ What do you reply?
i *No idea, I'm afraid.*
ii *I have to admit I don't know a great deal about Spain.*
iii *I'm sorry to say Spain is not a country I know much about.*
iv *Don't know the first thing about Spain.*
v *I have to say I know very little about Spain.*

Key a 1–8, 22–24 also possible **b** ii, iii, v (i and iv too informal)

5 Reminding

1 *(Please) don't forget ....*	0 1 6	7–9

At a hotel you have asked a receptionist for a 7am call. Later that evening, you see the night porter at the hotel desk.

2 *Can I remind you to call me at 7 tomorrow morning?*	1	7–9
It's all right, sir, I've got a note of it. Goodnight.		
3 *I'd like to remind you ....* **4** *Could I remind you ... ?*	1	7–9
5 *Will you (please) remember ... ?*	0 1	7–9
6 *You will remember to ..., won't you?*	0	17
7 *You won't forget to ..., will you?*	0	17
8 *You won't forget about ..., will you?*		16
9 *You will remember about ..., won't you?*		16
10 *I'd like to remind you about ....*	4–6 8	9
11 *Could I remind you about ... ?*	4–6 8	9
12 *You haven't forgotten about ..., have you?*		16

in other situations

13 *I wonder if you've remembered ....*	0 1	6–11
14 *You haven't forgotten to ..., have you?*	0	17
15 *(I think) you said you were going to ....* } [very polite]	0	17
16 *I expect you've already done it, but ....* }		33–35

I You want to make sure a friend, Ann, gives your best wishes to another friend of yours, Helen.

17 *Remember to give my best wishes to Helen.*	0 1	6–9
It's OK, I will.		

18 *You ↘are going to give her my best wishes, aren't you?/*
You ↘will give her my best wishes, won't you? [or any other
suitable statement + question tag]   35
19 *Remember about . . . .*   **20** *Don't forget about . . . .*   4–6

in other situations

21 *What about . . . ?*   4–6
22 *Hey, the toast!/That phone call!/Jill's birthday card!* [or another
suitable noun]   31

F You are in a meeting. It is taking longer than you expected, although the chairman knows you have to catch a plane. You address him.

23 *(Excuse me,) Mr Chairman, (I think) I should remind you that I*
must leave in twenty minutes.   1   7–9
Oh yes, of course. Well, shall I sum up our conclusions, then?
24 *May I remind you . . . .*   **25** *I should like to remind you . . . .*   1   7–9
26 *I must just remind you . . . .*   1   7–9
27 *Perhaps I ought to remind you . . . .*   1   7–9
28 *I hope you won't mind me/my reminding you . . . .*   0   1   7–9
29 *I'm sure you've remembered/you'll remember, but . . . .*   33
30 *If you recall/remember . . . .* [very formal]   33
31 *May I/I should like/I ought to remind you about . . . .*   4–6   8   9
32 *I hope you won't mind me/my reminding you about . . . .*
[extremely polite]   4–6   8   9

Practice

a You want to remind an acquaintance to telephone you next Sunday.
▶ What do you say?

b ▶ What does he say?

c ▶ Who would you say this to?
I ought to remind you about Mr Black's visit tomorrow evening.
  i   to an old friend
  ii to a colleague in the office, whom you work with every day
  iii to your boss, whom you don't know very well

Key **a** 1–12, 15 **b** 17–22 most appropriate, 5–9, 12, 15 also possible **c** iii

6 Asking about remembering

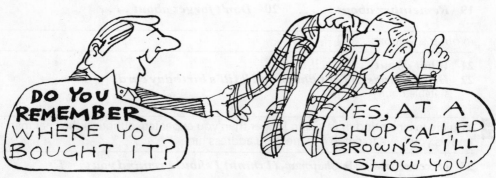

1 Do you remember . . . ?   0 4–10

You are at your hotel. Earlier in the day you asked the receptionist for some rail travel information.

2 I wonder if you remember *my asking for information about*
trains to Edinburgh?   0 4–6 8–10
Yes, sir. I've got a timetable for you here.
3 You remember . . . , don't you?   ♂ 16
4 You haven't forgotten . . . , have you?   0 16

in other situations

5 Don't you remember . . . ?   0 4–10
6 Perhaps you've forgotten 0 4–10

I You are talking to a colleague about people you've worked with in the past.

7 Remember *old Fred? He was always good fun.*   0 4–10
Yes, I wonder what he's up to these days.

in other situations

8 Surely you remember . . . ?   0 4–10
9 You must remember . . . ?   0 4–10
10 You can't have forgotten . . . ?   0 4–10
11 Can't you remember . . . ?   0 4–10
12 Have you forgotten . . . ?   0 4–10

F An executive of a company in Britain is ringing you to ask for some information you gave him but which he has forgotten.

13 *You mentioned a reliable export agency.* **Do you happen to**
remember *its name?*   0 4–10
Yes—Exportise, Kansas City. Shall I give you the full details?
14 I was wondering if perhaps you remember . . . ?   0 4–10
15 Could I ask if you remember . . . ?   0 4–10
16 Do you by any chance remember . . . ?   0 4–10

Practice

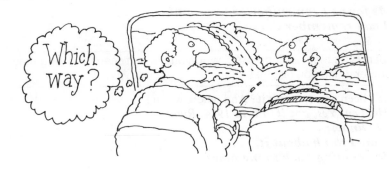

a ▶ What does the driver actually say?

b You want to re-introduce a friend of yours, John Simpson, to various people.

	who	where
i	your managing director	a formal reception
ii	your oldest friend	in a coffee bar
iii	a good friend	a formal reception

▶ What would you say in each case?

Key **a** 1, 3; 7–12, 13, 16 also possible   **b** i 13–16, 1, 2 also possible   **b** ii 7; 1, 3 also possible
b iii 7; 1, 3 also possible

7 Saying you remember

1 *I remember*	0 4–9

You are talking to someone about a visit to Scotland.

2 *It was wonderful.* **I remember especially** *the mountains and the lakes.*   .4–9
Yes, they're beautiful, aren't they?
3 *I'll never forget* ....   **4** *I'll always remember* 0 4–9
5 *I remember quite clearly* 0 4–11

in other situations

6	*As far as I remember/can remember, ...*	0	33	35	36	38
7	*I can remember ....*					4–9

I At a party you meet a friend, Bert, who you haven't seen for a long time. He can't remember when you last met.

It's been years, hasn't it? And where was it?

8	*Hold on. Yes, got it! Paris. 1974. Right?*	0
9	*↘I ↗know: .... !*	33–35 38
10	*Now I think about it, ...*	33–36
11	*It's coming back to me now: ....*	0 33–35

in other situations

12	*I can see ... now!*	16
13	*What I remember is ....*	4–6

F An executive in a British firm rings you up to find out if an important letter has arrived at your company's offices.

We sent it on the 18th. Has it arrived yet?

14	*Well, I haven't got it with me, but **if I remember correctly**, it arrived on the 23rd, yes.*	33	35	36
15	*If I'm not mistaken, ...*	33	35	36
16	*If my memory serves me right, ...*	33	35	36
17	*As I remember it/recall, ...*	33	35	36
18	*I seem to remember ....*			4–7
19	*I distinctly remember/recall/recollect ....*			4–7
20	*I have some recollection of ....*		4–6	8–9

in other situations

21	*What I shall never forget is/are ....*	4–9

Practice

a ▶ What does she say?

12

b You are talking to an old friend, Peter.
Peter: *When did you first come to Britain?*
You think: *First time? Can't remember. Oh, yes. 1968.*
▶ What do you actually say?

c ▶ What does she say?

Key **a** 1, 8 **b** 8–10, 1 equally possible **c** 1, 5, 6

8 Saying you have forgotten

1 *I've forgotten . . . , (I'm afraid).*	0 1 6 8–10

You are having lunch in a pub and talking to another customer. You tell him about another pub you went to recently.

2 *I was in a very nice pub last week, but **I can't remember** its name.*	0 4–6 8–11
3 *I don't remember . . . .*	0 4–6 8–11
4 *(I'm sorry,) I've completely forgotten . . . .*	0 1 4 6 8–11
5 *I (really) can't/don't remember . . . .*	0 4–6 8–11
6 *(I'm afraid) I forget . . . now.*	0 16

I An old friend, Mike, asks you for the telephone number of another friend of yours.

What's Jane's phone number? Any idea?
7 *Er, let me think. No, it's no good. **It's gone.** Better look it up in the book.*	0
8 *. . .'s slipped my mind.*	15
9 *(Sorry,) my mind's gone blank/gone a complete blank.*	0

13

F At a business conference the chairman asks you a question about the history of a product.

> Do you remember exactly how much it cost us to launch our PP model?

10	***(I'm sorry but) I have to/must admit/confess that I don't remember.***	0 4–6 8–10
11	***(I'm afraid) I have no memory/recollection of . . . .***	0 4–6 8–10
12	***(I'm sorry but) I seem/appear to have forgotten . . . .***	0 1 6 8–10
13	***(I'm afraid) . . . escapes me for the moment.***	15

Practice

a A colleague wants to know the name of a certain book. You've read it but you can't remember its name. He asks: *What was the book called?*
▶ What do you say?

b You are telling a good friend, Dick, about a very good restaurant you went to a few months ago. He says: *What's it called?* You can't remember.
▶ What do you say?

c You are talking to a close friend, Andy. He asks you for the address of a girl you both know well. You say: *I'm sorry, Andy, but I appear to have forgotten her address. Could I let you have it tomorrow?*
▶ Is this appropriate? If not, what would you say?

Key **a** 1–6 most appropriate, 7, 8, 9 also possible   **b** 7, 8, 9 most appropriate, 1–6 also possible
    c No, 7–9 most appropriate, 1–6 also possible

9   Asking if something is correct

1 ***Is . . . right, (please)?***	16

You have just filled in a booking form at a travel agency. But you are not sure you have understood all the questions. You show the form to the clerk.

2	***Have I got this right, (please)?***	16
	Yes, that's fine, thank you.	
3	***Could you tell me if . . . is right/correct, (please)?***	16
4	***Is . . . correct, (please)?***	16
5	***I'd like to check that I've got . . . right.***	16

14

   6 *Is it true/right that . . . ?*   7

I You met Tessa Jones at a party recently. Now you want to ring her. You think you remember her number, but you ring a friend, Peter, to make sure.

   7 *Hello, Peter . . . er . . . . Tessa's phone number—it's 74722,* **right?**   33
      No, it's 74724. Better write it down before you forget it again!
   8 *. . . , yes?*
   9 *That right?*   **10** *Am I right?*   33   0
 11 *It's 74722, isn't it?/I've got her number right, haven't I?*/etc
      [or any suitable statement + question tag]   29

in other situations

 12 *Is . . . OK, (or not)?*   16
 13 *Anything wrong with . . . ?*   6

F You have arranged several appointments at Smith & Co for tomorrow. You ring up Smith's to make sure you have noted down the times correctly, and to see if there have been any changes. You speak to a secretary.

 14 *I think I'm seeing Mr Green at 11 and Mr Smith for lunch at 12.30.*
      Would you mind telling me if *that's correct, please?*   16
      Mr Green at 11, yes, but Mr Smith isn't able to meet you until 1.
      He hopes that isn't inconvenient for you.
 15 *Am I right in thinking/supposing . . . ?*   7 14
 16 *I assume . . . .*   **17** *Is it true to say . . . ?*   7 14
 18 *Would that be right/correct?*   0
 19 *I'd like to check that . . .'s correct.*   16

Practice

a ▶ What does he say?

b Your friend, James, has asked you to his house tomorrow evening.
     James: *OK, then? See you tomorrow.*
     You: *. . . ?*
     James: *7.30, yes, that'll be fine. Look forward to seeing you.*
     ▶ What do you say?

c You are discussing a business meeting arranged for next week. You have not previously met the people you are discussing it with.

▶ What do you say?

i *Next Tuesday, 2 o'clock, right?*
ii *We meet at 2 o'clock next Tuesday. Would that be right?*
iii *2 o'clock on Tuesday, yes?*

Key **a** 1, 3, 4 most appropriate, 8, 9, 11 also possible **b** 7, 8, 11 most appropriate, 1 also possible
c ii (i and iii too informal)

10 Saying something is correct

1 *Yes, that's right.* 0

You are staying with a family. They want to take you to the British Museum. But they want to make sure that you haven't visited it before.

You haven't been there before, have you?
2 *No, I haven't. I'd very much like to go.* 0 33

in other situations

3 *Yes, ...* 0 33
4 *Yes, that's quite right.* **5** *Yes, that's correct.* 0
6 *Yes, you're quite right.* **7** *Exactly.* 0

I You are staying with a friend, John. You have written a letter but you aren't sure you've written the address in the right way. So you ask him.

John, is this the right way to put the address?
8 *That's fine.* 0
9 *Nothing wrong with that.* 0
10 *That's it/OK/all right.* 0

in other situations

11 *You're dead right.* **12** *Spot on.* 0

16

F You are at lunch with an important new client. He has a lot of interesting things to say, and you think many of them are correct.

The key word in the business vocabulary today is 'rationalization'.
13 *Absolutely*.   14 *Precisely*.   0

in other situations

15 *. . . is perfectly correct*.   15
16 *(Yes,) I can/should like to confirm . . . .*   6-7
17 *I should say . . . is perfectly correct*.   16

Practice

a ▶ What does Mr Kogo say?

b Your good friend, Ray, wants to take you to a film, but wants to find out if you've seen it already. You haven't. He says: *You haven't seen it before, have you?*
▶ What do you reply?

c ▶ When would you say this?
I should say that is perfectly correct.
In answer to:
  i *Jim, have I got this sales figure right? £23 567?*
  ii *Our estimates for sales in the coming year is of the order of £23 000.*
  iii *We'll sell £23 000's worth, surely?*
  iv *Would it be over-optimistic to talk in terms of sales worth £23 000 next year?*

Key   a 1, 3, 4, 6   **b** 2   **c** ii and iv (too formal an answer for i and iii)

II Saying something is not correct

1 *(Sorry,) ...'s not right.*   15

Another guest at your London hotel is going away for the day by train. She tells you about her plan.

I'm going to Brighton. Let me see—the right station for Brighton's Waterloo, isn't it?

2 *No, it isn't, **actually.***   36
3 *(I'm afraid) ...'s **wrong.***   15
4 *(I'm afraid) ... is/are not (quite) right.*   15
5 *I'm not sure you're right about ....*   4–6 9
6 *I don't think ....*   7 *I didn't think ....*   7 14

I You are having a friendly argument about animals with a friend, Chris.

I don't think you really like animals at all.

8 *No, **that's all wrong.***   15
9 *No, **you've got ... all wrong.***   16

---

in other situations

10 ***Have you got ... right?***   16
11 *... isn't right, is it?*   15
12 ***Nonsense/Rubbish.*** [only to close friends, or if you're angry or scornful]   0

F A British company is expecting delivery of some components from your factory. Someone from the factory rings you up to ask about them.

I'm afraid those KB components have simply not been sent off to us.

13 ***If I may say so,** that **is not the case.***   16
14 *I think I should point out ... is not correct/not the case.*   16
15 *If I may say so, you are mistaken/wrong (there).*   0
16 *I really do have to correct you (there).*   0
17 *I think the information you have must be incorrect.*   0
18 *I'm sorry, there is some/has been some misunderstanding (here).*   0
19 *It is not correct to say/to suppose that ....*   7

18

Practice

a   An acquaintance says to you: *The capital of Brazil is Rio de Janeiro*. He's wrong.
▶ What do you say?

b   Your friend John: *You'll get two dollars fifty to the pound with a bit of luck.*
You: . . . .
John: *Oh? Well, what's the right figure then?*
▶ What do you say?

c ▶ What does the man actually say?
 i   *That's rubbish!*
 ii *No, that's all wrong.*
 iii *If I may say so, you're mistaken.*

Key **a** 1–7   **b** 10, 11 most appropriate, 1–7 also possible   **c** iii

12   Correcting someone

1 *(Well,) in fact . . . .*	33 35 36

You are walking along the street with a colleague, talking about cars. He thinks he's rather an expert.

Look at that VW. Now that's a good car.

2 *Surely*, *it's a BMW, isn't it?*	33 35 36
3 *But . . . .* 4 *As far as I know, ...*	33 35 36
5 *(Well,) as a matter of fact, ...* 6 *(Well,) actually, ...*	33 35 36

19

I You are having a friendly argument about football with a friend, Adrian.

Brazil last won the World Cup in, let's see, 1974.
7 *No, 1970. West Germany won it in '74.*   33 35 36
8 *Hold on (a minute) . . . .*   9 *Hang on (a minute) . . . .*   33 35 36

F You are at a seminar on in-company training. During one session, a speaker says that in-company training is not compulsory in any country. When you get the opportunity to speak, you correct him.

10 *(If I may,) I'd like to correct one thing you said: in my*
   country, in-company training is compulsory by law.   33
11 *If I may correct you, ...*   33–35
12 *I think it might be more accurate/correct to say . . . .*   7

Practice

a ▶ What does the tall man actually say?

b   You are talking to a colleague.
   Colleague: *We agreed we'd get together in my office at 10.*
   You think: *10.30, that's what we said yesterday.*
   ▶ What do you actually say?

c   At an important meeting the sales manager makes a statement:
   Our exports have risen by some twenty per cent over the last financial year.
   You say: *Hold on a minute. It's only fifteen per cent.*
   ▶ What does the sales manager think?
   i   *That may be right, but he hasn't chosen his words very well.*
   ii *He's right. Fifteen per cent is nearer the truth.*
   iii *He may be right, but I'd prefer him not to talk like that in this sort of meeting.*

Key **a** 1, 5, 6 **b** 1–6, 7–9 also possible **c** i and iii (what you say is too informal for the situation)

13 Asking if someone is sure about something

1 *Are you sure about . . . ?*   4–6 9

You and a colleague, Andrew Lacey, have arranged to meet an acquaintance for a drink. But there is no sign of her. Andrew thinks she will arrive soon.

> She'll be here in a few minutes.

2 *Are you certain . . . ?*   0 7
3 *Are you certain about . . . ?*   4–6 9
4 *You're absolutely/quite sure . . . ?*   **5** *Are you sure . . . ?*   0 7 9
6 *You're absolutely/quite sure about . . . ?*   4–6 9
7 *Are you quite sure . . . ?*   0 7
8 *Are you quite sure about . . . ?*   4–6 9
9 *Definitely?*   0

I You are driving with your friend, Jasmine, to visit someone in another town. You think you're going to be late. Jasmine tries to reassure you.

> We'll be there in another ten minutes.

10 *You're sure?*   0 7
11 *Positive?*   **12** *Really?*   0

---

in other situations

13 *D'you mean to say . . . ?*   7

F You are having lunch with the managing director of Network Electronics, with which you have been negotiating a contract. He has some important information to give you.

> I can tell you now unofficially that you'll be getting the video contract.

14 *And there's no doubt in your mind about that?*   6 8 9
15 *Is there any doubt about . . . ?*   6 8 9
16 *Forgive me, but are you (really) sure/certain about . . . ?*   6 8 9
17 *And there's no doubt in your mind . . . ?*   0 7–9
18 *Perhaps I misunderstood, but are you quite sure . . . ?*   0 7–9

Practice

a ▶ What does she actually say?

b You take a punctured tyre to a garage to be mended. You need it urgently. You haven't been to this garage before.
Garage man: *We can't do this before tomorrow, I'm afraid.*
You: . . . .
Garage man: *I'm afraid that's the earliest. We've got a lot of work on at the moment.*
▶ What do you say?

c A clerk is talking to his manager in his manager's office.
Manager: *I have it on reliable authority that you will be transferred to our Hong Kong branch in the near future.*
Clerk: *Positive?*
▶ Is the clerk's reply appropriate? If not, what is?

Key a 1–9 **b** 1–9 **c** No, 14–18 (plus name of manager) most appropriate, 1–8 (plus name of manager) also possible

14 Saying you are sure

1 *I'm sure . . . .*   0 7

You and a colleague have arranged to meet a visitor, but he has not arrived.

Do you think he's forgotten to come?
2 *I'm quite sure he has.*   0 7
3 *I'm absolutely/fairly sure . . . .*   4 *I've no doubt . . . .*   0 7

22

5 *I'm absolutely/fairly certain*	0	7–9
6 *I know*	6	7
7 *...certainly/definitely*	33	35
8 *I'm sure/certain about* .... 9 *I've no doubt about*		6
10 *He must have.*		0
11 *He must have missed the bus/had an accident* etc.		0

in other situations

12 *He must be.* 13 *He must be here/there* etc.	0

You and a friend, Terry, are discussing a football match before watching it on television.

And you really think Holland are a better side?

14 *Yes.* 15 *Yes, really!* 16 *Absolutely certain/positive.*	0
17 *(Surely) that's obvious, (isn't it?)* [say with a smile, and only to friends] [could sound rude]	0

in other situations

18 *You can be sure*		7
19 *You can be sure about*		6
20 *I'm a hundred per cent certain*	0	7–9

F You are in a discussion with other members of management about one of the employees in your company, John Symes.

And you think Symes has been neglecting his work for some reason?

21 *I don't think there can be any doubt about* that.	4–6	8	9
22 *I don't think there can be any doubt*	0	7	8
23 *I don't think there can be any doubt as to*	6	8–11	
24 *There's no/very little doubt in my mind*	0	7	8
25 *There's no/very little doubt in my mind as to*	6	8–11	
26 *There's no/very little doubt in my mind about*	6	8	9
27 *There can't be any doubt*	0	7	
28 *There can't be any doubt as to*	6	8–10	
29 *There can't be any doubt about*	4–6	8	9
30 *It's quite certain*	0	7	
31 *It's my conviction*		7	
32 *I'm (quite) convinced*	0	7	
33 *That is my conviction.*		0	

Practice

a ▶ What does the businessman say?

b You are talking to a friend at work.
   You: *There are going to be some shake-ups in this company before long.*
   Your friend: *Do you really think so?*
   You: . . . .
   ▶ What do you say?

c At a government committee meeting you tell another delegate that a certain
   official is about to be dismissed. The other delegate asks you if you are sure
   about that.
   ▶ What do you say?
   i   *I know he is.*
   ii *I don't think there can be any doubt about it.*
   iii *Yes, really!*

Key   **a** 1–3, 5–8   **b** 14–16, 18–20 most appropriate, 1–9 also possible   **c** ii

15 Saying what you think is possible or probable

1 *. . . is going to . . . .*			25

You tell someone you are going to ring a friend in the U.S.A.

2 *That'll **probably** cost you at least ten pounds.*	33	35	36
Really? Well, I'll keep it as short as possible.			
3 *. . . **will/may/might/could well** . . . .*			25
4 *I expect . . . .*	1 2 7		14
5 *It's (quite) possible/probable . . . .*		0	7
6 *It's (quite) likely . . . .*		0 1	7

in other situations

7 *Maybe/Perhaps/Probably . . . .*	0 33	35	36
8 *. . . is/looks/seems etc (quite) possible/likely/probable.*			15

I You are at your friend, Carol's, house, ringing a shop to make an enquiry. It's 9.00 a.m.

There's no answer.
9 *If you ask me, they don't open until nine-thirty.*	33	35	36
10 *It looks like/looks as if . . . .*			12
11 *I shouldn't be surprised if . . . .*			12
12 *Could be . . . .* 13 *You can be sure . . . .*			7

24

14 *There's a good chance*	15 *I bet*	7
16 *I reckon*		7 14
17 *There's a good chance of*		4–6
18 *Surely*		33–36

F You are talking about general economic problems with Mr Lacey, a specialist you have just met at a conference.

19 *I think there is every possibility* that the economic situation will improve before long, don't you, Mr Lacey?	0 7
Yes, I think the evidence certainly points that way at present.	
20 *I assume/believe*	2 7 14
21 *It's my expectation/prediction*	7
22 *It's reasonable to believe/assume/expect*	6 7 14
23 *It's not out of the question*	0 7
24 *It's not unlikely*	0 7
25 *We/One can't rule out/exclude the possibility*	0 7
26 *We/One can't rule out/exclude the possibility of*	4–6
27 *There's always/certainly the possibility*	0 7
28 *There's always/certainly the possibility of*	4–6
29 *It's more than likely/probable*	0 7
30 *... is more than likely/probable.*	15
31 *... is bound to*	25
32 *In all probability/likelihood,*	33 35 36
33 *I predict*	6 7

Practice

a ▶ What does she say?

b You think the government of your country is about to increase its imports of cars from Britain. You want to tell various people about this.

who	*where*
i a close friend	at lunch
ii a colleague you work closely with	in your office
iii a colleague you don't know very well	in a board meeting

▶ What do you say to each one?

Key **a** 1–4 most appropriate, 10, 14, 17 also possible **b** i 9–17 most appropriate, 1–8 also possible
b ii 1–8 most appropriate, 9–17 also possible **b** iii 19–33 most appropriate, 1–8 also possible

16 Saying you are not sure

1	*(Sorry,) I'm not sure ....*	0	7–11

Someone has invited you to go and see a horror film. You only rarely like such films.

Would you like to come?
2	*I can't make up my mind whether to come or not.*	0	8–11
3	*I can't decide ....*	0 6	8–11
4	*I'm not really sure ....*	0	7–11
5	*I'm not really sure about ....*	4–6	8 9
6	*I'm in two minds ....*	0	9 11
7	*I'm in two minds about ....*	4–6	8 9

I Your friend, Mike's, mother has been taken to hospital. You ring Mike for news.

Sorry to hear about your mother. Is it serious?
8	*I can't say for certain.*	0 7	8 10
9	*I'm not too sure ....*	0	7–11
10	*I couldn't say, (really,) ....*	0	8 10

in other situations

11	*I wouldn't be too sure about ....*	4–6	8–11
12	*This is right off the top of my head, but ....*	33	35–37

F Your managing director wants to know about some negotiations you have been involved in.

Well, did you succeed in getting what we requested?
13	*I'm afraid I can't be certain about that until next week.*	4–6	8 10
14	*There's some doubt in my mind ....*	0 8	9 11
15	*There's some doubt in my mind about ....*	4–6	8 10
16	*I'm not at all convinced ....*		0 7
17	*I'm not at all convinced about ....*		6
18	*It's not at all certain ....*		0 7 8
19	*One can't say with any certainty ....*	0 7	8 10
20	*One can't say with any certainty about ....*		6
21	*There's still an element of doubt ....*		0 7 10
22	*There's still an element of doubt about ....*	4–6	8–11

23	*I find it difficult to reach a conclusion.*		0
24	*I find it difficult to reach a conclusion on*		6 10
25	*There is surely some doubt*	0 7 10
26	*There is surely some doubt about*	4–6 8–11
27	*There is surely some doubt as to*	6 8–11

Practice

a ▶ What does she say?

b Your friend, Pete, is talking to you.
Pete: *I hear you're jetting off to Venezuela next week.*
You: . . . .
Pete: *Oh? I thought it was all fixed.*
▶ What do you say?

c Your managing director is expecting your report on one of the company's investment plans. He asks to see you in his office and says: *I take it you've decided we should proceed with the plan?*
▶ What do you say?
i *I can't make up my mind.*
ii *Not too sure.*
iii *There's still some doubt in my mind about it.*

Key **a** 1, 9 **b** 8, 9, 11, 1–7 **c** iii (i and ii too informal)

17 Saying what you think is improbable or impossible

1 I don't think 7 14

You have taken some shoes for urgent repair.

Can I get them back sometime tomorrow?
2 (Sorry, but) it's not likely that they'll be ready before Friday. 0 7
3 I don't expect 1 2 7
4 It's not probable 0 7
5 It's unlikely 0 1 7
6 . . . is/are not likely. 15
7 . . . is/are not likely to 25
8 It's impossible/not possible 0 1 7
9 It's impossible/not likely for 2
10 . . . is impossible/not likely/not probable, (I'm afraid). 15

I You and your friend, Pete, are running to catch a train.

Do you think we'll make it?
11 Probably not! 0
12 Impossible, (I'm afraid). [could sound rude unless said with a smile or friendly intonation] 0
13 Perhaps not.   14 Maybe not. 0
15 Not a chance. 0
16 . . . is/are bound not to. 15
17 . . . is/are bound not to 25
18 I don't think/don't suppose 7 14
19 No way. 0
20 There's no way 7
21 It doesn't look like/as though 12
22 Surely not. 0
23 . . . (just) won't/can't. 15
24 . . . (just) won't/can't 25
25 I'd be surprised 0 1
26 I'd be surprised if 12

28

F Someone you do not know has rung you up about the delivery of some of your products.

> And we'd like to know if you could possibly get them to us two
> weeks early?

27	*(I'm afraid) there's very little likelihood of our being able to do that.*			4–6
28	*I consider . . . quite out of the question.*			16
29	*It's very doubtful . . . .*	0	7	10
30	*It's extremely unlikely/improbable . . . .*		0	7
31	*It's quite out of the question . . . .*	0	1	7
32	*It's quite out of the question for . . . .*		2	6
33	*It's my expectation/prediction . . . .*			7
34	*I cannot believe . . . .*		6	7
35	*I think there's very little chance/likelihood/probability . . . .*			7
36	*I think there's very little chance/likelihood/probability of . . . .*			4–6
37	*It is not reasonable/sensible etc to expect . . . .*	2	6	7
38	*It would not be sensible/wise etc to assume . . . .*		6	7
39	*I think we can rule out/discount the possibility of . . . .*			4–6
40	*I think there's absolutely no possibility of . . . .*			4–6
41	*The likelihood/probability/possibility of . . . is low/remote etc.*			16
42	*In all probability, ...*	33	35	36

Practice

a You go to a booking office to ask for some tickets for a play.
You: *Do you have any tickets for tomorrow night's performance?*
Booking clerk: *I'm sorry, sir, they're all sold. But there are two cancellations for tonight, if you're able to come.*
You think: *Probably not.*
▶ What do you say?

b At the office your friend, Steve, has some news to tell you.
Steve: *They say they're going to sack Ronnie Burton.*
You don't believe it.
▶ What do you say?

c At a company meeting the chairman asks members if they think it's possible to have a new range in production within six weeks. He gets various answers.
▶ Which is appropriate?
i *I consider that quite out of the question.*
ii *Impossible!*
iii *It's extremely unlikely, in my opinion.*
iv *That just can't be done.*
v *Not much chance of that.*

Key **a** 1, 8, 9 most appropriate, 12 also possible **b** 12, 15, 17–20, 22–26 most appropriate, 1–3; 5–8, 10 also possible **c** i and iii, other answers too informal

18 Talking about what might happen

This is our latest model, miss.

If I bought that, I wouldn't have enough money to pay for the petrol!

1 **If . . . .**	13

You are at an open-air theatre. At the end of the first act you notice storm clouds gathering. The person sitting next to you turns to you and says:

Getting cold, isn't it?

2 Yes, **I wonder** whether it's going to rain?	0 8 10
3 **Suppose**	13

in other situations

4 **Unless**	13

I You and your friend, Dave, are choosing some numbers in a lottery.

5 **What if** we won, Dave. What would we do with all that money? Stop dreaming! Just pick some numbers.	12
6 **(Just) imagine**	4–7
7 **(Just) imagine if**	12

in other situations

8 **If only**	13

F You are at a management training course, listening to a lecture. The lecturer puts a question to his audience.

9 **Let us imagine** that a strike suddenly occurs. What would be the most appropriate course of action? Presumably one would want to get some kind of dialogue going between management and the unions.	4–7
10 **Let us suppose**	2 7 14
11 **Let us assume**	2 6 7 14
12 **If I may speculate for a moment,**	33 35
13 **Speculating for a moment,**	33–35
14 **Let us take a hypothetical case:**	33

in other situations

15 **On the assumption (that)/the supposition (that)**	13
16 **On condition (that)** . . . . 17 **Provided (that)**	13
18 **Allowing (for the fact that)** . . . . 19 **Given (that)**	13

Practice

a ▶ What does she say?

b You and your girlfriend, Jane, are reading the Sunday newspapers at her house. It looks as if it might rain, but you want some exercise outside. You say: *What about a nice walk in the country?*

▶ What does she say?

i *Let us imagine that it rained. That would rather spoil it.*
ii *Supposing it rained. That wouldn't be much fun.*
iii *What if it rains? That'd be pretty miserable.*

c You are addressing a conference on trade matters.

▶ What do you say?

i *Just suppose inflation shot up by 10%.*
ii *Let us assume an increase in the rate of inflation of 10% per annum.*
iii *Let us take a hypothetical case. We find that the rate of inflation is rising at 10% a year.*

Key a 1–3 most appropriate, 5 and 7 also possible **b** ii and iii (i too formal) **c** ii and iii (i too informal)

19 Asking how someone feels before something happens

1 *Are you all right . . . ?*

0

You are sitting in a hired car. You are not familiar with the controls. The hire firm representative is watching you.

2	*Is anything the matter?*		0
	Well, I haven't driven one of these before, you see.		
3	*Are you worried/happy etc . . . ?*		0 7
4	*Are you worried/happy etc about . . . ?*	4–6	8–10
5	*How do you feel?*		0
6	*How do you feel about . . . ?*	4–6	9

in other situations

7	*Are you looking forward to . . . ?*		4–6

I You are with your friend, Diana, who is about to take an exam.

8	*Are you OK?*		0
	Yes, this sort of thing doesn't worry me much.		
9	*Everything OK?* 10 *Sure you're OK?*		0
11	*You're not nervous/unhappy etc are you?*		0
12	*You're not nervous/unhappy etc about . . . , are you?*		16

F A secretary has brought you to a waiting room. You are about to have an important interview for a job. She smiles and says:

13	*If I may say so, you appear a little/somewhat nervous.*		0
	Yes, I must confess I find interviews rather nerve-racking.		
14	*I wonder if you aren't just a little worried/nervous etc.*		0
15	*I wonder if you aren't just a little worried/nervous etc about . . . .*	4–6	8–10
16	*Would I be right in supposing you were worried/nervous etc about . . . ?*	4–6	8–10

in other situations

17	*Would I be right in supposing you were worried/nervous etc?*		0
18	*Could I ask if you feel anxious about . . . ?*	4–6	8–10
19	*Could I ask if you feel anxious?*		0
20	*What do you expect your reaction will be?*		0
21	*What do you expect your reaction will be to . . . ?*		4–6

Practice

a ▶ What does he say?

b ▶ What does he say?

c At an important formal dinner, you are sitting next to someone you have just met. He is about to give a speech, and looks rather nervous.
▶ What do you say?
i *How do you feel about giving a speech on such an occasion?*
ii *Everything OK?*
iii *You're not worried about it, are you?*
iv *I wonder if you aren't just a little worried about your speech.*

Key a 2–4 (8–12 equally possible) **b** 6, 7, 11, 12 **c** i or iv (ii and iii too informal)

20 Saying you are curious

1 *I wonder . . . ?*		0 8 10

You are visiting a castle. Part of the castle is being excavated and there is much excitement beside a roped-off area. You go over to the excited group.

2 *Can someone tell me* what's going on? Yes, they think they've found a Roman temple.		0 6 8 10
3 *I'd be very interested to know . . . .*		0 8–11
4 *Can someone tell me about . . . ?*		4–6

in other situations

5 *I wish I knew more about . . . .*		4–6 8 10
6 *I wish I knew . . . .*		0 8–11
7 *Doesn't anyone know . . . ?*		6–11

33

8 *I'd like to know* . . . . **9** *I wish someone would tell me*	0 6	8–11
10 *I wish someone would tell me about*		4–6
11 *What I'd really like to find out is*	6	8–10

I   You are out with your friend, Pete, when you see a pretty girl.

12 *I wouldn't mind knowing* where she lives. Why not go and ask her then!	0 6	8–10
13 *I'd love to know* . . . . **14** *I'd give a lot to know*	0 6	8–11
15 *If only I knew*	0 6	8–11

in other situations

16 *If only I knew about*		4–6	8 9
17 *I'd love to know about* . . . . **18** *I'd give a lot to know about*		4–6	
19 *I wouldn't mind knowing about*		4–6	
20 *Penny for your thoughts.* **21** *What's on your mind?*		0	
22 *How on earth* . . . ?		34	

F   In a marketing meeting you are informed that your competitors have halved the wholesale price on their product. You wonder how this has been possible.

23 *I'd particularly like to know* how Brambram & Son have managed to do it.	6	8–11
24 *I'm rather/very keen to know*	6	8–11
25 *I'd particularly like to know about*		4–6
26 *I'm rather/most curious to know about*		4–6
27 *I'd be rather/very/most interested to discover*	6	8–10
28 *Is it possible to obtain any information on/about* . . . ?	4–6	8–10
29 *I'm rather/very/most curious about*		4–6

Practice

a   You are talking to an American you have recently met about politics in the United States. He says he has some inside information on the Watergate affair that has not come out yet.
> What do you say?

b   Your friend, James, is showing you some of his colour slides.
James: *What d'you think of them, then?*
You think: *How does he get such good photos?*
James: *Well, why don't you go to evening classes, like I did?*
> What do you actually say?

c   You've heard a rumour that your firm is moving its offices out of London to another town. You want to find out if this is true.
> What do you say?
   i   to a colleague you don't know very well
   ii   to your manager, when you happen to be in his office
   iii   to a close friend and colleague whom you meet in a corridor

Key   **a** 1, 3, 5, 6, 8–11 most appropriate, 12–19 also possible **b** 12–19, 22 most appropriate, 3, 5, 6, 8–10 also possible **c** i 1, 3, 5, 6, 8–11 most appropriate, 12–19 also possible **c** ii 22, 25, 27, 28 most appropriate, 3, 5, 6, 8–10 also possible **c** iii 12–19 most appropriate, 1, 3, 5, 6, 8–11 also possible

21 Saying what you hope will happen

1 *I hope . . . .*   1 7 14

You are expecting an important letter from your family. You mention this while chatting to someone you've met in your hotel lounge about delays in the post.

---

2 *Yes, I wish that letter would arrive soon.*   7
Mm, maybe there's been a postal strike somewhere.
3 *I'd like . . . .*   1 2 6
4 *I'm hoping . . . .*   1 7 14
5 *I'm hoping for . . . .*   2 6
6 *Hopefully . . . .*   0 33 36
7 *. . . , I hope.*   33 36

I You and your friend, Ray, are about to watch a programme on television. But the TV is old and not very reliable.

---

8 *Let's hope the old box doesn't go wrong again.*   1 7 14
Right, let's see what happens when I switch on.
9 *Keep your fingers crossed . . . .*   0 7
10 *Here's hoping . . . .*   0 7 14
11 *So/As long as . . . .*   13

---

in other situations

---

12 *Here's hoping for . . . .*   **13** *Let's hope for . . . .*   6
14 *If only . . . .*   13

F You are arranging a game of golf with a business associate who you do not know very well.

---

15 *We must hope the weather stays fine.*   7 14
Perhaps we'd better take our umbrellas, just in case!
16 *I do hope . . . .*   1 7 14
17 *We must hope for . . . .*   6
18 *I trust . . . .*   7 14

---

in other situations

---

19 *I do hope for . . . .*   6

Practice

a ▶ What does the customer say?

b It's Friday afternoon at the office, and a lovely summer day. You're working with a friend, Chris.

Chris: *Just the day for a round of golf.*
You think: *Can we leave early?*
Chris: *Oh, I don't think the boss will mind.*
▶ What do you actually say?

c You are at an important marketing meeting. The chairman remarks on the poor state of trading generally in the country, seeing little change ahead.
▶ What do you say?
  i *Here's hoping for better times.*
  ii *So long as things get better soon.*
  iii *We must hope for an improvement in the situation soon.*
  iv *I trust that things will take a turn for the better in the near future.*
  ▶ What else could you say?

Key **a** 1, 6, 7; 16 also possible **b** 1–3, 6, 7 most appropriate, 8–11, 14 also possible **c** iii and iv (i and ii are too informal), 15, 16, 19 most appropriate 1, 5, 6, 7 also possible

22 Saying what you want

1 *I'd like . . . .*

1 2 6

You've gone to a shop for a needle and some thread to mend a shirt you have torn.

2	***I need*** *a needle and some thread to mend this shirt with.*	1	2	6

Yes, of course. Here's a packet of needles. Now the thread.

3	***May I . . . ?***	0	3
4	***What I need is . . . .***	1	6

I It's a scorching day and you're out for a walk with a friend, Julie.

5	***I'm dying for*** *a long, cold drink.*		2	6

Well, there's a cafe over there. Let's go and get one.

6	***I want . . . .***	1	2	6
7	***I must have . . . .*** 8 ***I could use/could do with . . . .***			6
9	***I'm dying to . . . .***	0		3
10	***. . . would go down well.*** 11 ***. . . would just suit me.***			15
12	***I'd love . . . .***	1	2	6
13	***I wish I could . . . .*** 14 ***If only I could . . . .***	0		3
15	***I've got to have . . . .***			6

in other situations

16	***Why can't I . . . ?***	0	3

F You are on a special visit to a chocolate factory. The managing director asks you what you would like as a souvenir of your visit.

17	***I should very much like*** *some of your milk chocolates, if that is possible.*	1	2	6

But of course. Here is a box of our special selection.

18	***What I should really like is . . . .***		1		6
19	***I should really love . . . .***	1	2	4	6

in other situations

20	***I'm really longing . . . .*** 21 ***I very much wish . . . .***	1
22	***I'm really longing for . . . .***	2 6

Practice

a ▶ What does he actually say?

37

b ▶ What does she actually say?

c Your directors have invited you and some other colleagues for a drink in the boardroom. One of the directors asks you what you would like to drink.
▶ What do you say?
  i *I could use a gin and tonic.*
  ii *I should very much like a martini.*
  iii *A vodka would go down well.*
  iv *May I have a tomato juice?*

Key a 1, 2, 4 most appropriate, 6–8, 13–15 equally possible **b** 10, 12, 15 most appropriate, 1, 4 also possible **c** ii and iv (i and iii too informal)

23 Saying you are looking forward to something

1 *I'm looking forward to . . . .*   4–6

You have been invited to join a family for a trip to the seaside.

Don't forget to bring your swimming costume, will you?
2 *It'll be nice to swim in the sea again.*   0 1
3 *It'll be good/interesting/pleasant etc . . . .*   0 1
4 *. . . is going to be nice/wonderful etc.*   15

I A friend, Paul, has invited you to a concert this evening.

5 *I can't wait for this evening.*   2 6
   Yes, it should be really great.
6 *Looking forward to . . . .*   4–6

You are waiting to listen to a lecture at a conference. You are talking to your neighbour.

7 ***I must say I look forward to*** *hearing Professor Brown.*   4–6
   Yes, so do I—although I can't say I agree with some of his views.

in other situations

8 ***I look forward to hearing from you.*** [often used at the end of a letter]   0
9 ***In eager/keen anticipation of your reply/visit*** etc. [often used at the end of a letter]   0

Practice

a ▶ What does he say?

b You are writing a letter to an old friend, Lena, whom you haven't seen for a long time.
   ▶ How do you end your letter?
   i *In keen anticipation of your visit.*
   ii *I look forward to your visiting us.*
   iii *Looking forward to seeing you again.*
   iv *It'll be very good to see you again.*

Key **a** 1–4 (5, 6 equally possible), **b** iii or iv (i and ii too formal)

24 Saying you are optimistic

1 ...*'ll* .... [with optimistic words]   25

A colleague is saying goodbye to you as you are about to go off on a short holiday. You are not convinced you are going to enjoy yourself.

2 *(I think) you're going to have a marvellous time.*   3
I certainly hope so. I'll tell you when I get back!
3 *(I think) you're going to have fine weather/a good holiday* etc.
[or other optimistic words]   0
4 *You're bound to enjoy it/have a good time* etc. [or other optimistic words]   0
5 *...is bound to be successful/enjoyable* etc. [or other optimistic words]   15
6 *...will be good/nice/wonderful* etc, *(I'm sure).*   15

I A friend of yours, Marina, is going to have an operation. You want to cheer her up.

7 *Everything'll be fine.*   0
Thanks. Come and see me, won't you?
8 *It'll all turn out OK/fine.*   0
9 *(You wait and see.) It's all going to be OK.*   0

in other situations

10 *Things'll work out fine/all right.*   0
11 *... can't go wrong.*   15
12 *I don't see how ... can fail.*   16
13 *...'ll be great, (I'm sure).*   15
14 *... is bound to win/do it/get there* etc.   15

F At a board meeting the directors are talking about sales.

15 *I am confident that sales next year will increase significantly.*   7
Yes, I must say I share your confidence.
16 *I am very optimistic ....*   0 7
17 *I am very optimistic about ....*   4–6
18 *I have every confidence ....*   19 *I feel quite sure ....*   7
20 *I have every confidence in ....*   5 6
21 *I feel quite sure about ....*   4–6
22 *I anticipate success in ....*   4 6
23 *My expectation is ....*   1 7

Practice

a ▶ What does she actually say?

40

b Your friend, Bill, is going for a job interview. He's a bit nervous about it.
▶ What do you say?
  i *Everything'll be fine.*
  ii *It'll all turn out OK.*
  iii *I feel quite sure you will succeed.*

c At an embassy reception you are talking to someone you do not know well. He asks you what you think of prospects for improvements in trade relations between your countries.
You say: *They're going to be OK.*
▶ What does the other person think?
  i *That's a funny way to express an opinion on an important topic.*
  ii *Does he really know me well enough to talk like that?*
  iii *How extraordinarily rude!*

Key a 1–6, 13   **b** i or ii (iii too formal)   **c** i or ii (not iii, the words used are not rude, just very informal)

25 Saying you are pessimistic

| 1 *I'm not so sure . . . .* | | 0 | 7 | 10 |

You have got to catch a plane, but have been delayed. A colleague thinks you will still be able to catch it.

You'll get it all right if you leave at once.

2 *I rather doubt that.*		6	7	10
3 *I'm rather doubtful . . . .* 4 *I'm not at all sure . . . .*		0	7	10
5 *I'm rather doubtful about . . . .*		4–6	8	10
6 *I'm not at all sure about . . . .*		4–6	8	10
7 *I don't really believe . . . .* 8 *I don't think . . . .*			6	7

in other situations

9 *I'm not too happy about . . . .*				4–6
10 *I don't hold out much hope for . . . .*				6
11 *. . . am/is/are bound to fail/lose etc.* [or other pessimistic words]				15

I   A friend at work, David, has shown you his new design for a product, but you know the management is not going to like it.

Do you think the boss will go for this?

12	*No, (sorry,) can't (really) see* him accepting it.	5	7
13	*Fat chance . . . !* 14 *No way!/There's no way . . . .*	0	7
15	*. . . is bound to reject it/hate it/ditch it* etc. [or other pessimistic words]		15
16	*Fat chance of . . . !*		4–6
17	*. . . is bound not to . . . .*	0	3

in other situations

18	*Can't be done.*	0

F   You are having coffee with a fellow delegate to an international trade conference.

What are the prospects of reaching agreement today?

19	*(Actually,/In fact,/To be honest,/To tell the truth,/I have to say) I'm not all that optimistic . . . .*	0	7
20	*(Actually,/In fact,/To be honest,/To tell the truth,/I have to say) I'm fairly pessimistic . . . .*	0	7
21	*(Actually,/In fact,/To be honest,/To tell the truth,/I have to say) I'm fairly pessimistic about . . . .*	4–6	8
22	*I'm (rather) sceptical about . . . .*	4–6	8
23	*I have to admit to doubts about . . . .*	4–6	8
24	*I suspect . . . .* [with pessimistic words]	6 7	14
25	*I'm wondering . . . .* [with pessimistic words]		8–10
26	*(I don't want to sound too pessimistic, but) I'm afraid . . . .* [with pessimistic words]		7

Practice

a   A colleague thinks you will pass your English driving test easily. You feel pessimistic about your chances.
   ▶ What do you say?

b   You are talking to your friend, Chris, in the office.
   Chris: *D'you think the boss'll give us a bonus this month?*
   You think: *No.*
   Chris: *Well, damn it, we've earned one!*
   ▶ What do you say?

c   At a sales review, the manager wants to know if sales can be increased by 10%
   ▶ What do you say?
   i   *I rather doubt that.*
   ii   *Fat chance of that happening!*
   iii   *No way we can do that!*
   iv   *I don't hold out much hope for an increase of that size.*

Key   **a** 1–11   **b** 12–17 most appropriate, 1–8, 10 also possible   **c** i or iv (ii and iii too informal)

26 Saying you are worried or afraid

How do you find driving in London?

Well, **I'm worried about** getting lost. It's so big.

1 *I'm worried about . . . .*	4–6	8–10

A colleague you know is ill and has been in bed for several days.

2 *I find her condition (very) worrying.*		16
Yes, I think maybe she's going to need an operation.		
3 *I'm (very) worried/uneasy . . . .*	0	7
4 *I'm afraid . . . .*	0 1	7
5 *I'm (very) worried/uneasy about . . . .*	4–6	8–11

---

in other situations

6 *I'm frightened . . . .*	0 1	7
7 *I'm (really) frightened of . . . .* 8 *I'm afraid of . . . .*		8
9 *I'm (really) terrified . . . .*	0 1	7
10 *I'm (really) terrified of . . . .*	4	6

I You are at the zoo with some friends and their young child, Polly.

11 *I'm scared that we'll lose Polly somewhere.*	0 1	7
Well, so long as she doesn't try and climb in with the lions!		
12 *I'm scared (stiff) of . . . .*	4	6
13 *I'm worried sick . . . .*		7
14 *I'm worried sick about . . . .*	4–6	8–11
15 *I'm worried sick by . . . .*	4	6

---

in other situations

16 *I'm (really) in a flap.* 17 *I've got the wind up.*		0
18 *I'm (really) in a flap about . . . .*	4–6	8–11
19 *I've got the wind up about . . . .*		4–6
20 *. . . gives me the creeps/jitters.*		15

F Your managing director is talking to you about a building contract.

21 *I'm (very) concerned that we may not meet the deadline on this.*	0	7
Well, there will be a few problems, certainly, but I'm sure we can manage it.		
22 *I'm (very) concerned about . . . .*	4–6	8 10
23 *I have (serious) misgivings/qualms about . . . .*		4–6

24	*I'm (very) anxious . . . .*	0 1	7
25	*I'm (very) anxious about . . . .*	4–6 8	10
26	*I'm (rather) apprehensive about . . . .*	4–6 8	10
27	*I fear . . . .*	6	7

in other situations

28	*. . . gives some cause for anxiety/concern/worry.*	15
29	*I'm extremely nervous of . . . .*	4–6

Practice

a ▶ What does she say?

b A close friend, Don, is taking you by car to an important job interview. The car is caught in a long traffic jam.
▶ What do you say?
  i *I'm very concerned that I will arrive late.*
  ii *I'm worried sick we won't make it.*
  iii *I fear that I may create a bad impression by arriving late.*
▶ What else could you say?

c You are at a one-day conference in Scotland and have just met a businessman. He offers to fly you back in his private plane to London where you are staying at a hotel.
▶ What do you say?
  i *Oh no, flying gives me the jitters.*
  ii *Oh no, I'm scared stiff of flying.*
  iii *Well, actually, I'm extremely nervous of flying.*
▶ What else could you say?

Key **a** 4, 7, 8 most appropriate **b** ii (i and iii too formal) 11, 14 most appropriate, 1, 3–5 also possible **c** iii (i and ii too informal) 23, 26, 29

27 Asking how someone feels after something happens

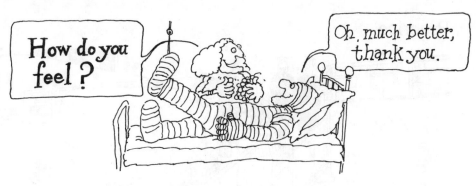

1	***How do you feel?***	0

Someone has invited you to go and see a film. Afterwards he asks you about it.

2	***Did you like*** that?	4–6
	Well, I thought it wasn't too good actually.	
3	***Did you enjoy . . . ?***	4–6
4	***What did you feel about . . . ?***	4–6
5	***What were your feelings about . . . ?***	4–6

in other situations

6	***Are you all right/disappointed/better*** etc?	0

I Your friend, Carol, has taken you to a fair ground. You've just been with her on the big dipper.

7	***(Hey,) what about that?***	0
	That was fun!	
8	***Well?***	0
9	***How did . . . grab you?***	16
10	***Liked/Enjoyed/Hated*** etc ***. . . , did you?***	16
11	***Didn't you like/enjoy*** etc ***. . . ?*** ⎫ [if you don't think the other	4–6
12	***Was . . . awful/unpleasant*** etc? ⎭ person enjoyed the experience]	16

F On the first day of a business trip to England, you have been to a concert with your host.

13	***Did you find*** that ***enjoyable?***	16
	Yes, indeed, I enjoyed it very much, thank you.	
14	***Did you find . . . exciting/worthwhile?***	16
15	***Was/Wasn't . . . to your liking?***	16
16	***What is/are your reaction/reactions?***	0
17	***What is/are your reaction/reactions to . . . ?***	4–6
18	***How did you react to . . . ?***	4–6
19	***Can I ask what your reaction/reactions was/were to . . . ?***	4–6
20	***Do I sense that you didn't much enjoy . . . ?*** [if you don't think the other person enjoyed the experience]	4–6

Practice

a ▶ What does she say?

b You have just taken your friend, Sally, to see the Chamber of Horrors at
a waxworks.
Sally: *Phew!*
You: . . . .
Sally: *It was horrible, but nice.*
▶ What do you say?

c A business colleague, whom you do not know well, tells you that he recently
received a letter informing him he would soon be made redundant.
▶ What do you say?
  i   *How did you react to that?*
  ii *How did that grab you?*
  iii *Can I ask what your reactions were to that?*
▶ What else could you say?

Key **a** 1, 6 most appropriate, 11, 12 also possible **b** 7–12 most appropriate, 2, 3, 6 also possible
c i and iii (ii too informal) 18 (1, 4 and 5 equally possible)

28 Expressing surprise

1 *(Well,) that's very surprising.* 0

You are talking to a fellow guest in the lounge of your hotel about a famous pop singer, Blondie.

Did you know that she's staying here?

2	ゝ *Really?*	0
3	*Here?/Blondie?/Is she?* [or any similar echo question]	32
4	*What a surprise!* 5 *That ˋis a surprise!*	0
6	*(Oh,) that's amazing/extraordinary* etc!	0
7	*Good heavens!* 8 *My goodness!*	0
9	*Good lord!*	0

I A close friend at your office, Charlie, has some news for you.

That old fool Pete Jones has got the sales manager's job.

10	ゝ *What?*	0
11	*No! I don't believe it!* 12 *ˊNever!* 13 *ˊOh, ˋno!*	0
14	*Are you serious?* 15 *You must be joking!*	0
16	*Well, I never!* 17 *Well, I'm blowed/damned* etc.	0
18	*Fantastic/Crazy* etc! 19 *You don't say!*	0
20	*Who'd have thought it?* 21 *Fancy that!*	0
22	*Fancy . . . !*	4 5
23	*You're kidding!*	0

F You have made a formal recommendation that your company should diversify its products. Your managing director has asked to speak to you.

I'm afraid the board hasn't accepted your recommendation.

24	*I find that very surprising.*	16
25	*I must say . . . surprises me/comes as a (total) surprise.*	16
26	*I find it astonishing/extraordinary/incredible* etc	0 7
27	*Indeed?* 28 *How very surprising/amazing* etc.	0
29	*I must say . . . surprises me.*	16

in other situations

30	*I must say . . . has taken me completely by surprise.*	16

Practice

a ▶ What does he say?

47

b Your holiday in Britain with your friend, Nino, is just finishing. Nino suddenly says: *I've decided I'm not going back home. I'm going to join a rock group in Coventry and live here for a year or two.*
▶ What might you say?

c At a board meeting, the investments manager states that the firm has just invested a large sum of money in another company. You know that that company is about to collapse.
▶ What do you say?
i *You must be joking!*
ii *Well, I'm blowed!*
iii *I must say your statement surprises me.*
▶ What else could you say?

Key a 1, 5–9 (16, 17 possible)   **b** 10–19, 21–23 (2–9 also possible)   **c** iii (i and ii too informal)
24–28, 30 most appropriate, 1, 2; 5–9 also possible

29 Saying you are pleased

1 *I'm very pleased with ....*   6

Someone you have just met has just received a telegram from her son-in-law.

It says my daughter has just had a son, and they're both doing well.
2 *(Oh,) how marvellous!*   0
3 *(Oh,) ...'s wonderful/marvellous etc.*   15
4 *(Oh,) ... is good news.*   15
5 *I'm (very) pleased/(really) delighted.*   0
6 *I'm (very) pleased/(really) delighted about ....*   4–6
7 *...'s good/wonderful/splendid etc news.*   15

---

in other situations

8 *...'s the best thing/news I've heard for a long time/I've heard in years.*   15

I A friend, Jon, has been trying to get tickets for the Wimbledon tennis championships.

Phew! I had to queue for hours, but I got them.
9 *Great!*   **10** *Terrific!*   **11** *Fantastic!*   **12** *Super!*   0
13 *Smashing!*   **14** *Hey, that's terrific/great etc.*   0

48

You are at a reception. Your host, whom you do not know very well, informs you that his son has just become engaged to be married.

> Yes, they plan a June wedding and a honeymoon in Sicily.

15	*(Oh,) I'm delighted to hear that.*	6 7
16	*(Oh,) I'm delighted to hear about . . . .*	5 6
17	*It gives me great pleasure to hear . . . .*	6 7

in other situations

18	*It gives me great pleasure/satisfaction . . . .*	0 1
19	*I can't ˅say how pleased/delighted I am . . . .*	0 1 7
20	*I can't ˅say how pleased/delighted I am about . . . .*	4–6

Practice

a ▶ What does she say?

MR COOPER   MR DOWNES

b ▶ Who is saying something inappropriate? What should he say?

c You have been staying in England for some time. Your friends buy you a large bottle of champagne for your birthday and your immediate reaction is one of delight.
▶ What do you say?

Key **a** 2, 4, 7 most appropriate, 9–14 also possible   **b** Mr Downes. 2–8   **c** 9–14 most appropriate, 2, 3, 5 also possible

30 Saying you are displeased or angry

1 *I'm very annoyed ....*	0 1 7

You have gone to collect your car from a garage where it has been for repairs. You want to leave at once to drive to the seaside.

I'm afraid it won't be ready until tomorrow.

2 *Oh no!* 3 *Oh dear!* 4 *Oh bother!* [very mild]	0
5 *What a nuisance!* 6 *How infuriating/irritating* etc*!*	0
7 *... really makes me cross/angry* etc.	15
8 *... annoys/irritates* etc *me.*	15
9 *... really isn't ˋgood enough.*	15

in other situations

10 *... isn't very nice/pleasant* etc.	15
11 *I really hate ....* [very strong]	4–6

I You are staying with friends, Mike and Steve. Steve has borrowed your expensive camera without asking you. Mike tells you this.

Steve's just rung up. It's been stolen.

12 *Oh, that's great!* [sarcastic]	0
13 *Oh, hell, no.* 14 *Oh bloody hell!* [swear words]	0
15 *Oh damn!/blast!/hell!* [swear words] 16 *Hell's bells!*	0
17 *Oh no, what next?*	0
18 *... (really) makes me mad.*	15
19 *... (really) makes me see red.*	15
20 *... (really) makes my ˋblood boil.*	15
21 *What an idiot/fool* etc.	0
22 *Why on earth/Why the hell didn't he ... ?*	3
23 *I've had (just about) enough of ....*	4–6
24 *I can't stand ....* 25 *I'm fed up with ....*	4–6

in other situations

26 *That's the last straw!*	0
27 *Look here, ...*	33–37

F You were expecting one of your employees to submit an important report today, but he has arrived without it.

28 *This **is extremely irritating.***	15
Yes, I'm sorry, but there have been unforeseen problems.	
29 *... is most/very/extremely* etc *annoying/exasperating* etc.	15
30 *I'm extremely/very/most* etc *displeased/unhappy/angry* etc	0 1 7
31 *I'm extremely/very/most* etc *displeased/unhappy/angry* etc *about ....*	4–6
32 *I can't say I'm at ˅all pleased ....*	0 1 7
33 *I can't say I'm at ˅all pleased about ....*	4–6
34 *I can't say I'm at ˅all pleased by ....*	4–6

---

in other situations

35 *I find ... most/extremely* etc *offensive/objectionable* etc.	16
36 *I must say I resent/object to ....*	4–6
37 *I will not put up with ....*	4–6
38 *I take great/considerable* etc *exception to ....*	4–6

Practice

a ▶ What does he say?

b You get home one evening with your friend, Pete, and find you've left your front door key at work—twenty minutes' walk away.
▶ What do you say?

c Your employer tells you that, owing to difficulties in the firm, you will have to work longer hours, with no increase in salary or holidays.
▶ What do you say?
  i *Hell's bells!*
  ii *I'm extremely unhappy about this.*
  iii *Bloody hell!*
▶ What else could you say?

Key a 1, 2, 6–9, 28–31, 26, 27 also possible **b** 12–16, 21 most appropriate, 2–6 also possible
c ii (i and iii too informal), 32–34

51

31 Saying you are relieved

1 *(Oh,) that's a relief.*   0

You fill up your car with petrol at a filling station. Suddenly you discover you have no cash to pay for it. You ask the cashier if she will accept a cheque.

Yes, certainly.
2 *(Oh,) thank goodness for that.*   0
3 *Thank goodness for . . . .*   6
4 *Thank goodness!*   **5** *Thank heavens!*   0
6 *(Oh,) good/marvellous!*   **7** *(Oh,) what a relief!*   0

I You have been shopping with your friend, Dolores, and are coming back to your car. It has been parked in a parking space for over two hours. You are worried you may have got a parking ticket. Dolores gets to the car before you.

It's OK, there's no ticket.
8 *(Oh,) that's all right, then.*   0
9 *(Oh,) that's a weight off my mind.*   0
10 *That had me worried (for a moment).*   0
11 *(Hm,) am I glad . . . !*   0   1   7
12 *Boy, am I glad about . . . !*   4–6
13 *Whew!*   0
14 *Thank God for . . . .*   6

F An important business letter has been delayed by a postal strike. Before a marketing meeting starts, your managing director says to you:

Oh, you'll be glad to know that letter from TL, Oslo, has arrived.
15 *That's a great relief.*   0
16 *It's a great relief . . . .*   1   7
17 *I'm (very/most) relieved to hear . . . .*   6   7
18 *I'm (very/extremely etc) glad to hear . . . .*   6   7
19 *I'm (very/most) relieved to hear about . . . .*   5   6
20 *I'm (very/extremely etc) glad to hear about . . . .*   5   6

Practice

a ▶ What does she say?

b You borrowed your friend, Steve's, new video-recorder. It suddenly stopped working. You have taken it back to him.
You: *I'm terribly sorry, I think I've broken it.*
Steve: *It's OK. The mains plug's come out, that's all.*
▶ What do you say?

c You have decided to keep a large sum of your firm's cash in Swiss francs. One morning you see a newspaper headline: SWISS FRANC TO BE DEVALUED BY 20%. You are horrified. Later, a business associate telephones you from Switzerland.
Associate: *The rumours about devaluation are completely unfounded.*
▶ What do you say?

Key **a** 1–7 **b** 8, 9, 11–14, (1–7 equally possible) **c** 15–20, 1–7 also possible

32 Saying you are disappointed

1 *(Oh,) I ⌄am disappointed ....*   0 1 7

You booked a ticket for a day trip from London to Brighton. But the agent has just told you that the trip has been cancelled.

I'm very sorry, but there haven't been enough bookings for the trip.
2 *That's very disappointing, (I must say).*   0
3 *I'm rather/very etc disappointed ....*   0 1 7
4 *I'm rather/very etc disappointed about ....*   4–6

53

5 *...'s a great pity/disappointment.* 15
6 *What a pity/disappointment.* 0
7 *(Oh dear,) I've/I'd been looking forward to ....* 4–6

in other situations

8 *(Oh dear,) I was hoping/I'd been hoping ....* 1 7
9 *(Oh dear,) I was hoping for ....*   10 *I'm sorry to hear ....* 6
11 *I'm sorry to hear about ....* 5 6

I You have arranged with your friend, Ted, to go out for a picnic. But it is pouring with rain

Look at the weather. No chance of a picnic today.
12 *Oh, no!*   13 *That's too bad.* 0
14 *That's a real shame/pity/let-down.* 0
15 *It's a real shame/pity ....*   16 *Just our luck ....* 0 1 7

F At a meeting of senior executives the sales results for the past year are announced. Sales are up by only 5.3%. The company chairman asks for your views.

Are you satisfied with these figures?
17 *No, I have to say I'm very disappointed. We'd been hoping for 8% at least.* 0 1 7
18 *... comes as a great disappointment.* 15
19 *I must say I had hoped ....* 1 7
20 *I must say I had hoped for ....* 6

Practice

I'M AFRAID THE TRIP TO HOLLYWOOD'S BEEN CANCELLED

a ▶ What does he say?

b   You offer a job in your firm to an excellent candidate. However, he telephones you next morning and says: *I'm afraid I shan't be able to accept the post after all.*
You think: *Oh, no!*
▶ What do you actually say?

c Peter Coles has some bad news for you and your wife: *I'm really sorry, but I can't make it to your party tonight.*

▶ Who is saying something inappropriate?

You: *This comes as a great disappointment.*

Your wife: *Oh, that's a real shame.*

▶ What else could they say?

Key **a** 1–10 **b** 2, 5, 6, 8, 10 **c** You (too formal). 12–15, 5–10 also possible

33 Saying you are excited

1 . . .'s *very exciting.*   15

Someone you have just met is talking about a famous athlete from your country.

Did you know Knutsen broke the world record yesterday?

2 ✓*Really? Oh, that's wonderful.*		0
3 . . . *is exciting/thrilling/sensational* etc.		15
4 *How exciting/marvellous/wonderful* etc	0 1	7

---

in other situations

5 *I find . . . very exciting/interesting* etc.   16

I You are talking to a friend and work colleague, Sabrina.

Have you heard? The boss says we all worked so hard to get the JP project finished yesterday, he's giving us tomorrow off!

6 *Great!*	0
7 *(Hey,) . . .'s terrific/great!* etc.	15
8 *Fantastic!* **9** *Terrific!* **10** *Smashing!* **11** *Super!*	0
12 *Hooray!* **13** *Yippee!* **14** *What a great idea!*	0

---

in other situations

15 . . . *sounds like fun.*   15

F Your company has designed a new product. Your managing director wants your opinion on it.

---

16 *I'm (really) very enthusiastic about* it.	4–6
17 *I'm very enthusiastic.*	0

18 *I'm very excited/fascinated* etc *by . . . .*   5 6

19 *. . . is most exciting/fascinating* etc.   15

20 *I can't deny my enthusiasm for . . . .*   4–6

Practice

a ▶ What does she say?

b A friend tells you that an old friend whom you haven't seen for many years will be arriving in a few minutes.
▶ What do you say?
  i *Hey, that's terrific!*   ii *Oh, how exciting!*
  iii *I can't deny my enthusiasm at the prospect of seeing him again.*

c You are participating in inter-governmental talks.
Your opposite number: *What do you think of the proposal that we collaborate to find new sources of natural energy?*
You think: *Exciting!*
▶ What do you say?

Key **a** 1–4, (6–11 equally possible) **b** i and ii (iii is too formal for the situation) **c** 16–19, 1 and 5 also possible

34 Saying you are bored

1 *I don't find . . . very interesting, (actually).*   16

Another student at an English language school is telling you about the programme of evening lectures at the school.

I don't think I'll go to tonight's lecture. It's on Anglo-Saxon pottery.

2 *Really.*	[only if you	0
3 *How boring/unexciting.*	know the other	0
4 *... looks/sounds/seems etc rather boring, (I think).*	person also isn't	15
5 *(I'm afraid) I'm rather bored by ....*	interested]	4–6
6 *I'm sorry, but ... rather bores me.*		16
7 *I'm sorry, (but) I'm really not terribly interested in ....*	4–6	8–10
8 *I don't think ... is very exciting/interesting, (actually).*		16

I You and a friend are walking past a record shop. The sound of loud pop music is coming out of the shop.

What d'you think of modern pop?

9 *(Actually,) it bores me stiff.*	[only if you	15
10 *... is a (total) bore/drag.*	know the other	15
11 *... leaves me cold.*	person also isn't	15
12 *... really turns me off.*	interested]	15
13 *... is deadly/awfully/incredibly etc boring.*		15
14 *Can't work up much enthusiasm for ....*		4–6
15 *I'm not all that keen on ....*		4–6

---

in other situations

16 *I'm fed up with ....*	4–6

F You are at a formal dinner party, talking at table to your neighbour whom you have not met before this evening.

Did you follow the election at all?

17 *(I'm afraid) I find it difficult to be enthusiastic about politics.*		4–6
18 *To be quite frank, I find ... rather/very etc tedious.*	[only if you know the other	16
19 *I should like to say I find ... interesting, but quite honestly I can't.*	person also isn't interested]	16
20 *Actually, I find ... rather/very/totally etc uninteresting.*		16
21 *I can't honestly say I'm all that interested in ....*	4–6	8–10

Practice

a ▶ What does she actually say?

b You offer to take a representative of a foreign government to see a sculpture exhibition in your capital city. He says: *Sculpture bores me stiff*.

▶ What do you think?

i *You bore me stiff, but I don't say so.*
ii *What a pleasant person!*
iii *Perhaps, but can't you say so politely?*

c A friend asks you what you think about space travel. You find it extremely boring and you know he does too.

▶ What do you say?

Key **a** 1, 7, 8 **b** i or iii **c** 9–16 most appropriate, 1, 4, 5, 8 also possible

35 Calming or reassuring someone

1 (Please) don't worry. 0

Someone you've just met is talking about an English exam that he has to take tomorrow.

I'm certain I'm going to fail it.
2 There's nothing to worry about. *Your English seems very good to me.* 0
3 There's (really) no need to worry/to get upset about 4–6 9 10
4 You (really) needn't worry about 4–6 8 10
5 I shouldn't worry/get upset, if I were you. 0
6 I'm sure things'll turn out all right. 0

---

in other situations

7 I'm sure things'll turn out fine in the end. 0

I You find a secretary in your firm in tears. You ask her what the matter is.

Oh, it's Mr Black. He's been telling me off again about my work.
8 Now, now, take it easy. 0
9 Now, don't get upset/worried about 4–6 8
10 There, there. 11 Steady on. 12 Relax. 13 Don't worry. 0
14 Don't let ... worry you. 16
15 ⌄Cheer ⌐up! 16 ⌄Come ⌐on! It's OK/all right. 0
17 ⌄It's all ⌐right. 18 Try and look on the bright side. 0
19 ... is not as bad as all that. 15

in other situations

20	**The best thing is to keep cool.** ⎫ [especially when the	0
21	**No need to get so worked up.** ⎬ other person is angry	0
22	**No need to get so worked up about . . . .** ⎭ but not with you]	4–6 8–11

F One of your junior executives has come to talk to you about his career.

I didn't get the promotion I was hoping for, and I'm not sure now that I have a future with the company.

23	**Let me reassure you** *that your work is very satisfactory. We just think that you need a little more experience.*	0	7
24	**I assure you . . . .**		7
25	**You need have no fears . . . .**	0	7
26	**You need have no fears about . . . .**	4–6	8–11
27	**There's really no reason/cause to be worried/alarmed** etc.		0
28	**There's really no reason/cause to be worried/alarmed** etc **about . . . .**	4–6	9

in other situations

29	**You may rest assured . . . .** ⎫	7
30	**May I assure you . . . .** ⎬ [often used in writing]	7
31	**May I assure you of . . . .** ⎭	6

Practice

a ▶ What does she say?

b Your friend, Frank, comes into the office, where you and other colleagues are working.
Frank: *God, I'm fed up! Failed my driving test again.*
He gets these replies:
You: *No need to get so worked up, Frank. Try again and you'll pass.*
Bob: *Cheer up! You'll do it next time.*
Sheila: *I assure you that you'll pass next time.*
▶ Who is saying something inappropriate? What would be more appropriate?

c You have just been employed as a translator and have submitted a piece of work to your rather strict employer. He has looked at it and called you in to see him
You: *I'm afraid the English may not be perfect, Mr Evans.*
Mr Evans: *Relax. It's OK.*
▶ Is this appropriate? If not, what is appropriate?

Key **a** 1–5, (13, 14 equally possible) **b** Sheila (too formal), 11, 13, 14, 18, 19, 22 most appropriate, 5, 7 also possible **c** not appropriate, 23–28, 1–4 also possible

36 Asking about likes

1 ***Do you like . . . ?***   1 2 4–6

You are with someone you've just met, wandering in a London street market.

2 ***Do you enjoy*** *spending time in these markets?*   4 6
Yes, I do. I find it very relaxing.
3 ***Are you keen on . . . ?***   4–6
4 ***Don't you like . . . ?***   1 2 4–6
5 ***. . . is nice/pleasant*** etc, ***isn't it?***   15

I Your friend, Jethro, and you are in a record shop listening to the latest album of a popular rock group, Zilch.

6 ***D'you go for*** *Zilch?*   4–6
Well, I can't say it's really my thing.
7 ***Isn't/Aren't . . . great/fantastic*** etc?   16
8 ***Don't you love . . . ?***   1 2 4 6

F At a formal dinner party, you are talking to your hostess.

9 ***May I ask if you are fond of*** *this country?*   4–6
Very much so. It feels like a second home to me.

---

in other situations

10 ***What are your feelings about . . . ?***   4–6
11 ***Don't you find . . . very exciting/enjoyable*** etc?   16

Practice

a ▶ What does he say?

b ▶ What does she say?

   i   *Isn't this scenery great?*   ii   *Are you keen on this scenery?*

   iii   *Are you fond of this sort of scenery?*

c ▶ What does he say?

Key   **a** 1–5 most appropriate, 6–8 also possible   **b** i   **c** 9–11 most appropriate, 1–5 also possible

37 Expressing likes

1 *I like/love . . . .*   1 2 4 6

In a country hotel, two guests are looking at the brochure of activities offered by the hotel.

2 *I'm very keen on pony-trekking.*   4–6

   Mm. I think I enjoy fishing more.

3 *I (really) enjoy . . . .*   4–6

4 *I've always liked/loved . . . .*   1 2 4–6

5 *I do like/love ....*   1 2 4–6
6 *... is wonderful/very enjoyable* etc.   15
7 *... is a lovely/marvellous* etc *way to pass the time/of
  spending an evening/a day off* etc.   15
8 *There's nothing I like/enjoy more than ....*   1 4–6
9 *I adore ....* [very strong]   4–6

I You are at a restaurant with a close friend and business colleague. You are discussing the menu together.

10 *I (really) go for shellfish. But it's so incredibly expensive here.*   6
   Yes, that's the trouble. I think I'll settle for the steak and kidney
   pie, myself.
11 *You can't beat ....*   4–6
12 *I'm (absolutely) crazy/mad/nuts/wild about ....*   4–6
13 *... is (really) terrific/great* etc.   15

in other situations

14 *I'm (really) sold on ....*   4–6
15 *I'm head over heels/over the moon about ....* [very strong]   4–6

F At a trade conference reception, the chairman's wife is talking to you.

And what do you do in your spare time—if you have any?
16 *I'm (really) very fond of sailing.*   4–6
17 *What I particularly/most/greatly* etc *enjoy is ....*   4–6
18 *I have a particular/special fondness for ....*   4–6
19 *... is one of my favourite pastimes.*   15

Practice

a You are talking to a fellow guest you have recently met at your hotel.
Guest: *People seem to like the strangest things. Some of these new films, for example.*
You: *Well, ... the new horror movies.*
▶ What do you say?

b ▶ When would you say this?
You can't beat hang-gliding.
i   A friend asks what your favourite way of spending a weekend is.
ii You are asked what your interests are at a formal interview.
iii Your host at a formal dinner asks you what your pastimes are.

c ▶ What does he say?

Key a 1–5, 8 **b** i (ii and iii not informal enough for these words) **c** 16–19 most appropriate, 1–7 also possible

38 Expressing dislikes

1 *(I'm afraid) I don't like ....*   1 2 4–6

Someone you've met at your hotel suggests that you go to the cinema together.

There's a very good John Wayne film on near here.
2 *I've never liked John Wayne, (I'm afraid).*   1 2 4–6
3 *... is not one of my favourite ....*   24
4 *I (really) hate ....*   1   4–6
5 *I think ... is pretty awful/really unpleasant* etc.   16
6 *I'm not (really) very keen on ....*   4–6
7 *I can't work up any enthusiasm for ....*   4–6
8 *There's nothing I like less.*   0
9 *There's nothing I like less than ....*   1   4–6

---

in other situations

10 *I find it difficult to get on with ....* [for people]   6

I Your friend at the office, Carrie, is telling you about the company outing next week.

It's on Thursday. To Brighton. I think we're all sort of expected
to go.
11 *Oh, I can't stick those outings.*   4–6
12 *I can't bear ....* [emphatic]   1 2 4–6
13 *I can't stand ....*   4–6
14 *... is ghastly/rubbish.*   15
15 *Oh no!*   **16** *Oh God!*   **17** *Oh hell!*   0
18 *Oh, how awful!*   0
19 *I never could put up with ....*   4–6

F One of your directors is discussing a marketing seminar that you have helped to organize.

And, of course, we're expecting you to make the speech of welcome.
20 *Oh dear, I can't say making speeches appeals to me very much.*   16
21 *I have to admit I rather dislike ....*   4–6
22 *I must say I'm not too/particularly fond of ....*   4–6
23 *I especially dislike ....*   4–6
24 *I have a particular dislike of ....*   4–6
25 *I have a particular aversion to ....*   4–6
26 *I'm not over-enthusiastic.*   0
27 *I'm not over-enthusiastic about ....*   4–6

28 *I don't think . . . is particularly/(really) very*
    pleasant/enjoyable.   16
29 *I find . . . particularly/distinctly* etc *unpleasant/unattractive* etc.   16

Practice

a ▶ What does the customer say?

b You are with a group of friends at the zoo, looking at some large spiders.
    ▶ Which of these is inappropriate?
    i   *Ugh, I can't stand spiders.*
    ii *Let's go. Spiders leave me cold.*
    iii *Personally, I have a particular aversion to spiders.*

c The president of a firm you are visiting in Detroit wants to provide some
    entertainment for you.
    President: *How would you feel about going to a baseball game tonight?*
    You think: *Don't like baseball . . . .*
    President: *Well, that's fine. We'll find something you really do like.*
    ▶ What do you actually say?

Key **a** 1–3 **b** iii (too formal) **c** 20–22, 26, 27

39 Asking about preference

1 *Do you prefer . . . or . . . ?*   18

You are at a travel agent's, planning a trip to the U.S.A., and have just booked your flight.

2	***Would you rather** I paid now **or** later?* As you like, sir. It's entirely up to you.	19
3	***Would you prefer** . . . **or** . . . ?*	18
4	***Do you like** . . . **better/more than** . . . ?*	18
5	***Which would you prefer:** . . . **or** . . . ?*	18

in other situations

6	***Do you prefer** . . . ?*	1 2 4 6
7	***Would you prefer** . . . ?*	1 2 6
8	***Would you rather** . . . ?*	3 7
9	***Do you like** . . . **better?***	16
10	***Which seems better/the best, (as far as you're concerned)?***	0
11	***Which would you prefer?***	0

I An old friend, Ray, is arranging a visit for you to his factory. He wants to know what you want to do first.

12	***We can** go for a drink first, **or** have a look at the factory first. **What's it to be?***	21
13	***We can** . . . **or** . . . . **What do you say?***	21

in other situations

14	***What's your favourite** . . . ?*	6

F You are with a visiting sales manager, and want to give him a good lunch.

15	***The choice is yours,** Mr Ojowemi—an English pub **or** a French restaurant?* Oh, I think a pub, since we're in England—if that's all right?	18
16	***We could** . . . **or** . . . . **I leave it to you** (to decide).*	21
17	***Do you find** . . . **or** . . . **more enjoyable/interesting/to your taste** etc?*	20
18	***Which appeals more:** . . . **or** . . . ?*	18

in other situations

19	***Can we establish your preference on the question of** . . . ?* [very formal]	4–6 8–11
20	***How do** . . . **and** . . . **compare, in your opinion?***	20

Practice

You asked for your bill, sir.

...settle the bill now, or when I leave after lunch?

a ▶ What does he say?

65

b An old friend, Tessa, has come to visit you. You are wondering what she would like to do this evening.
You : *We could watch television or go for a walk along the river. I leave it to you to decide.*
▶ What might Tessa think?
i   *He's being very formal—I thought we were old friends.*
ii *How kind and considerate he is!*
iii *Why is he so pompous all of a sudden?*

c You are on the telephone to the director of a firm who is coming to visit your company. He is potentially a very important customer.
You think : *He can either stay in a motel or a traditional British inn.*
You describe both places to him. Then you ask him which one he prefers.
▶ What do you ask?

Key **a** 2, 3, 6, 9 **b** i or iii **c** 16–19, (1–4, 6–9, 11, 12 equally possible)

40 Saying what you prefer

1 *I'd prefer ..., (if possible).*   1 2 4 6

You are talking to someone you have just met, about the sort of holidays you both like.

I enjoy touring around in a caravan.
2 *I'd rather take a tent and camp, (myself).*   3
3 *I like ... more/better than ....*   18
4 *I enjoy ... more/better than ....*   18
5 *I (tend to) prefer ....*   1 4 6
6 *(On the whole,) I find ... more interesting/enjoyable etc than ....*   18
7 *(As far as I'm concerned) ... is more pleasant/fun etc than ....*   15
8 *My choice/preference would always be ....*   1 6

I A friend at work is talking about places he'd like to live in.

I wouldn't mind living in New York.
9 *Oh no, give me San Francisco every time.*   16
10 *I'd go/plump for ... (every time).*   4 6
11 *If it was up to me, I'd ....*   3
12 *I'd rather ... any time.*   17

F Your personnel officer is talking about methods of selecting people for jobs in your company.

Of course, some of these new psychological tests are excellent.

13	*(Well,) I (much/really) prefer the personal interview.*	1 2 4 6
14	*I would (usually/generally etc) choose . . . in preference to . . . .*	18
15	*Rather than . . . , I'd (much/really) prefer to . . . .*	19
16	*I (usually/generally etc) find . . . much more satisfactory/ enjoyable etc than . . . .*	18
17	*(I must say) I have a strong preference for . . . .*	4–6
18	*(On balance,) . . . appeals to me more than . . . .*	18

Practice

a ▶ What does the customer say?

b ▶ What does she say?

c You are phoning the director of a language teaching school whom you've never met, to arrange a course of English lessons for yourself. The director asks if you would like private tuition.
▶ What do you say?
  i *On balance, classes appeal to me more than private lessons.*
  ii *Rather than private lessons, I'd prefer to join a class, if that's possible.*
  iii *Oh no, give me a class every time. More fun.*

Key **a** 1, 2 most appropriate; 13 also possible **b** 9, 10, 12 most appropriate, 2, 3, 5 also possible
c i or ii (iii too informal)

41 Asking if someone approves

1 **Do you think** *they're all right?*   16

At your language school, you have planned an end-of-term party. You speak to your teacher about the arrangements.

2 *We think we might hold it in the big classroom downstairs.* **Would you be in favour of** *that?*   4–6
    Yes, I would.
3 **Do you think . . . will work?/is a good idea?** *etc.*   16
4 **Is . . . all right, d'you think?**   16
5 **Are you in favour of . . . ?**   4–6
6 **You** ↘ **are in favour of . . . , aren't you?**   16
7 **You** ↘ **would be in favour of . . . , wouldn't you?**   16

I You have accidently broken a plate at a friend's house, but have been able to glue it together again.

8 **Is this OK** *now?*   16
    Looks good as new. Thanks.
9 **D'you reckon . . . is OK/all right** *etc?*   16
10 **Have I made a mess of . . . ?** [but hoping for approval]   4 6

---

in other situations

11 **Are you for . . . ?**   4 6

F You want your managing director's opinion on a new manufacturing project.

12 **Could I ask if you approve of** *the project?*   4–6
    I'd like rather more time to study it, if you don't mind.
13 **Do you approve of . . . ?**   4–6
14 **Do you approve?**   0
15 **Is . . . acceptable/satisfactory** *etc?*   16
16 **What is your attitude towards . . . ?**   4–6
17 **Does . . . meet with your approval?**   16
18 **I hope . . . has your approval/support.**   16
19 **I take it . . . has your approval/support.** [expecting approval]   16
20 **Could I ask for your reaction to . . . ?**   4–6
21 **I take it you are not opposed to . . . ?** [expecting approval]   4–6
22 **. . . has your approval, hasn't it?** [expecting approval]   15

Practice

a You and your colleague meet in the foyer after having booked in at a hotel that you have selected. You hope he is happy with your choice.
  ▶ What do you say?

THAT'S FINE, LOVE.

b ▶ What does the driver ask?

c You are responsible for organizing an important reception to be held at a famous hotel. You are having a final look at the room where the reception will take place. The hotel manager says: *D'you reckon everything's OK in here?*
  ▶ What do you think?
  i *That's a rather casual way of asking it.*
  ii *I would have expected a bit more respect in a hotel like this.*
  iii *Nice, friendly chap, this manager.*

Key **a** 1, 4 most appropriate, 8, 9, 13, 14 also possible **b** 8–10 most appropriate, 1, 4 also possible
c i or ii (the words are too informal in this situation to be friendly)

42 Saying you approve

Yes, that's very good.

1 . . .'s very good.   15

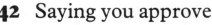

You are having a conversation with an old man you've met in a post office.

They say that we pensioners are going to get a bigger pension soon.
2 *(Oh) good. I'm very much in favour of* that.   4–6
3 . . . *is quite/absolutely etc right.*   15

69

4 *I'm very pleased/happy about*   4–6
5 *That's the way it should be.*   0
6 *What a good/an excellent* etc *idea/arrangement* etc.   0 1

---

in other situations

---

7 *. . . is just what I wanted/hoped for/had in mind.*   15
8 *. . . seems/sounds* etc *just right/fine* etc.   15

I You and some friends are planning a party, but you want to do something unusual.

I know! Let's hire a boat and have our party on that!
9 *That's a great idea!*   15
10 *Terrific!/Smashing!/Fantastic!*   **11** *Fine!*   **12** *Great!*   0
13 *OK!*   0
14 *. . .'s great/fine* etc.   **15** *. . .'s just the job!*   15
16 *I'm all for*   4–6

---

in other situations

---

17 *How terrific!/smashing!/fantastic!* etc.   0

F The possibility has arisen of a merger between your company and a well-known American one. The merger is being discussed at a meeting.

Well gentlemen, can we have your opinions on this proposal?
18 *(Personally,) I entirely approve of the plan.*   4–6
19 *I would certainly give . . . my backing.*   16
20 *I think we can/should* etc *give . . . our full/complete* etc *approval.*   16
21 *(In my opinion,) . . . is the proper/correct* etc *course to take.*   15
22 *(I must say) I find . . . quite satisfactory/acceptable* etc.   16
23 *. . . has my full support.*   15
24 *I can see no reason to oppose*   4–6
25 *I would like to endorse*   6
26 *I can thoroughly recommend* 2 4 6

Practice

a You are booking a long distance flight at a travel agency.
Assistant: *Of course, if there are any delays, the airline will pay for you to stay in a hotel overnight.*
You: . . . .
Assistant: *Yes, well, it's the usual thing to do.*
▶ What do you say?

b You are with a group of friends talking about another friend, Sharon, who loves flying, and whose birthday is next week.
Vanessa: *Let's give her a surprise. Let's book a helicopter flight over London for her!*
▶ Who is saying something inappropriate?
Jim: *I would certainly give that idea my backing.*
You: *That's a great idea!*
Carol: *Terrific!*
▶ What else would be possible?

c At a managerial meeting, it is suggested that Mr French, who works under you, should be promoted to chief sales executive. You approve.
▶ What do you say?
i *Great!*
ii *That suggestion has my full support.*
iii *I can thoroughly recommend Mr French for the position.*
▶ What else could you say?

Key **a** 1, 6 **b** Jim (too formal), 9–11, 13, 14 most appropriate, 6 also possible **c** ii or iii (i too informal), 18–26 most appropriate, 1–8 also possible

43 Saying you do not approve

1 *I don't think . . .'s very good.* 16

In a train your neighbour shows you a newspaper headline: GOVERNMENT TO CLOSE TEN HOSPITALS.

2 *I'm (certainly) not in favour of that. What do you think?* 4–6
I don't know the details, but it sounds bad.
3 *I'm (really) not pleased/displeased/upset etc about . . . .* 4–6
4 *It's wrong to . . . .*   5 *It isn't right to . . . .* 0   3
6 *I can't approve of . . . .*   7 *I (really) don't approve of . . . .* 4–6
8 *I'm not (very) happy about . . . .* 4–6
9 *Is it really necessary . . . ?* 0   1
10 *. . . needn't . . . .*   11 *. . . shouldn't . . . .* 25
12 *How dreadful/appalling etc!* 0

I You run across a friend, Tessa, who seems very upset.

Hey, you know Sheila—she borrowed my car for two days last week, and when I got it back there was melted ice-cream all over the back seat and ground out cigarette ends all over the floor!
13 *(Well,) I don't think much of that.* 4–6   8
14 *. . .'s a rotten/mean etc thing to do/trick etc.* 15
15 *How rotten/mean etc!* 0
16 ⤴*Really!*   17 ⤴*Surely not!* [say with a frown or grimace] 0

in other situations

18 *. . .'s all wrong.* 15
19 *I'm dead against . . . .* [usually to an idea or suggestion] 4–6

F At a board meeting, a director puts forward a suggestion for dealing with the problem of falling sales.

> As I see it, the only solution is to lay off twenty per cent of the labour force.

20 *(Well,) I'm (definitely) opposed to such a move. Perhaps we'd do better to look at our sales staff.* 4–6
21 *(I must say) I disapprove of . . . .* 4–6
22 *I should like to say how much/greatly etc I disapprove of . . . .* 4–6
23 *I feel I must register my disapproval of . . . .* 4–6
24 *I (really) don't feel I can give my approval to . . . .* 4–6
25 *I (certainly) cannot give my approval/support to . . . .* 4–6
26 *(In my opinion,) . . .'s quite wrong.* 16
27 *I would find it difficult to recommend . . . .* 2 4 6
28 *(I must say) I find . . . (quite/completely etc) unsatisfactory/ unacceptable etc.* 16

Practice

a ▶ What does he say?

b ▶ What does she say?
  i *Surely not!*
  ii *I must say I find that very unsatisfactory.*
  iii *I don't think much of that.*
  ▶ What else could she say?

c At a meeting of an international association the member organizations are asked to increase their financial support in order to solve the association's financial problems.

Delegate: *I'm dead against that idea. There must be other ways of working this thing out.*

▶ Is this appropriate? If not, what is appropriate?

Key a 3, 4, 10, 11 most appropriate, 13–16 also possible **b** i or iii (ii too formal), 14–16 most appropriate, 5, 11, 12 also possible **c** not appropriate, 20–28 most appropriate, 2, 5–11 also possible

44 Comparing

1 *...than...*	26

You have met an American and are talking about the prices of various things.

Well, I'll tell you something. Petrol sure is expensive over here.

2 *Yes, but **compared to** other prices in Western Europe, it's really quite reasonable.*	22
3 *If you compare ... and ... , ...*	23
4 *On the whole, ...*	33 35 36

You are visiting an old friend who lives in New Zealand and you are talking about the country.

Which of the two islands d'you reckon is nicer?

5 *Oh, I think South Island **has the edge over** North Island.*	24
6 *You just can't compare ... and ...*	18
7 *I don't see how you can talk about ... and ... in the same breath.*	20
8 *There's no way ... is better/worse etc than ....*	18
9 *... isn't a patch on ....*	24

You are interested in furniture and have met an expert at a dinner party.

What's your opinion of nineteenth century furniture? It seems to be coming back into fashion now.

10 *Yes, some people like it, but **I consider** it to be (greatly) **inferior to** that of the eighteenth century.*	18
11 *(My own assessment is that) ... is (greatly) superior/inferior etc to ....*	24
12 *There's (absolutely) no comparison between ... and ....* [i e one is superior]	18

13 ...*is (incomparably) more interesting/valuable* etc
   than   24
14 ...*is less interesting/valuable* etc *than*   24
15 *I don't consider* ... *to be (in any way) more/less*
   attractive/interesting etc *than*   18
16 *On balance,* ....   17 *By and large,* 33 35 36
18 *All in all,* 33 35 36

Practice

a ▶ What does he say?

b ▶ What does the boy say?

c ▶ When might you say this?
   There's absolutely no comparison between San Francisco and Los Angeles.
   i   when you are having a chat with an old friend from the States
   ii when your employer is asking you about your recent trip to the west coast
       of the U.S.A.
   iii when you have just met another delegate at an architectural conference and
       are talking about cities in the States.

Key a 1–4 most appropriate, 5, 6, 8, 9 also possible **b** 6–9 most appropriate, 1–3 also possible
c ii and iii

45 Saying something is not important

1	... *doesn't matter.*	15

You have got into conversation with another traveller at an airport about different ways of travelling and how safe each one is.

I find that the staff on some airlines can be very unhelpful.
2 **I don't think** *that's (so) important.* At least planes have the best safety record.   16

in other situations

3	... *doesn't (really) make any difference.*	15
4	... *has got nothing to do with it, (surely).*	15
5	*I don't think ... matters.*	16
6	*Does ... matter?*	16

I   You and a friend are planning to drive from London to Glasgow.

It said on the radio that there are long hold-ups on the M1.
7	**What's** *that* **got to do with it?** *We're going by the M6.* ⎫	16
8	*It's/That's neither here nor there.*	0
9	*It/That doesn't make a blind bit of difference.*	0
10	*It's/That's beside the point.*	0
11	... *doesn't matter one bit/a damn.*	15
12	*How does ... come into it?*	16
13	*So what?* ⎭	0
14	*You don't have to worry about ....*	4–6 8–11
15	*I shouldn't let ... worry you.*	16

[emphatic—could sound rude]

F   You are chairing an executive meeting to discuss ways of improving your firm's products. The production chief speaks first.

Well, I think our marketing techniques need looking at.
16	*That* **shouldn't concern us** *(at this point).*	15
17	*I think ... is something we can ignore (for the time being).*	16
18	... *doesn't affect the issue/question under discussion (at the moment).*	15
19	... *is of no great consequence.*	15
20	*I really can't see what relevance ... has, (I'm afraid).*	16
21	... *(just) not the issue/point/question, (as I see it).*	15

Practice

a Someone you have met recently, Phil Turner, has invited you to a party. You are worried because you won't know anyone at the party. Phil Turner doesn't think that is important.
▶ What does he say?

b A very close friend, Bob, wants to go fishing at the weekend, but is worried about the weather. You are very keen to go.
▶ What do you say?

c You are at a company meeting, trying to decide the best way to advertise your products. Someone says:
I hear our usual advertising agency, S & S, are raising their prices in the near future.
▶ Who is saying something inappropriate?
Ms James: *So what?*
Mr Gordon: *That's neither here nor there.*
Mr Felton: *I really can't see what relevance that has at the moment, I'm afraid.*
▶ What else could they say?

Key a 1 and 2; 14, 15 possible **b** 7–15 most appropriate, 1–6 also possible **c** Ms James and Mr Gordon.(their words are too informal); 16–19, 21; 1–6 also possible

46 Asking for someone's opinion

1 *What do you think about . . . ?*   4–6

You are attending a language school in England. Your class has been asked to interview people in the street about their attitude to the existence of language schools in their town.

2 *Excuse me, madam, **what do you feel about** the language schools in Oxford?*   4–6
   Oh, I think they're very good. Excellent, in fact.
3 *What are your views . . . ?*   4–6
4 *What do you think of/about . . . ?*   4–6
5 *What's your opinion of . . . ?*   4–6
6 *What are your feelings about . . . ?*   4–6

in other situations

7 *What's your view/opinion?*   0
8 *What do you think/feel?*   0

76

I You are chatting over coffee to a friend at work, Mick, about recent government financial measures.

9 **What d'you reckon to** *the tax increases?* 4–6
Well, I'm not too worried, but some people I know will be hit
pretty hard.
10 **What about . . . ?**   11 **How d'you feel about . . . ?** 4–6
12 **How d'you see . . . ?** 6
13 **I don't think much of these tax increases, do you?/The tax
increases are pretty awful, aren't they?** [or other suitable
statement with question tag] 29

in other situations

14 **What d'you reckon?** 0

F One of the items on the agenda of an executive meeting you are attending concerns promotions within your organisation.

15 **Have you got any comments on** *the proposed promotion of young
Baker?* 6 10
Well, I'm not convinced he's ready for it yet, but I'm prepared to
listen to other opinions.
16 **What is your reaction to . . . ?** 4–6
17 **Could I know your reaction to . . . ?** 4–6
18 **Do you have any particular views on . . . ?** 4–6 8 9 10
19 **Do you have any opinion on . . . ?** 4–6 8–10
20 **I'd be glad/grateful to have your view/opinion on . . . .** 4–6 10 11

in other situations

21 **How would you react to . . . ?** 4–6
22 **What would you say to . . . ?** } [to a hypothetical proposal] 4–6

Practice

Nuclear power stations?
Well, I wouldn't like to live
near one.

a ▶ What does she say?

b You are a junior executive in a large company which has announced pay
increases for its employees. You ask various people for their opinion of the
increases.
▶ What do you ask each one?
i a friend who shares your office   ii a colleague you don't know very well

iii the head of another department of the company
iv your secretary

c You work for a financial journal. You ring up a Mr Blake, managing director of a large textiles firm, whom you have never met, to ask him about rumours that another firm is making a takeover bid for his firm. You ask: *What about these takeover rumours, Mr Blake?*

▶ Is this appropriate? If not, what is appropriate?

Key **a** 1–6 **b** i 9, 11, 13|most appropriate, 1–6 also possible **b** ii 1–6 **b** iii 16–18 most appropriate 1–6 also possible **b** iv 9, 11, 13 most appropriate, 1–6 also possible **c** No, too informal, 15–20 most appropriate, 1–6 also possible

47 Giving your opinion

| 1 *I think* .... | | | | | 7 | 14 |

You are at the theatre. Before the performance starts, you are having a conversation with the person who happens to be sitting next to you.

What do you think of the theatre in London?

2 *As I see it, it's probably the best in the world.*					33	36
3 *In my view/opinion,*					33	36
4 *(Personally,) I believe*		2	6	7		14
5 *(Personally,) I feel*		2	6	7		
6 *It seems to me*		1		7		14

in other situations

7 *Well, I must say* .... [for strong opinions]			7
8 *Don't you think* ... ? [very polite]		7	14
9 *I'd just like to say*			7
10 *From my point of view,* .... ⎫ [this emphasizes that it		33	36
11 *As far as I'm concerned,* .... ⎭ is *your* point of view]		33	36

I You run a section of a small company. You are holding an informal meeting with a close colleague, Jim Richards, to assess the performance of your staff.

How d'you think Tim Smith's been doing in the last six months?
12 *Well, **to my mind**, he's a bit of a square peg in a round hole.*	33	36
13 *The way I see it,* .... 14 *From where I stand,*	33	36

15	*If you ask me, ...*		33 36
16	*I reckon . . . .*		2 7 14
17	*What I reckon is, ...*		33
18	*I'd say . . . .*		6 7 14

in other situations

19	*You know what I think? (I think) . . . .*	33

F You are attending a scientific conference on energy, and talking to another delegate

20	*I'm convinced that solar power will eventually solve many of our present energy problems.*		7
21	*I consider . . . .*		2 7
22	*I'm of the opinion/view . . . .*		7
23	*It's my opinion/view/feeling . . . .*		7
24	*I hold the view/opinion . . . .*		7
25	*My own view of the matter/problem etc is . . . .*		7
26	*Personally, I consider . . . .*		2 7
27	*It's my considered opinion that . . . .*		7

in other situations

28	*To be quite/perfectly frank/honest etc, ...* ⎫	[usually before	33 36
29	*With all due respect, ...* ⎬	you make an	33 36
30	*If I may say so, ...* ⎭	adverse criticism]	33 36

Practice

a ▶ What does she say?

b The government has just announced an increase in income tax. You think this move is a mistake. You want to tell various people your opinion.
   ▶ What do you say to each person?

	who	*where*
i	your managing director	in the staff canteen
ii	a close friend's wife	at your house
iii	the postman	outside your house

c You are reporting back to a meeting of senior executives at the retail firm where you work, after attending a fashion show. You do not think this year's fashions are going to be popular.

▶ What do you say?

  i *Personally, I consider the fashions I saw unlikely to sell well in the retail trade.*

  ii *It's my considered opinion that these fashions won't succeed in the sort of shops that we represent.*

  iii *I reckon just about everything I saw'll flop. I'm against buying any, that's for sure.*

Key a 1 most appropriate, 16, 18 also possible **b** i 1, 3–8, 11 most appropriate, 13, 18, 20, 28, 30 also possible **b** ii 12, 13, 15–19 most appropriate, 1–8 also possible **b** iii 12–13, 15–18; 1–8, 10, 11 equally possible **c** i or ii (iii too informal)

48 Saying you have no opinion

1 *I really don't have any opinion about . . . .*   4–6 8

You are staying at a hotel in Scotland and talking to one of the staff. He asks:

And what d'you think about the question of Scottish independence?

2 *I (really) couldn't say, (I'm afraid) . . . .*   0 8 10

3 *I've no strong feelings about . . . .*   4–6 8 10

4 *I (really) don't know what to say.*   0

5 *It doesn't (really) affect me/matter to me, (I'm afraid) . . . .*   0 8 10

6 *I (really) don't know what to think about . . . .*   4–6

I At work, there is a rumour that the canteen will be closed because it is uneconomic. A friend of yours, Pete, is annoyed about this.

You don't really think they'll do that, do you?

7 *Your guess is as good as mine.*   0

8 *I don't know.*   0

9 *It makes no odds to me . . . .*   8 10

F You are at a trade conference in Los Angeles, talking to your neighbour just before a seminar begins.

What is your reaction to the recent government paper on international law?

10 *It is not something I've considered a great deal, (I'm afraid).*   15

I'm primarily concerned with the home market.

11 *I can't say I have/hold any (particular) views on the subject/
question,* etc.   0

12 *I don't hold any (particular) position on that matter/issue* etc.   0

Practice

a ▶ What does he say?

b Your firm has announced the introduction of flexible working hours in the near
future. A colleague you know well asks: *How d'you see this flexible hours thing
working out?*
  ▶ What do you say?
  i *I can't say I have any particular views on the subject.*
  ii *It makes no odds to me.*
  iii *It's not something I've considered a great deal, I'm afraid.*
  ▶ What else could you say?

c You are attending a conference on environmental conservation. You ask the
chairman's opinion on a rather obscure and difficult point. The chairman says:
It's not something I've considered a great deal, I'm afraid.
  ▶ What do you think?
  i *That's a strange way to talk to me.*   ii *How unfriendly he is.*
  iii *At least I received a polite answer.*

Key a 2, 4 (7, 8 equally possible)   **b** ii (i and iii too formal) 7, 8 most appropriate, 2, 4, 6 also
possible   **c** iii

49 Avoiding giving an opinion

1 *I'd rather not say anything about ....*   4–6 8

81

Your fellow passenger on a train from New York to Boston is talking about an announcement made recently by the President.

Well, I'd say he was a damned fool to talk like that.

2 *D'you think so?*		0
3 *Was he?*		32
4 *It's difficult to say*	0	7–11
5 *I suppose it depends on your/one's point of view.* 6 *Really?*		0

in other situations

7 *I'd have to think about*	4	6	8–11
8 *I'm sorry I can't answer*		0	6
9 *I'd prefer not to say anything about*	4–6	8	10
10 *No comment, (I'm afraid).*			0
11 *Is it?/Was it?/Would they?* [or other echo question]			32

I There has been a row in your company about policy and one executive has resigned. A friend, Paul, is talking to you about this.

Don't you think Frank was right to resign?

12 *Well, I don't know (really)*	0	8	10
13 *Well, now you're asking.* 14 *It/That all depends.* 15 *Maybe.*			0
16 *Perhaps.* 17 *Could be.* 18 *Can't say, (really).*			0
19 *That's ˅your opinion,˥ is it?* 20 *Search me!*			0

in other situations

21 *Not my department, I'm afraid.*	0

F You have heard a rumour that expense accounts in your company are to be closely investigated. You meet your immediate boss, Mr Bremner, in the corridor.

Excuse me, Mr Bremner, could I ask you what you think about the director's decision to investigate our expense accounts?

22 *(I'm afraid) I can't comment on* that at the moment.	5	6	8	10
23 *It's difficult to give an opinion right now/at the moment* etc.				0
24 *I don't (think I) have anything to say on*		4–6	8	10
25 *I'd rather not commit myself on* ..., *(if you don't mind).*		6	8	10
26 *I'm not in a position to say anything about*		4–6	8	10
27 *(I'm afraid) you'd have to ask* ... *about that.*				16

Practice

a   The young man doesn't want to give an opinion.
▶ What does he say?

b   A friend, Liz, is talking about a book which both she and you have read.
Liz: *Didn't you think it was the greatest book ever?*
You think: *No—but I don't want to say so directly.*
▶   What do you actually say?

c   ▶   What does the executive say?

Key   a 2, 4, 5, 11 most appropriate, 13, 15–17, 19 also possible   **b** 12–17 most appropriate, 2, 4–6, 11 also possible   **c** 22–27 most appropriate, 1, 8–10 also possible (10 best answer for this situation)

50   Trying to change someone's opinion

1   *But don't you think . . . ?*

Someone sitting next to you in a bus shows you a newspaper headline: TEN KILLED IN CLIMBING DISASTER.

You know, I think all climbing should be stopped. Too many people get killed.

2 *(Yes, but) do you really think* it would be possible to stop it?	6 7 14
3 *(Yes, but) surely you don't think/believe* etc	6 7
4 *(Yes, but) is/isn't it possible that . . . ?*	7
5 *(Yes, but) another way of looking at it would be (to say) that . . . .*	7
6 *Surely not, I mean . . . .*	33 35–37
7 *(Yes, but) on the other hand . . . .*	33–35 37

I At your friend, Bert's, house you have just watched England being beaten 3–0 in an international match.

> God, they were rubbish. No idea at all. It makes me weep.

8 *Hold on, they weren't that bad. After all, they were playing the best team in the world.*   33–37

9 *No, but look, ...*   33–37

10 *Well, think of it this way, ...*   33–35

11 *But look at it like this, ...*   33–35

12 *You don't really think . . . ?*   6   7

13 *Are you kidding? . . .*   33   35–37

14 *You can't mean that, surely?*   0

F You are at an international symposium on fishing rights. One delegate is complaining to you about a certain country.

> I really think they had no right to extend their fishing limits to 200 miles.

15 *But seen from another angle, one might say they are totally dependent on fish for their economic survival.*   7

16 *But if we look at it in another light, ...*   33–35

17 *Of course, an alternative view/opinion might/would be that . . . .*   7

18 *But there are other considerations. For example, ...*   33–35   37

19 *I wonder if you have taken everything into account/consideration. For instance, ...*   33–35   37

20 *Yes, but if we look at the whole picture, ...*   33–35   37

21 *I wonder if that view/opinion is justified in the light of . . . .*   5   6

22 *I respect your opinion/view, of course. However, ...*   33–35   37

23 *Well, I think others might say . . . .*   7

Practice

a   You are on a visit to London and are talking to another guest in your hotel.
He says: *I think all these parks are a waste of space. They should build houses and office-blocks instead.*
You like the parks.
▶   What do you say?

b ▶   What does she say?

c You are at an informal party. The conversation is about education and one guest says that the English system of comprehensive schools has been a total failure.
▶ Who is saying something inappropriate?
Sally: *Hold on a minute, it's too early to say that yet.*
Michael: *Well, I think others might say that is a premature judgement.*
Peter: *Surely you don't think it's possible to generalize in that way?*

Key   a 1–7   **b** 8–14 most appropriate, 1–7 also possible   **c** Michael (too formal)

51 Asking if someone is interested

1 *Are you interested in . . . ?*		4–6 8–10

You are in Sydney, Australia, and talking to someone about music.

2 *They're doing 'Carmen' at the Opera House. **Does** opera **interest** you (at all)?*	16
Oh, yes, it does. How can I get a ticket for it?	
3 *Are you interested in . . . at all?*	16
4 *Do you find . . . interesting (at all)?*	16

in other situations

5 *What are your interests?*	6 *What are you interested in?*	0

I You are thinking of buying a chess set and wonder if your friend, Rob, is interested in the game.

7 *Are you keen on chess (at all)?*	4 6
I've never played it. But I'd like to try.	
8 *Are you a . . . fan?*	16
9 *Do you go for . . . (at all)?*	4 6
10 *Does . . . grab you (at all)?*	16

F You are at the start of a Mediterranean cruise and talking to your neighbour at dinner. You have just met.

11 *I wonder if you have any interest in Greek archaeology (at all)?*	4 6
Up to a point, but I've really come for health reasons.	

Practice

a ▶ What does he ask?

b You want to get a group together to go on a weekend camping trip.
▶ What do you ask each of these people?

	who	where
i	a colleague	at the office
ii	a close friend	at your home

c Your boss sends for you in his office. He introduces a very important client to you. Suddenly he has to leave and you have to keep the conversation going. You wonder if he is interested in the English theatre.
▶ What do you say?

Key a 1–4 **b** i 1–4 most appropriate, 7–9 also possible **b** ii 7–9 most appropriate, 1–4 also possible **c** 11–13 most appropriate, 1–4 also possible

52 Saying you are interested

1 *I'm interested in . . . .*   4 6 8–10

You are talking to another guest at a hotel with whom you are sharing a table.

And what do you do when you're not working?
2 *Well, **my particular interest is** collecting antiques.*   4 6
3 *... **interests me a lot/a great deal** etc.*   15
4 *I **have some/a great** etc **interest in** ....*   4 6
5 *My **main interest is** ....*   4 6
6 *I **find** ... **quite/very** etc **interesting**.*   16
7 *My **hobby is** ....*   4 6

I You are telling a work-mate about your private interests.

8 *Well, **I'm (very) keen on** modern jazz.*   4 6
   Oh? I prefer the traditional stuff myself.
9 *I'm a ... **fan**.*   10 *I **go for** ... **in a big way**.*   16
11 *... **is what grabs me/turns me on**.* [usually more 'unusual' interests] 15

F You are visiting an associate company in Chicago. Tonight you are the guest of the company vice-president at dinner.

Well, and how do you like our city?
12 *I'm delighted to be here, **I find** Chicago **(quite/extremely)**
    fascinating.*   16
13 *... **fascinates/intrigues me (a great deal)**.*   15
14 *... **has always interested/fascinated** etc **me**.*   15
15 *I'm **(quite/extremely) fascinated/intrigued** etc **by** ....*   4 6

in other situations

16 *I **have a passion for** ....*   4 6

Practice

a ▶ What does he say?

b You and a close colleague at work are chatting about leisure activities. Your favourite pastime is bridge.
    ▶ What do you say?
    i   *I'm a bridge fan.*
    ii *I go for bridge in a big way.*
    iii *I find bridge quite fascinating.*
    ▶ What else could you say?

87

c You are representing your company at an important reception. You are talking to another representative whom you have just met.

Representative: *And what are your interests apart from work?*

You: *The history of medicine is what turns me on, actually.*

▶ Is this appropriate? If not, what is?

53 Saying you are not interested

1 *I'm not very interested in . . . .*	4 6 8 10

You have gone into the television room at your hotel with another guest. You find that there is nothing but sport on the TV.

I wish they wouldn't always show sport in the afternoons.

2 *Yes, I must say **I don't find** sport **very interesting** either.*	16
3 ***Actually, I don't have any/much interest in** . . . .*	4 6
4 *I find . . . **rather uninteresting/boring**, I'm afraid.*	16
5 *. . . **isn't all that interesting as far as I'm concerned**.*	15

I You are in Britain for some time and a friend, Susie, is talking about various activities that might interest you.

Don was saying you might be keen on joining the local amateur choir.

6 *No, actually, **that sort of thing isn't for me**.*		16
7 ***I just can't get worked up about** . . . .*		4–6 8 10
8 *(I'm afraid) . . . **leaves me cold**.*		16
9 *(I'm afraid) . . . **just isn't my cup of tea**.*		16
10 *(I'm afraid) **I couldn't care less about** . . . .*	[sounds rude unless	4–6
11 *(I'm afraid) **I don't give a damn about** . . . .*	used to close friends	4–6
12 ***What's so interesting about** . . . ?*	who wouldn't be	4–6 8 10
13 *. . . **bores me stiff**, I'm afraid.*	easily offended]	15

F You are acting as a consultant to an engineering firm. On your first day you meet the firm's chairman who broaches the subject of finance.

I see your currency has fallen against the pound again.

14 *Well, as an engineer, (I must admit) I don't take any great interest in international finance.*	4 6 8 10
15 *I can't say I find/consider etc . . . so very interesting/ fascinating etc.*	16
16 *I can't say . . . concerns me a great deal.*	15

in other situations

17 *(Actually), . . . is a matter of some indifference to me.*	[only use if you wish to be very	15
18 *Nothing interests me less than . . . , (as a matter of fact).*	emphatic—verging on rude]	4–6 8 10

Practice

a ▶ What does he actually say?

b Bill, a friend of yours, suggests that the two of you go to a pop festival.
You say: *I must admit I don't take any great interest in pop music.*
▶ What does Bill think?
  i *Well, that's not very polite.*
  ii *Why is he being so pompous?*
  iii *Right, I'd better think of something else.*
▶ What could you say?

c A junior employee of yours has met you in the lift. He asks you if you have read a certain journalist's review of the economic situation in today's newspaper.
You reply: *I couldn't care less about the man's views.*
▶ Is this appropriate? If not, what is?

Key **a** 1–4 **b** ii, 6–9 most appropriate, 1–5 also possible **c** not appropriate; 5, 15, 16

54 Giving reasons

1 *(Well,) because . . . .*   12

You are having dinner with a fellow guest at your hotel by the seaside.

> I didn't see you at breakfast. Why was that?

2 *(Well,) I got up early (so as) to* have a walk along the beach before
it got crowded.

3 *. . . so that . . . .*   13

4 *Well, you see, ...*   33   35

5 *The reason was that . . . .*   7

6 *Let me explain. You see, ...*   33

in other situations

7 *But the point is, ...*   33   35

8 *But surely, ...*   33   35

9 *The simple reason was that . . . .* [could sound impatient]   7

I Your friend, Jane, is going out with Fred. But she is cross.

> I'm fed up. Fred won't let me drive his car. And there's nothing
> wrong with my driving.

10 *Well, the thing is,* it's not insured for you.   33   35

11 *Fred's got a point. You see, ...*   33   35

12 *But surely Fred's dead right: . . . .*   33   35

in other situations

13 *It's like this; you see, ...*   33

F Your employer has called you into his office to talk to you about your colleague,
Hank Perry.

> I don't understand. Perry has turned down the Hong Kong job.
> I thought it would be a marvellous opportunity for a young man.

14 *If I could explain:* his wife doesn't want to go overseas. It's as
simple as that.   33

15 *The main/basic* etc *reason is that . . . .*   7

16 *I think there's actually a good case for . . . .*   4–6

17 *I think . . . is right/justified for the following reasons: . . . .*   18
18 *I think . . . warrants/justifies . . . .*   18
19 *I believe John Jones/Mrs Sims etc is fully justified in saying/suggesting etc that . . . .*   0 7
20 *John Jones/Mrs Sims etc has every justification for his/her decision/opinion etc.*   0

Practice

a ▶ What does the leader actually say?

b ▶ What does the other man say?
  i   *But surely John's right. There's no budget for it.*
  ii *I believe John is fully justified in his opinion.*
  iii *Well, it's like this, you see. The money for new projects has run out.*

c ▶ When would you say this?
  In my opinion, Mr Scott has every justification for his conclusion that the company is overproducing.
  i   You are having a conversation with your secretary.
  ii You are chatting with a close colleague at work.
  iii You are talking to the head of the department in which you are employed.

Key a 1, 4, 6 **b** i or iii (ii too formal) **c** iii, situations i and ii not sufficiently formal

55 Asking if someone agrees

1 ***Don't you agree?***   0 7

You are in the television lounge at your hotel in Dallas, Texas, with another guest.

---

2 *There are far too many commercials on American TV,* ***wouldn't you say?***
    Yes, they ruin the programmes completely.   33

3 ***There are too many commercials on American TV, aren't there?/***
    American TV has too many commercials, doesn't it?
    [or other statement + question tag]   29

4 ***Wouldn't you say so?***   0

5 ***You'd agree with . . . , wouldn't you?***   16

6 ***. . . , don't you think?***   33

7 ***Don't you think so?***   0

8 ***Don't you feel/think . . . ?***   7

9 ***. . . , or am I talking nonsense?***   33

I At work you and a friend, Jim, have a complex problem to solve.

---

10 *I think this is something for the computer to look at.* ***Right?***   0

11 ***Yeah?***   **12** ***OK?***   **13** ***OK/All right with you?***   0

14 ***OK by you?***   **15** ***D'you go along with that?***   0

---

in other situations

---

16 ***. . . , or is that a load of rubbish/nonsense?***   33 35

17 ***. . . , or am I talking through my hat?***   33 35

F At a formal union meeting you are discussing proposals to put forward to your
management.

---

18 *And next, it has been suggested that we ask management to improve*
    the employees' pension scheme. ***Would you agree*** *that that is*
    justified?   0 7
    Oh, certainly. And long overdue, as far as I'm concerned.

19 ***Do/Would you agree with . . . ?***   6

20 ***Is . . . agreed?***   16

21 ***You don't/wouldn't disagree, do/would you . . . ?***   0 7

22 ***You don't/wouldn't disagree with that (view*** *etc),*
    do/would you?   0

23 ***I wonder if you would agree . . . .***   0 7

24	*Can I ask you if you (would) agree . . . ?*	0 7
25	*I wonder if you would agree with . . . .*	6
26	*Can I ask if you (would) agree with . . . ?*	6
27	*Would you concur with such a proposal/suggestion etc?*	0

Practice

a You are attending English classes in England. Another student you have just met has just said that English is easy to learn. She wants to know if you agree.

▶ What does she ask you?

b ▶ What does he actually say?

c At an executive meeting someone has a proposal to make: *With the recent increase in staff, we should do something about improving recreation facilities. Would you agree with that suggestion?*

▶ Is this appropriate? If not, what is?

Key **a** 1–9 **b** 10–17 most appropriate, 1, 2, 4, 6–9 also possible **c** appropriate

56 Agreeing

| 1 | *Yes, I agree . . . .* | 0 7 |

You are visiting a small town in Canada and talking to another visitor.

I suppose it's too much to expect to find a decent restaurant in a town like this.

| 2 | *True enough. But it's only a small place, isn't it?* | 0 |
| 3 | *That's (quite) right/true.*   4 *I can't help thinking the same.* | 0 |

5 *That's (just) what I was thinking.*　　**6** *I couldn't agree more.*　　　　0

---

in other situations

7 *How true.*　　**8** *How right you are/that is.*　　　　0
9 *I (absolutely/entirely etc) agree ....*　　　　0 7
10 *Oh, exactly/definitely/absolutely/quite etc.*　　　　0

I　At work, you are talking to a friend, Dave, about another colleague, Tony, who has been sacked.

> Tony was stupid. He should never have tried to fiddle the books. It was too obvious.

11 *Well, that's the thing. He couldn't hope to get away with it.*　　　　0
12 *Well, this is it/that's it, (isn't it)?*　　　　0
13 *Yes.*　　**14** *Yeah.*　　**15** *Right.*　　**16** *Dead right.*　　　　0
17 *Too true.*　　**18** *I'd go along with you there/with that.*　　　　0
19 *I'm with you there.*　　**20** *You're (so) right.*　　　　0

F　You are at a book trade fair and discussing the future with a representative from another firm.

> I think the prospects for medium-priced hardbacks are definitely promising.

21 *Oh, I agree entirely. That's just what our marketing people have been saying.*
22 *I agree entirely/absolutely etc with ....*　　　　6
23 *My own view/opinion etc exactly/precisely etc.*　　　　0
24 *That's exactly/precisely etc my own view/opinion etc.*　　　　0
25 *I'm of exactly the same opinion.*　　　　0
26 *I'm of exactly the same opinion as ....*　　　　6
27 *I think I'd accept ....*　　　　6
28 *I don't think anyone could/would disagree ....*　　　　0 7
29 *I don't think anyone could/would disagree with ....*　　　　6

---

in other situations.

30 *I'd like to endorse that/your view/opinion etc.*　　　　0
31 *Hear, hear.* [at a public meeting or debate]　　　　0

Practice

a ▶ What does he actually say?

b You are talking to a friend, Richard, at work, about the oil industry.
Richard: *The point is, we can't rely on oil for ever.*
You think: *.... agree ....*
▶ What do you actually say?

c ► What does he actually say?

Key a 1, 3, 6, 9, 10; 13–16, 18–20 also possible **b** 11–20 most appropriate, 1–10 also possible
c 21–26, 28, 29 most appropriate, 1, 5, 6, 9, 10 also possible

57 Disagreeing

1	*(Oh,) I don't agree.*			0

You are in an airport lounge, waiting to leave on a delayed flight. Your neighbour is complaining.

It'll be the fault of the unions again. It usually is.

2	*(Well,) as a matter of fact, they said it was due to technical problems.*	33	35	36
3	*I'm not (at all) sure, actually/in fact.* **4** *Not really.*			0
5	*(Oh,) I don't know . . . .*	0	7	10
6	*(Oh,) I don't know about . . . .*			4–6
7	*No, I don't think . . . .*		7	14
8	*Actually/In fact, I think . . . .* [followed by a different opinion]		7	14
9	*I disagree, (I'm afraid,) . . . .*		0	7
10	*That's wrong/not right, surely.* **11** *I don't think that's right.*			0
12	*That's not the way I see . . . .*			6
13	*I can't agree . . . .*		0	7
14	*I can't agree with . . . .*			6
15	*I can't help thinking . . . .* [followed by a different opinion]		6	7
16	*But isn't it more a matter/question of . . . ?*		4–6	8–11
17	*But isn't it more to do with . . . ?*		4–6	8 10
18	*Do you really think . . . ?*		7	14
19	*I think that's nonsense, (I'm afraid).* [for very strong disagreements]			0

I You have been watching a TV programme on America's space programme with your friend, Bill.

Hm! I think the whole thing's a complete waste of money.

20	**(Oh,) surely not!** *It's given us all sorts of knowledge and new technology. Besides, it's been exciting!*		0
21	**I don't see why.**		0
22	**I can't go along with ....**	6	8
23	**(Oh,) come off it!**		0
24	**Rubbish!** 25 **Nonsense!**		0
26	**No way!** 27 **Never!**		0
28	**You can't mean that!**		0
29	**You can't be serious!**		0
30	**You must be joking!**		0

F Your board is considering the installation of automated processes for some of the production lines in your factory. Not everyone is in favour.

Well, personally, I think that these processes have yet to prove themselves.

31	**I really must take issue with you (there).** *It's quite clear that they are efficient and highly cost-effective in the long run.*		0
32	**(I'm afraid) I entirely disagree ....**	0	7
33	**(I'm afraid) I entirely disagree with ....**		6
34	**(I'm afraid) I can't accept ....**	6	7
35	**I can't say that I share that/your view/assessment ....**	0	7
36	**I can't say that I share that/your view/assessment of ....**		6
37	**I'm not at all/entirely etc convinced ....**	0	7
38	**I'm not at all/entirely etc convinced by ....**	6	8
39	**I see things rather differently myself.**		0
40	**Well, my own opinion, (for what it's worth), is that ....**		7

in other situations

41	**Personally, I'd be more inclined to agree with ....**	[when you are agreeing with one	6
42	**Personally, I tend to agree with ....**	of several speakers]	6

Practice

a ▶ What does she say?

b ▶ What does she say?

c At a board meeting, the chairman expresses the view that there is no point in discussing future investment levels as any future investment at all is out of the question. You feel this is not so.
  ▶ What do you say?
  i *You can't mean that!*
  ii *I can't say I share that view.*
  iii *I disagree, I'm afraid.*
  ▶ What else could you say?

Key **a** 1–19 most appropriate, 20–30 also possible   **b** 20–30 most appropriate, 1–8, 18 also possible
c ii or iii, 31–42 most appropriate, 1–19 also possible

58 Saying you partly agree

1 *I don't entirely agree with ....*   6

You have been listening to the news with your landlady. One item concerns the sale of an important British painting to a foreign buyer. Your landlady is upset.

If only they charged for entry to art galleries and museums, we
could stop our art collections going abroad. Don't you think so?

2 *I see your point, but there were lots of protests when the government tried to introduce charges before.*	33–35	37
3 *I see what you mean, but ....*	33–35	37
4 *To a certain extent, yes, but ....*	33–35	37
5 *There's a lot in what you say, but ....*	33–35	37
6 *Yes, maybe/perhaps, etc but ....* 7 *Agreed, but ....*	33–35	37
8 *I couldn't agree more, but ....*	33–35	37

9 *Yes, up to a point, but . . . .*	33–35	37
10 *That's one way of looking at it, but . . . .*	33–35	37
11 *Yes, but on the other hand, ...*	33–35	37
12 *Yes, but we shouldn't forget . . . .*	6	7
13 *Yes, but don't you think . . . ?*		7
14 *That's all very well, but . . .* [argumentative]	33–35	37

in other situations

15 *I agree with much of/most of what you say, but . . . .*	33–35	37

I You work for an engineering firm. You are talking to a friend there, Stan.

Well, I think most of us will have an electric car in ten or fifteen years' time.

16 *Could be, but they don't seem any nearer solving the problem of the batteries for electric cars yet, as far as I can see.*	33–35	37
17 *OK, but . . . .* **18** *Yes, but . . . .* **19** *Mm, but . . . .*	33–35	37

in other situations

20 *I can see that, but . . . .*	33–35	37
21 *I'd go along with a lot of/most of that, but . . . .*	33–35	37
[when someone has made several points]		

F Your company is looking for new export markets, and you are at a meeting called to discuss the matter. Your chairman says:

There can't be any doubt that Australia offers great export potential for our products.

22 *Well, while I agree with you on the whole, there are problems when you examine the Australian markets in depth.*	33–35	37
23 *There's some/a lot of truth in what you say. Still/However, ...*	33–35	37
24 *I agree in principle, but . . . .*	33–35	37
25 *I take your point, but . . . .*	33–35	37
26 *I think we're very much in agreement on this. However, ...*	33–35	37
27 *That may be so, but . . . .* **28** *Granted, but . . . .*	33–35	37
29 *Personally, I wouldn't go so far as (to say) that.*		0
30 *In spite of what you say, I think perhaps . . . .*		7

Practice

a ▶ What does he actually say?

b You and a friend, Ted, are discussing a new pay offer your management has made.

Ted: *I think their offer's pretty fair.*

You: *Yes, but it's less than we asked for.*

▶ Is this appropriate?

c You are in a business seminar with a number of people whom you have not met before. One of them, a company director, states that the standard of living has risen considerably in the past forty years.

▶ Is anyone saying anything inappropriate?

You: *That may be so, but is the distribution of wealth as it should be yet?*

Sales Manager: *OK, but it's risen a lot more for some than for others.*

Works Manager: *Could be, but I still think there's too much profit in too few hands.*

Key **a** 6–8, 11, 13 most appropriate, 18, 19 also possible **b** yes **c** probably not, although the Sales Manager and the Works Manager are being a little informal; 22–27 most appropriate, 1–15 also possible

59 Saying you are wrong and someone else is right

1 *(Yes,) sorry. You're (quite) right.*		0

You are watching television in your hotel lounge with another guest. You don't like the programme you are watching.

I don't think English TV is very good, really.
Oh, I don't know. They do some excellent documentaries, and their news and sports coverage is first class.

2 *(Yes,) perhaps I'm wrong (there). But I certainly don't like this programme.*		0
3 *(Yes,) you may/could well be right . . . .*	0	7
4 *(Yes,) perhaps you have a point (there).*		0
5 *Yes, now I (come to) think about it, ...*	33	35
6 *Yes, I hadn't thought of/remembered . . . .*	6	7

in other situations

7 *Yes, of course.*	0
8 *Yes, I don't know what I was thinking of.*	0
[If you have said or done something rather silly]	

I You have been playing a game with some friends, and keeping the score.

> *I make it 23 to Fred, 18 to Pat, 19 to Jim and 21 to me.*
> Hey, hold on, you only got five that time. So you're 20, not 21.

9 *My mistake. 20 it is.* **10** *Sorry, I got it/that all wrong.* 0
11 *Sorry, slipped up there.* **12** *Of course.* **13** *Yes, silly of me.* 0

in other situations

14 *OK, you win.* [at the end of a discussion or argument] 0

F You have submitted your departmental budget recently. Now the chief accountant has asked to see you.

> *I'm afraid these figures don't quite work out. I think you may
> have omitted a figure for depreciation.*

15 *May I see the figures again? Hmm. Yes, I must admit you are right.* 0
16 *Yes, I may well have been in error over . . . .* 6
17 *Yes, I must have overlooked . . . .* 6
18 *Yes, I'm afraid I didn't take . . . into account.* 16

in other situations

19 *Yes, I take your point entirely/completely etc.* [in a discussion] 0

Practice

a You have bought some things in a shop. You tell the assistant that she has charged too much.
Assistant: *No, V.A.T. went up 5% on Thursday.*
You think: *. . . she's right . . . .*
▶ What do you actually say?

b ▶ What does he say next?

c You have been making some travel arrangements for your boss and have given him a schedule.
Boss: *It says I leave here at eight and arrive in Montreal at three. That's GMT—I asked for local times on my schedule.*
You think: *. . . . I've got it wrong . . . .*
▶ What do you actually say?

Key a 1, 7, 8 most appropriate, 9, 11–13 also possible **b** 9–12 most appropriate, 1, 7, 8 also possible **c** 1, 6–8 (10–13, 17, 18 equally possible)

60 Saying you have reached agreement

1 *Right, we agree.* 0

You are at a restaurant with some people you have met recently. You have agreed to share the cost of the meal. The waiter brings the bill.

Let's see now. The drinks cost about the same as the food.
Right, I'll pay for the food and you pay for the drinks.

2 *(Good), that's agreed then.* 0
3 *Well, that's settled, (then/isn't it?).* 0
4 *So we're agreed, (then/aren't we?).* 0

---

in other situations

5 *(Well, basically,) we seem to be saying the same thing.* 0

I You and two friends are planning a trip to the States. You are trying to decide your route.

I know, let's fly to the west coast and work our way eastwards.
Yes, good idea.

6 *That's it, then. Now let's work out the cost!* 0
7 *That's that/OK, then.*   **8** *That seems to be that/OK, then.* 0
9 *Good/Well/Right, etc that wraps . . . up.* 16
10 *Looks like we're agreed . . . .* 0 7–9
11 *Everyone's happy about . . . , then.* 16
12 *Looks like . . . is OK/taken care of.* 16

---

in other situations

13 *So what are we arguing about?* [to bring an argument to an end] 0

F The question has arisen at a managerial meeting of whether your company should submit a tender for a certain contract. After discussion, you are all in favour.

---

14 *We seem to be in complete agreement that we should submit a tender immediately.* 0 7
Good. Now we can get down to details.
15 *We seem to be in complete agreement on . . . .* 6 8–11
16 *So, we appear to agree . . . .* 0 7
17 *So, we appear to agree on . . . .* 6 8–10
18 *We are agreed . . . , then.* 0 16

19 *We are agreed on ..., then.*   16
20 *Can I take it that ... is agreed/settled?*   16
[when full agreement has not yet been clearly expressed]   16
21 *That seems to be agreed, then.*   0

Practice

a   You are with a group of tourists in the States. Your guide suggests that tonight
        you go and see the Niagara Falls by moonlight. You all agree.
        ▶ What does the guide say next?

b   You are holding an informal meeting at work. You suggest that your department
        apply for an increased budget for its current project. Everyone agrees.
        You say: *Right, we seem to be in complete agreement on that question.*
        ▶ Is this appropriate? If not, what is?

c   You are chairman at a meeting between your trade association and a trade
        delegation from another country. You suggest that you move on to the
        next item on the agenda. Everyone agrees.
        ▶ What do you say?
        i   *Everyone's happy about moving on, then?*
        ii   *Looks like we're agreed on that.*
        iii *We are agreed that we should move on to the next item, then?*

Key   a 1–4 most appropriate, 6–8, 10, 11 also possible   **b** not appropriate, 1–4 most appropriate, 6–12
also possible   **c** iii (i and ii too informal)

6I Offering to do something for someone

Can I help?   Oh, thank you.

1 *Can I help?*   0 1–3 6

A young man is trying to push his car. The battery is flat.

2 *Let me help you push it.*   0 3
       Thanks! I can't move it.
3 *Shall I ... ?*   **4** *If you like I could ....*   0 3
5 *I'll ....*   3
6 *What can I do to help ... ?*   0 1–3 6
7 *Would you like any help ... ?*   0 1 4
8 *Is there anything I can do ... ?*   0 1

102

I At a bar, your friend, Ted, is having trouble picking up a lot of drinks to carry back to your table. You go over to him.

9	*Need some help, Ted?*	0	1	4
	Cheers. Could you take those?			
10	*(Here,) I'll do it for you.*			0
11	*You look like you could do with some help ....*	0	1	4
12	*Want a hand ... ?*	0	1	4
13	*Can I help out?*			0

F Your company is holding an exhibition of its products. A stranger, who you think might be an important client, is looking very lost.

14	*May I be of assistance?*	0
	Oh, thank you, yes. I wanted to enquire about ordering in bulk.	
15	*Might I help at all?*	0
16	*Perhaps I could assist in some way?*	0

in other situations

17	*If we can be of any assistance, (please) do not hesitate to contact us again.* [often written].	0

Practice

a You are going through customs. The man in front of you in the queue cannot speak English very well. He is trying to explain to the customs officer that he has lost his passport. Your English is better than his.

▶ What do you say?
  i *May I be of assistance?*
  ii *Would you like any help?*
  iii *Let me explain!*

b You have just been introduced to an important business client, at a reception. Someone has bumped into him causing him to drop his drink and a plate of food on the floor.

▶ What do you say?

c ▶ What does he say?

Key **a** ii most appropriate, i also possible **b** 14–16 most appropriate, 1–3, 5–8 also possible
c 9, 11–13 most appropriate, 1–8 also possible

62 Accepting an offer of help

1 Thank you.   0

You are in a bookshop. You want a book on the top shelf but can't reach. The assistant comes up with a step-ladder.

Let me get it for you.
2 That's very kind (of you).   3 (Oh,) yes please.   0
4 If you're sure it's no trouble (for you) 0 1

I You are underneath your car trying to repair it. You're trying to loosen a nut, with a torch in one hand and a spanner in the other. Your sister sees you are in difficulty.

Let me hold the torch.
5 Cheers!   0
6 Thanks (very much)!   7 Lovely!/Great!/Terrific! etc.   0
8 Just what I needed . . . !   0 1

F You are attending an important meeting in England which has overrun. You are anxious not to miss your plane back home where you have another important meeting to attend. The chairman offers to help you.

I'll see that my chauffeur gets you to the airport in time for your flight.
9 You are most kind.   0
10 That's extremely good/kind/thoughtful etc (of you) 0 1

---

in other situations

11 I'd be delighted 0 1
12 I'd be delighted if   12

Practice

a   You are waiting outside a railway station. You have a lot of luggage, you want a taxi, but you don't know how to phone for one. A stranger offers to phone for a taxi for you.
▶   What do you say?

104

b ▶ What does he say?

c You and your wife are at the theatre. It is full inside except for two seats on either side of an old lady. The lady offers to move so that you and your wife may sit together.

▶ What do you say?

  i *Cheers!*

  ii *Thanks very much.*

  iii *That's extremely good of you.*

Key a 1–4 most appropriate, 6, 10 also possible **b** 1–3 (4 rather *too* polite for this situation), 6 also possible **c** ii and iii (i too informal)

63 Refusing an offer of help

1 *No, thank you.*	0

You are on a train. An old man is trying to get his heavy case down from the luggage rack.

Would you like any help?	
2 *No, really, I can manage (thanks).*	0
3 *That's very kind of you, but . . . .*	33–37
4 *I don't think so, thank you.* 5 *No, don't bother, really.*	0
6 *No, it's all right, really.*	0
7 *Thank you for offering, but . . . .*	33–37

I A friend offers to post a letter for you, but you can quite easily post it yourself.

> I'll post that letter for you.

8 *(No,) it's OK, thanks. I can do it on the way home.*	0
9 *Thanks a lot, but . . . .* 10 *Nice thought, but . . . .*	33–37
11 *(No,) don't worry.*	0
12 *(No,) don't worry about . . . .*	4–6

F You have just been introduced to an important business client. After a meeting at your firm he offers to drive you home, but your wife is picking you up at the office in ten minutes.

> Can I drive you back home?

13 *It's very good of you to offer, but I'm expecting my wife.*	33–37
14 *Please don't trouble yourself about . . . .*	4–6
15 *That's extremely kind of you, but . . . .*	33–37
16 *I'm very grateful for your offer. However . . . .*	33–37

in other situations

17 *I'm afraid I find myself unable to accept your offer. . . .*	[often written]	0 1
18 *I regret (to say) (that) I am not in a position to accept your (kind/thoughtful) offer. . . . .*		0 1

Practice

a ▶ What does he say?
  i *No, don't bother, really.*
  ii *No, it's OK, thanks.*
  iii *That's extremely kind of you, but I believe I can manage.*

b You are visiting a friend who is having trouble taking his lawn mower to pieces. You offer to help: *Want a hand?*
  ▶ What does he say?

c You are at a party given by an important person whom you don't know at all. It has become very late and he offers you a bed for the night. You feel you must go home, however.
  ▶ What do you say?

Key a i and ii (iii too formal)   **b** 8–12 most appropriate, 1–7 also possible   **c** 1–7 most appropriate, 13–16 also possible (16–18 too formal for this situation)

64 Saying what you think you ought to do

1 *I must . . . .*   0 3

You have bought an English colleague a birthday card, but you haven't posted it yet.
His birthday is tomorrow, Saturday. Another colleague asks you:

Did you buy a card for Ted Burgess, in the end?
2 *Yes, and I ought to send it today, if I want it to get there tomorrow.*   0 3
3 *I should . . . .*   **4** *I'd better . . . .*   0 3

I You are in a pub drinking with your friend, Pete. He suggests a game of darts, but
suddenly you realize it's later than you think.

Don't go now! A quick game won't take us long!
5 *(Sorry, I) can't stay! I'm meeting someone at nine.*   0 3
6 *(Sorry,) got to . . . .*   **7** *(Sorry,) must . . . .*   3
8 *(Sorry,) better . . . .*   3

F You are chairing a meeting of your subsidiary company in England. Everyone
disagrees completely with your point of view and you take it very seriously.

I'm afraid you have no support whatsoever for that point of view,
Mr Chairman.
9 *In that case I feel it is my duty to offer my resignation.*   0 3
10 *I have no alternative but to . . . .*   0 3
11 *There appears to be no alternative to . . . .*   4–6
12 *I have an obligation to . . . .*   0 3 6
13 *I am/I feel obliged to . . . .*   0 3
14 *I feel it is absolutely necessary (for me) to . . . .*   0 3

in other situations

15 *I have no alternative.*   0
16 *There appears to be no alternative.*   0
17 *I feel it is absolutely necessary.*   0
18 *I have an obligation.*   **19** *I feel it is my duty.*   0
20 *We are committed to . . . .*   3–6

Practice

a ▶ What does he say?

b At a board meeting you have to inform your co-directors that there will be redundancies in the near future unless sales figures improve.
▶ What do you say?

c Your best friend has phoned you at work about something unimportant. You are late for an important meeting.
▶ What do you say?
i *I feel it is my duty to go now.*
ii *Sorry, can't stop to talk now!*
iii *I'd better go now.*

Key **a** 1–4 **b** 9–11, 13, 14, 16 most appropriate, 1–3 also possible **c** ii and iii (i too informal)

65 Saying what you think you ought not to do

1 *I mustn't ....*   0 3

You have gone to a shop to buy a new suit. There are two that you like particularly but they are very expensive.

> Would you like to take both of them, sir? They look really good on you.

2 *(No,) I shouldn't (really).*   0 3
3 *(No,) I oughtn't to ....*   **4** *(No,) I can't possibly ....*   0 3
5 *(No,) I couldn't possibly ....*   0 3
6 *(No,) I'd better not ....*   0 3

108

I You are visiting England and have gone to a football match with some friends. Afterwards, they suggest you go back with them for a meal, but you've promised the person you're staying with you'll be home immediately after the match.

> There's plenty of time. Come back for a meal!
> 7 ***Better not.*** *I said I'd be back at six.*   0   3

in other situations

> 8 ***No way!*** [very strong, could sound rude]   0

F In a meeting of the directors of the theatre company that you work for, you give the information that a cheque for a large amount of money has been received from an anonymous sponsor.

> Surely you can tell us the sponsor's name?
> 9 *I'm afraid **I'm obliged not to** reveal the name.*   0   3
> 10 ***I feel obliged not to*** *. . . .*   0   3
> 11 ***I have an obligation not to*** *. . . .*   0   3
> 12 ***I'm committed not to*** *. . . .*   0   3
> 13 ***I feel it is my duty not to*** *. . . .*   0   3
> 14 ***It would be wrong of me to*** *. . . .*   0   3

Practice

a ▶ What does the customer say?

b   In your office, an important business client, whom you know only slightly, asks you whether your board has agreed to sign a draft contract with his company. You don't want to commit yourself at this stage.
     ▶ What do you say?

c   Your doctor has advised you to stop smoking completely. That evening one of your friends offers you a cigarette.
     ▶ What do you say?
     i   *No way!*
     ii   *I feel it is my duty not to.*
     iii *I'd better not.*

Key   **a** 1–6   **b** 9–14 most appropriate, 1–6 also possible   **c** i and iii (ii too formal)

66 Saying you intend to do something

1 *I'm going to . . . .*   0 3

You are in your office at work. Outside, children have been playing football noisily against your office wall. A colleague complains.

It's impossible to work with all that noise!

2 *(Yes, I think) I'll stop them.*   3
3 *(Yes, I think) I will . . . .*   0 3
4 *I've decided . . . .*   0 1 7
5 *I'll see if I can't . . . .*   0 3
6 *I'm going to make sure . . . .*   0 7

---

in other situations

---

7 *I'm planning to . . . .*   **8** *I plan to . . . .*   0 3
9 *I'll make an effort to . . . .*   0 3
10 *I'll do all I can . . . .*   0 1

I Your friend, Jeremy, comes to see you and admires your car, which you have been cleaning up.

It looks great!

11 *As a matter of fact **I'm thinking of** selling it.*   4 6
12 *I reckon I'll . . . .*   3

---

in other situations

---

13 *I reckon I will . . . .*   0 3
14 *I'll . . . or bust!*   17

F You are visiting your firm's subsidiary company in England to reassure the board officially that a move to take over your company will be resisted.

We'd be most grateful for a statement as to the present position.

15 *Then let me say clearly that **I have every intention of** preventing any possible moves for a take-over.*   4
16 *I (fully) intend . . . .*   1 2 4
17 *My intention is to . . . .*   **18** *It is my intention to . . . .*   3

110

Practice

It's a lovely camera.

a ▶ What does he say?

b The chairman of your company has asked you to sort out the financial problems that your subsidiary company in England is undergoing. In a meeting the English manager, disheartened, says: *I really don't feel you'll find any answers to our problems.*
▶ What do you say?

c You are chatting to a friend in a café. He asks you about your plans for a holiday this year.
▶ What do you say?
   i *I intend to go to France.*
   ii *I'm thinking of going to France.*
   iii *I've decided to go to France.*

Key **a** 1–4 **b** 15–18 most appropriate, 1–3, 6, 10 also possible **c** ii and iii (i too formal)

67 Saying you do not intend to do something

THAT'S EXPENSIVE.

OPEN

SUITS FROM £250

YES, I'M NOT GOING TO PAY £250 FOR A SUIT!

1 *I'm not going to ....* 0 3

You have recently arrived in England, and your landlady is talking to you.

If you don't see all of England now, you can see the rest next year.
2 *Well, **I won't be** visiting England next year.* 0 4
3 *I've decided not to ....* **4** *I won't ....* 0 3
5 *I don't plan to ....* 0 3
6 *I'm not planning ....* 1 6

111

in other situations

7	*Nothing could be farther from my mind.*	0
8	*Nothing could be farther from my mind than . . . .*	4–6

I Your friend, Sandy, tells you a very good job has been advertised, but you are not interested.

Have you seen this job?

9	*Yes, but **I don't reckon I'll** bother.*	3
10	*I'm not thinking of . . . .*	4

in other situations

11	*I don't reckon I will . . . .*	0	3
12	*It never entered my head . . . .*	0 1 7

F At a formal meeting you are asked if you have any intention of resigning as chairman.

Could you tell us if there is any truth in these rumours of your resignation?

13	*I have no intention (whatsoever) of resigning.*	4	5
14	*Nothing would/will induce me to . . . .*	0	3
15	*I don't intend to/propose to . . . .*	0	3

Practice

a ▶ What does the driver say?

b At an inefficiently run hotel, you have had to change your room. You are asked by the manager to change rooms yet again. You politely, but firmly, state your point of view.
▶ What do you say?

c You are chatting to a friend at work during the coffee break. He asks you if you've thought any more about the possibility of leaving your job.
▶ What do you say?

i *I'm not thinking of leaving, now.*
ii *I have no intention whatsoever of leaving now.*
iii *I'm not going to leave.*

Key   a 1, 4 most appropriate, 13–15 also possible   **b** 13–15 most appropriate, 1, 4 also possible   **c** i and iii (ii too formal)

68 Asking if someone is able to do something

Can you see England?

1	***Can you . . . ?***		0 3

On holiday, your car breaks down miles from the nearest town. Another car stops and the driver offers to help. He appears to know a lot about cars and locates the problem as an electrical fault.

2	***Do you know how to*** *repair electrical faults?*		0 3
	Yes, this one's easy. One of the leads has come loose.		
3	***Do you think you can . . . ?***		0 3
4	***Do you know anything about . . . ?***		4 6

I Your friend, Joe, has suggested you lend another friend, Ted, your car for the weekend. Ted has only just passed his driving test.

Go on! Let him borrow it!

5	***Think he could*** *manage?* 6 ***D'you reckon he could . . . ?***		0 3

in other situations

7	***I bet he couldn't . . . , could he?***		0 17
8	***Is he any good?***		0
9	***Is he any good at . . . ?***		4 6
10	***What's he like?***		0
11	***What's he like at . . . ?***		4 6

F You are interviewing someone for a responsible job as manager of a department in your company.

12	***Would you say you were capable of*** *reorganizing a department?*		4 6
13	***Are you capable of . . . ?*** 14 ***Do you feel capable of . . . ?***		4 6
15	***Are you able to . . . ?***		0 3
16	***Do you have the experience/qualifications/abilities***		
	necessary . . . ?		0 1
17	***Do you have any experience?***		0
18	***Do you have any experience of . . . ?***		4–6

Practice

a In the street you meet a man you have seen once or twice before. He has just arrived in Britain and wants to use a phone box. You think he may have problems.

▶ What do you say?

b ▶ What does the Englishman say?

c Your company is under the threat of being taken over by a bigger company. Your present employer calls you into his office to inform you officially of the possibility.

▶ What do you say?

i *Do you think they can do this?*

ii *Do they have the experience necessary to do this?*

iii *I bet they couldn't do it, could they?*

Key **a** 1–4 **b** 1 and 2 **c** i and ii (iii too informal)

69 Saying you are able to do something

1 I can . . . .

All the lights go out in the house of an acquaintance you are visiting. He doesn't know what to do.

Oh, no! What's happened?

2 *It's probably the fuses. It's all right.* **It's not too difficult** *to mend them.*

0 1

114

3	*... is/are not too difficult.*		15
4	*I know how to ....*		0 3
5	*I know ....*		8 9
6	*I know something about ....*	4 6	8 9
7	*I might be able to ....*		0 3

I You are with your friend, Tom, in a car that won't start. You think you know why and offer to help.

Do you really think you can start it?

8	*(Yes,) I reckon I can ....*	0 3
9	*I'm not too bad at ....* ⎫ [sounds modest]	4 6
10	*There's just a chance I can/could ....* ⎭	0 3
11	*(Yes, it's) easy as pie!* **12** *Sure.*	0
13	*(Yes, it's) a cinch!* **14** *(Yes,) no problem.* ⎫ [could sound	0
15	*(Yes, it's a) piece of cake!* ⎬ boastful]	0
16	*(Yes,) I'm pretty good at ....* ⎭	4 6

F At a job interview, you are asked if you could deal with complaints from angry clients.

Would you find dealing with complaints a problem?

17	*I'd say I was capable of doing that.*	4 6
18	*I'm capable.* **19** *I feel capable.*	0
20	*I'm capable of ....* **21** *I feel capable of ....*	4 6
22	*I don't think that would prove too difficult ....*	0 1
23	*I have experience of ....*	4–6
24	*I'd say I was able to ....* **25** *I'm able to ....*	0 3
26	*I feel able to ....*	0 3
27	*(I think) I have the qualifications/experience (necessary) ....*	0 1
28	*(I think) I have the ability/abilities (necessary) ....*	0 1

---

in other situations

29	*I'd say I was capable.*	0

Practice

a ▶ What does she say?

b Your company has got into legal difficulties with a business client. Your superior asks you in a meeting if you need help to deal with the situation.
  ▶ What do you say?

c Your friend, Penny, challenges you to swim ten lengths of a swimming pool. You're a very good swimmer.
▶ What do you say?
  i *I can do it easily!*
  ii *Piece of cake!*
  iii *I don't think that would prove too difficult.*

Key a 1 **b** 17–21, 23–26 most appropriate, 1–5 also possible **c** i and ii (iii too formal)

70 Saying you are not able to do something

1 *I can't ....*	0	3

You want to insure your car and the clerk has given you a very complicated form to complete. Your English isn't quite good enough to understand it.

Have you filled the form in yet, sir?
2 *No, I don't know how to fill it in.*	0	1
3 *I'm not sure I can/know how to ....*	0	3

in other situations

4 *I don't know anything about ....*	4	6	8	9

I Your friend, Bill, is trying to persuade you to have a game of golf with him. You have never played before.

Come on! You'll enjoy it!
5 *But I haven't got a clue how to play.*	0	1
6 *I've no idea how ....*	0	1
7 *I haven't the faintest/foggiest idea how ....*	0	1
8 *There's no way I can ....* **9** *I don't reckon I can ....*	0	3
10 *I wouldn't know where to begin/start ....*	0 4	6
11 *I'm hopeless.*		0
12 *I'm hopeless at ....*	4	6
13 *I'm no good.*		0
14 *I'm no good at ....*	4	6

116

in other situations

15	*It's no good.*	0
16	*(Sorry,) can't manage*	1 6

F Your managing director suggests in a formal meeting that you should double turnover in a year. You see this as very optimistic.

17	*I'm not sure I'm capable of doing that.*	4 6
18	*I'm not sure I'm capable.*	0
19	*I don't feel capable of*	4 6
20	*I don't feel capable.*	0
21	*(I think) that would prove (too) difficult*	0 1
22	*I don't feel able to*	0 3
23	*I wouldn't say I was able*	0 1
24	*(I'm afraid) . . . might be beyond me.*	15
25	*(I'm afraid) . . . might be beyond my capabilities/abilities.*	15

in other situations

26	*I have no experience.*	0
27	*I have no experience of*	4-6
28	*I don't think I have the qualifications/experience (necessary)*	0 1
29	*I don't think I have the ability/abilities (necessary)*	0 1
30	*(I'm afraid) I can't cope with*	4-6
31	*(I'm afraid) I can't cope.*	0

Practice

a ▶ What does she say?

b A friend challenges you to a game of chess. You have played only once before, a long time ago, and have forgotten the rules of the game.
   ▶ What do you say?

c You boss has signed a contract with an important new client. Some hours later the client phones, asking you to persuade your boss to cancel the contract. He says you are the only person who can do this.
   Client: *I really would be most grateful for your help.*
   ▶ What do you say?

Key **a** 1 and 2 **b** 5–7, 9–14 most appropriate, 1–4 also possible **c** 17–19, 21, 22, 24, 25

117

71 Asking for permission

Can I leave at 4 o'clock, **please**, mr Telford? I've got to be at the dentist's at a quarter past.

1 *Can I . . . , please?*	0	17

You are buying a pullover in a shop. You want to see if it fits you before you buy it.

2 *Excuse me, do you think I could try this one on?*	0	3
Yes. There's a fitting room over there.		
3 *Would it be possible . . . ?*	0	1
4 *Could I . . . ?* 5 *I wonder if I could . . . ?*	0	3
6 *I was wondering if I could . . . ?*	0	3
7 *Do you mind if . . . ?*		12

I You are going on holiday and have discovered that your camera is broken. You remember your friend, Jackie, has an old camera that she probably isn't using. You telephone her.

8 *Hello? Jackie? **Any chance of** borrowing that old camera of yours for a few days?*	4–6
9 *Any chance?*	0
10 *Mind . . . ?*	4–6
11 *OK . . . ?*	0 1
12 *Mind if . . . ?* 13 *OK if . . . ?* 14 *All right if . . . ?*	12
15 *All right . . . ?*	0 1
16 *Let me . . . , would you?*	17

in other situations

17 *Can I have the OK/go-ahead . . . ?*	0	1
18 *Have I got the OK/go-ahead . . . ?*	0	1

F At a board meeting it is felt that you have not provided sufficient information for the board to come to a decision about launching a new product.

19 *May/Might I commission a further market survey and notify the board of the results?*	0	3
20 *Do/May/Might I have your permission . . . ?*	0	1
21 *With your permission I should like to . . . .*	0	3
22 *Do you have any objection to/if . . . ?*	4–6	12
23 *Do you have any objection?*	0	
24 *Is there any objection to/if . . . ?*	4–6	12
25 *Is there any objection?*	0	

[carries the assumption that you expect permission to be given]

118

Practice

a ▶ What does he say?

b You are with a good friend watching a horse race. He has a pair of binoculars.
You do not. You want to borrow them for a moment.
   ▶ What do you say?
   i   *Mind if I borrow your binoculars a moment?*
   ii *Could I borrow your binoculars a moment?*
   iii *With your permission I should like to borrow your binoculars a moment.*

c ▶ What does she say?

Key **a** 1–7 most appropriate, 8, 11–16 also possible   **b** i and ii (iii too formal)   **c** 1–7 most
appropriate, 8, 11–15, 19 also possible

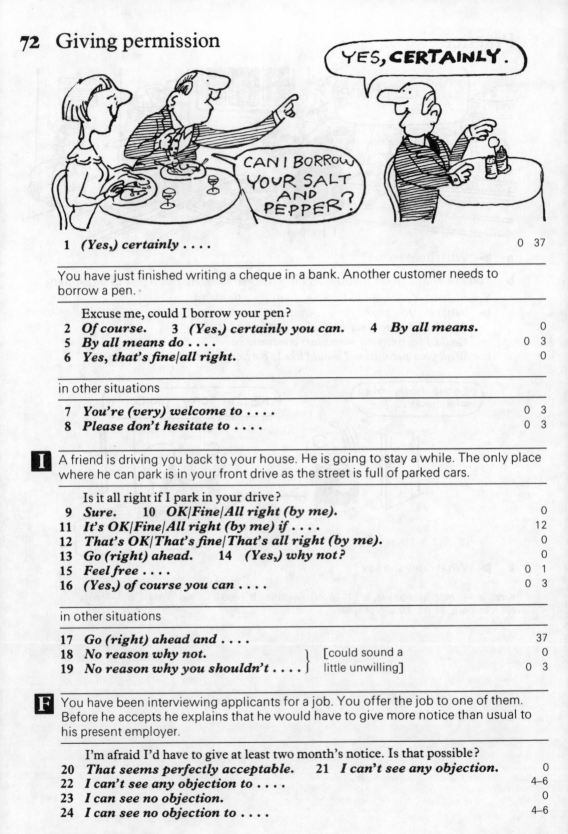

1 *(Yes,) certainly ....*   0   37

You have just finished writing a cheque in a bank. Another customer needs to borrow a pen.

    Excuse me, could I borrow your pen?
2 *Of course.*   **3** *(Yes,) certainly you can.*   **4** *By all means.*   0
5 *By all means do ....*   0   3
6 *Yes, that's fine/all right.*   0

---

in other situations

7 *You're (very) welcome to ....*   0   3
8 *Please don't hesitate to ....*   0   3

I A friend is driving you back to your house. He is going to stay a while. The only place where he can park is in your front drive as the street is full of parked cars.

    Is it all right if I park in your drive?
9 *Sure.*   **10** *OK/Fine/All right (by me).*   0
11 *It's OK/Fine/All right (by me) if ....*   12
12 *That's OK/That's fine/That's all right (by me).*   0
13 *Go (right) ahead.*   **14** *(Yes,) why not?*   0
15 *Feel free ....*   0   1
16 *(Yes,) of course you can ....*   0   3

---

in other situations

17 *Go (right) ahead and ....*   37
18 *No reason why not.*   } [could sound a   0
19 *No reason why you shouldn't ....* } little unwilling]   0   3

F You have been interviewing applicants for a job. You offer the job to one of them. Before he accepts he explains that he would have to give more notice than usual to his present employer.

    I'm afraid I'd have to give at least two month's notice. Is that possible?
20 *That seems perfectly acceptable.*   **21** *I can't see any objection.*   0
22 *I can't see any objection to ....*   4–6
23 *I can see no objection.*   0
24 *I can see no objection to ....*   4–6

25	*(Yes,) that's quite in order.*	0
26	*There seems to be no reason why you shouldn't . . . .*	0 3

in other situations

27	*(Yes,) indeed you may . . . .*	0 3

Practice

a ▶ What does the passenger say?

b In the park, a stranger asks if he can pat your beautiful dog.
▶ What do you say?

c You are on a coach tour abroad with a good friend. After a few days he asks you if you would mind changing seats.
▶ What is appropriate?
i *Of course.* ii *Yes, that's quite in order.* iii *That's OK.*

d You are in an important meeting negotiating for a contract. You are asked if there would be any objection to a penalty clause being written in to ensure delivery dates are met.
▶ What do you say?

Key **a** 1, 2, 4, most appropriate, 9, 10 also possible **b** 1–6 most appropriate, 9–14, 16 also possible
c i and iii (ii too formal) **d** 20–27 most appropriate, 1–8 also possible

73 Refusing permission

1	*(Sorry,) I'm afraid . . . .*	7 14

You are on business in England with a recently employed colleague from your own country, who will be taking over from you shortly, and has agreed always to speak in English. You are driving with him to a business appointment some miles away. Your colleague will have to travel a lot in England and asks you if he can drive as he needs the practice. However, he is not insured yet.

Can I drive back?

2	*I'm afraid you can't, you're not insured.*	0	3
3	*I'm afraid not.*		0
4	*I'm afraid I can't let you ....*	0	3
5	*I'm afraid that's not/it's not possible ....*	0	1
6	*I'm afraid that's not/it's not possible for you ....*		3
7	*I'm sorry, that's not/it's not allowed.*		0
8	*I'm sorry, I'm not supposed to/not allowed to let you ....*	0	3
9	*You're not really supposed to/allowed to ....*	0	3
10	*I don't really think you should/ought to ....*	0	3
11	*I'm sorry, I'm/You're not supposed to/allowed to ....*	0	3

in other situations

12	*(I'm afraid) we can't have ....*	4–6

I In a pub a good friend, Jenny, suggests you hold a party that evening for everyone sitting at your table. You don't think it's a good idea.

Come on! Let's go back to your place and have a party!

13	*I'd like to, but I'm feeling too tired this evening.*	33–37	
14	*I can't possibly ....*	0	3
15	*Sorry ....*	0	1
16	*(Sorry,) that's not on.*		0
17	*That's not on, (I'm afraid).*		0
18	*(Sorry,) no way.*		0
19	*No way, (I'm afraid).*		0
20	*(Sorry,) out of the question.*		0
21	*Out of the question, (I'm afraid).*		0

[emphatic]

F An employee of yours wants to change his working hours.

Would it be possible to work from eight o'clock to four o'clock instead of nine to five?

22	*(I'm afraid) we can't/couldn't allow/permit that. Everybody might want to do the same.*	2	4	6
23	*(I'm afraid) no one is allowed/permitted to ....*		0	3

in other situations

24	*(I'm afraid) we don't have the authority ....*	0	1
25	*(I'm afraid) we don't have the authority to allow/permit you to ....*	0	1

Practice

a You have been put in charge of organizing a party at your language school. A student you don't know well suggests hiring a disco group. You know the director won't allow this.
▶ What do you say?

b An employee you have just engaged comes to see you in your office to ask for five days' unpaid leave for no very good reason and at a very busy time.

▶ What do you say?

c Pete, a very good friend of yours, asks to borrow your brand new expensive camera. You know he drops things easily.

Pete: *Can I borrow your camera this afternoon?*
You: *. . . . It's brand new!*

▶ What do you say?

Key a 1–12 most appropriate, 13–21 also possible (12, 14–19 too informal)   **b** 1–12 most appropriate, 14, 15, 20–23 also possible   **c** 15, 18, 19 most appropriate, 1 (if 'sorry' is used), 3 also possible

74 Asking if you are obliged to do something

1 *Do I (really) have to . . . ?*	0 3

At a bank you have made out a cheque rather badly, as you are in a hurry. You have changed the figures and put the wrong date.

Could you write out another cheque, sir, please?	
2 *Do I (really) need to . . . ?* 3 *Need I . . . ?*	0 3

in other situations

4 *Am I/Aren't I supposed to/meant to . . . ?*	0 3
5 *Am I/Aren't I expected to . . . ?*	0 3

I You have driven with a good friend into town and parked. You are both late for an appointment. Your friend suddenly sees a 'No Parking' sign.

You'd better park somewhere else.	
6 *Oh no, have I got to?*	0 3
7 *(Surely) I haven't got to . . . , have I?*	0 17
8 *I suppose I've got to . . . .*	0 3

in other situations

9 *Am I the one that's got to . . . ?*	0 3
10 *Must I . . . ?/Mustn't I . . . ?*	0 3

F The firm you work for exports cars. Two cars have been damaged, because they fell on being lifted into the cargo vessel. You are in a formal meeting of your board to discuss whether your firm or the customer is liable.

11	*The question is, **are we under any obligation** to replace the damaged cars?*	0 1
12	*Are we/Aren't we obliged to/required to . . . ?*	0 3
13	*Is/Isn't the onus upon us . . . ?*	0 1
14	*Is it (really)/Isn't it necessary for us . . . ?*	1

in other situations

15	*Is/Isn't . . . compulsory/obligatory?*	16

Practice

a ▶ What does the client say?

b You and your sister are renting a cottage in England. Your sister has decided that you need to slim and has placed two raw eggs in a glass in front of you as your dinner.

▶ What do you say?

c You have had bad toothache for several days, but don't want to go to the dentist. Finally, your friend, Ted, tells you he has rung up the dentist and made an appointment for you.

▶ What do you say? .
  i   *I suppose I've got to go.*
  ii *Is the onus upon me to go?*
  iii *Do I have to go?*

Key **a** 1–5 **b** 6, 7, 10 most appropriate, 1 (4 and 5 with positive verb) also possible **c** i and iii (ii too formal)

75 Saying someone is obliged to do something

1 *I think you have to ....*   0 3

You are at the head of a queue at a cinema in the West End of London. A foreigner who is in England for the first time is puzzled by the queue and approaches you.

Can I go straight in?

2 *(I think) you're supposed to queue.*   0 3
3 *(I think/I'm afraid) you/you'll have to ....*   0 3
4 *(I think) you're meant to ....*   0 3
5 *(I'm afraid) you're supposed to/meant to ....*   0 3
6 *(I think/I'm afraid) you should/ought to ....*   0 3
7 *(I think/I'm afraid) you're expected to ....*   0 3

---

in other situations

---

8 *(I'm afraid) you must ....*   0 3
9 *(I'm afraid) you can't avoid ....*   4 6
10 *I don't think you can avoid ....*   4 6

I You and your friend, Jill, have promised another friend, Brian, that you will visit him in hospital. Brian is particularly looking forward to seeing Jill, but Jill is now saying she doesn't really want to go.

I don't really have to go, do I?

11 *I'm afraid you've got to. He'll be terribly disappointed.*   0 3
12 *I'm afraid you can't (just) not ....*   3
13 *I'm afraid you can't get out of ....*   4 6
14 *I don't see how you can get out of ....*   4 6

---

in other situations

---

15 *I'm afraid you can't get away with ....*   4 6
16 *I don't see how you can get away with ....*   4 6

F You have gone to a shop to complain about a television you have bought which does not work properly. Eventually you speak to the manager who is not very helpful.

There's nothing I can do about it.

17 *I'm afraid/I think you are under an obligation to provide me with a satisfactory television set.*   0 1
18 *I'm afraid/I think you are under an obligation to ....*   0 3

19 *I'm afraid/I think the onus is upon you . . . .* 0 1

20 *I'm afraid/I think the onus is upon you to . . . .* 0 3

21 *I'm afraid/I think you are obliged to . . . .* 0 3

in other situations

22 *I'm afraid/I think . . . is compulsory/obligatory.* 16

Practice

a ▶ What does he say?

i *I think you have to come between nine and five-thirty.*

ii *I'm afraid you'll have to come back tomorrow.*

iii *The onus is upon you to come back tomorrow.*

b Your friend, Bill, has just driven into the back of a police car. The policeman is not pleased, Bill has two endorsements on his licence already and does not want to show it to the policeman.

May I see your driving licence, please sir? I said, may I see your driving licence, sir?

▶ What do you say to Bill?

c *I'm sorry but the onus is upon you to declare any additional income you may have.*

▶ In which situation is this appropriate?

i *You to a friend you are visiting in England.*

ii *The tax collector to you in his office, while you have a temporary job in England.*

iii *You to your friend in an English pub.*

Key a i and ii **b** 11–16, 3, 8–10 **c** ii

126

76 Saying someone must not do something

1 *I don't really think you should ....*   0 3

You have asked your taxi driver to hurry. He hurries a little too much and you think he is going to go the wrong way down a one-way street.

2	*I don't think you should go down there.*	0 3
3	*I don't (really) think you ought ....*	0 1
4	*You oughtn't (really) ....*	0 1
5	*You shouldn't (really) ....*	0 3
6	*... is not (really) allowed.*	15

I You are wrapping your friend, Sue's, birthday present, when she suddenly comes into the room.

7	*(For goodness sake) don't look!*	0 3
8	*Whatever you do, don't ....*	3
9	*You're not meant to ....* **10** *You mustn't ...!*	0 3
11	*You can't ...!*	0 3
12	*Stop!/Wait!/*[or other suitable imperative]	30
13	*You're not to ....* [usually to children]	0 3

in other situations

14	*Let go!/Leave that alone!* [or other suitable imperative]	30
15	*You'd (really) better not ....*	0 3
16	*You're not (really) supposed to ....*	0 3

F You and your boss have just interviewed a very good candidate for the job of sales manager. Your boss doesn't want to interview any other applicants, but you disagree.

Well, there seems little point in interviewing anyone else now.

17	*Possibly, but **I think you're under an obligation not to** offer the job until we've seen all the candidates.*	0 3
18	*You owe it to ....*	2

in other situations

19	*On no account must you ....*	0 3

Practice

a ▶ What does the passer-by say?

b ▶ What is the appropriate situation for you to say this?
Whatever you do, don't forget to post that letter!
 i *to your friend, Bill, at his house*
 ii *to your new boss in the office*
 iii *to a travel agent in his office*

c In a quarterly meeting you are anxious to impress upon your marketing department the importance of not losing the GTR Motors contract.
 ▶ What do you say?

Key a 1–5 most appropriate, 7–12, 15, 16 also possible **b** i **c** 19

77 Telling someone to do something

1 . . . , *please.*	37

You have just hailed a taxi and are telling the driver where to go.

2 *Will you take me to Victoria Station, (please).*	0 3
3 *Would you . . . , (please).*	0 3
4 . . . , *will/would you, please.*	37
5 *I'd like you to . . . , (please).*	0 3

in other situations

6 *I must ask you to . . . , please.*	0 17

128

I You are on holiday with a good friend and have just climbed a mountain. The view is splendid.

> 7 ***Come and look!/Just look at this!*** [or any other suitable imperative]   30

F At a board meeting it emerges that your firm will be unable to fulfil its contract to Telford Ltd. You feel strongly that action must be taken.

> 8 *Telford Ltd **should** be informed immediately.*   25

in other situations

> 9 ***Would you be so kind as to . . . .***   3
> 10 ***I have to ask you to . . . , (I'm afraid).***   0 3
> 11 ***It is my duty/obligation to ask/to tell you to . . . .***   0 3
> 12 ***Would you mind . . . , (please).***   0 4

Practice

a ▶ What does the owner of the house say?

b You are in the garden with a friend who is standing next to you. Suddenly you see a plane travelling low and fast.
> ▶ What is appropriate?
> i   *Come and look!*
> ii *Look!*
> iii *Would you be so kind as to look?*

c ▶ When would you say this?
Would you wait a moment, please!
> i   to an old friend in the street who is walking too quickly for you
> ii to a man in a bus queue who is pushing in front of you
> iii to your managing director as he is about to close a meeting

Key a 1–4 b ii c ii most appropriate, iii also possible

78 Saying someone need not do something

> It's all right, **you needn't** move. I can reach it.

1 **You needn't** 0 3

You are at the end of a long queue in the Post Office. There is another much shorter queue for passports only, but you want stamps. A man holding a passport joins your queue.

> Long queue this, isn't it?
2 *Yes, but **you don't have to** queue here, you know—they deal with passports over there.* 0 3
3 **There's no reason why you should** 0 3
4 **You don't need to** . . . .   **5** **There's (really) no need to** 0 3

---

in other situations

6 **It's for you to decide** 0 6 8–11
7 **You can choose for yourself** 0 8–11
8 **I leave it up to you** 0 8–11
9 **I leave . . . up to you.** 16

I You and your friend, Diana, have been invited to a party in a few days' time.

> But I won't know anyone there!
10 *It's all right, **you haven't got to** come.* 0 3
11 **It's up to you** 0 8–11

---

in other situations

12 **Don't/Can't see why you should/shouldn't** 0 3

F You have just interviewed an excellent candidate for a job in your department. You want him to accept the position, but know that he has other interviews.

13 *Of course, **you are under no obligation** to accept now, but we hope you will come to a decision soon.* 0 1
14 **You are not obliged to/required to** 0 3
15 **The decision is yours** 0 8 10 11
16 **I shouldn't see . . . as something you must/have to do.** 16

---

in other situations

17 **You are free to decide for yourself** 0 8–11
18 **I leave it in your hands** 0 8 10
19 **I leave . . . in your hands.** 16

Practice

a ▶ What does the Englishman say?

b You have taken your fiancée out to an expensive restaurant.
She says: *I really don't know whether I fancy the steak or the fish.*
▶ What is appropriate?
i *Well, the decision is yours.*
ii *Well, I leave the decision in your hands.*   iii *Well, it's up to you.*

c ▶ When would you say this?
I leave it in your hands what course of action to take.
i to a committee in a formal meeting
ii to your wife in a clothes' shop
iii to a new, important client in your office

Key **a** 1–5 **b** iii **c** i and iii (ii too informal)

79   Telling someone how to do something

1 *(First) you . . . (then you . . .).*   3

Someone in a public call box is having trouble trying to use the phone.

Excuse me, could you show me how to make a phone call?
2 *Yes, of course.* **This is how you do it: (first) you** *lift the receiver,*
wait for the dialling tone, dial the number, listen for the pips and put in 5p.   3
3 **You do it like this: you** *. . . .*   3
4 **Lift/Pick up/Raise** *etc.* [or other suitable imperative]   30
5 **It's like this: (first) you** *. . . .*   3

6 *(First) you have to/should*   3
7 *Let me show you. (First) you*   3

I You are on holiday with your friend, Pete, who has bought a new camera, but doesn't know how to put the film in.

> I can't see how it works.
8 *(Look,) all you do is* press that button, slide the film in this way round,
   push it in and it's ready to use.   3
9 *Watch. (First) you* . . . .   **10** *Make sure you*   3
11 *It's (quite/very/dead etc) easy. (First) you*   3

F You are attending a meeting of your firm to discuss how to deal with the problem of delays in meeting orders caused by a supply shortage. You are the marketing manager and are addressing the meeting.

12 *Mr Chairman, **the first step is to** contact our foreign customers—who*
   represent over 70% of our market—and assure them that they have priority.   3

in other situations

13 *The following procedure should be adopted:*   33   37
14 *You should follow this procedure:*   33   37
15 *The job/process etc **should be done/performed/carried out** etc*
   according to the following procedure: 33   37

Practice

a ▶ What does he say?

b ▶ When would you say this?
It's dead easy : first you . . . .
   i   telling a subordinate in a sales meeting how best to increase turnover
   ii telling your friend, Bill, how to operate a pocket calculator he has bought
   iii telling a stranger in the street how to operate a ticket machine in a car park

c You are lecturing at a training seminar on dealing with trade unions.
▶ What would you say?
   i   *All you do is make sure you know your facts.*
   ii *Make sure you know all your facts.*
   iii *You should be fully acquainted with all the relevant facts.*

Key a 1, 3, 5 (e g *Take* . . .), 8 **b** ii **c** ii most appropriate (i and iii possible, according to how formal/informal the seminar is)

30 Asking for advice

Do you think I should try a larger size?

1	***Do you think I should . . . ?***		0	3

Your car needs a new engine. You are not sure whether it might be better to sell the car as it is and buy a new one. You ask the garage mechanic.

2	***Do you think I ought to** sell it?*			0	3
	It's difficult to say.				
3	***Ought I to . . . ?*** **4** ***Should I . . . ?***			0	3
5	***What should I/ought I to . . . ?***				3
6	***What would you advise?***				0
7	***What would you advise me to do?***				0
8	***What would your advice be?***				0
9	***Would you advise me to . . . ?***			0	3
10	***I'd like your/some advice on/about . . . .***	4	6	8–11	
11	***Can/Could you give me some advice on/about . . . ?***	4	6	8–11	
12	***What would you do (in my position)?***				0
13	***What/How/Where/When/Who would you . . . ?***				3
14	***Which one would you . . . ?***				3

I   You are with a friend at home when a telegram arrives for your brother who is returning from holiday in two days' time. You don't know whether to open it or not.

15	***What d'you reckon I should do?***		0
	Why not ring him and tell him a telegram's arrived?		
16	***What would you do if you were me?***		0
17	***What would you do if you were in ˅my shoes?***		0
18	***Reckon I should . . . ?***	0	3

---

in other situations

19	***How do you see . . . ?*** **20** ***What do you make of . . . ?***	5	6
21	***Can you sort me out on . . . ?***		6
22	***Can you help me sort . . . out?***		16

F   At your monthly departmental meeting you want some advice from your boss about an order.

	Was there anything else we had to discuss?			
23	***Well, I would appreciate your advice on** how to deal with the Hedley project.*	4	6	8–11
24	***I would appreciate your advice.***			0

25	*I would appreciate some advice on/about*	4	6	8–11
26	*Could I ask for your/some advice on/about* ... ?	4	6	8–11
27	*Could I ask for your/some advice?*			0
28	*I should like to ask*			8–11
29	*What course of action would you recommend* ... ?		0	2

---

in other situations

30	*Would you recommend* ... ?	2	4	6
31	*What would you recommend* ... ?		0	2
32	*I was wondering/I'd like to know what your reaction(s) would/be?*			0
33	*Could I ask what your reaction(s) would be to* ... ?			4–6

Practice

a ▶ What does she say?

b You and your friend, Sally, are at home, and about to cook fish for dinner. Sally notices that the fish is not fresh.
This fish smells a bit funny!
▶ What do you say?
  i *Yes—should I take it back?*
  ii *Yes—what course of action would you recommend?*
  iii *Yes—reckon I should take it back?*

c ▶ When would you say this?
What course of action would you recommend?
  i to your boss in a formal meeting about an orders problem
  ii to a friend in a restaurant about a girlfriend problem
  iii to a railway ticket clerk in a station about a timetable problem

Key **a** 1–12 (using various elements in the Thought Bubble), 13 (with *What* and *How*) **b** i and iii (ii too formal) **c** i (situations ii and iii not sufficiently formal for what is said)

81 Advising someone to do something

1 *I think you should . . . .*   0 3

A foreigner at the end of a very long taxi queue at Victoria Station stops you and asks how far away Radford Street is. You know it is only about 10 minutes' walk from the station.

Excuse me, how far away is Radford Street?
2 *Not very far.* **If I were you, I'd** *walk.*   3
3 *I'd . . . , if I were you.*   17
4 *It might be an idea to . . . .*   0 3

---

in other situations

5 *I think you ought to . . . .*   0 3
6 *I would . . . .*   0 3

I Your friend, Tessa, is engaged to marry Jim. But she has lately met and fallen in love with another man. She doesn't want to upset Jim. She asks you for advice.

What do you think I should do?
7 *You'd better* tell Jim as soon as you can!   0 3
8 *If I were in your shoes, I'd . . . .*   3
9 *I'd . . . , if I were in your shoes.*   17
10 *Tell him now/Warn Jim/Break it off with Jim.*
  [or other suitable imperative]   30
11 *I reckon you should . . . .*   **12** *Why don't you . . . ?*   0 3
13 *It mightn't be a bad idea . . . .*   0 1
14 *Take my advice and . . . .*   **15** *Just . . . .*   37
16 *The way I see it, you should . . . .*   0 3

F An important new client has asked your advice about money he has invested in stocks and shares.

I really have no idea which way the market will move.
17 *Well,* **my advice would be** *to sell immediately.*   1 37
18 *If you follow my advice, you'll . . . .*   3
19 *I would advise . . . .*   **20** *I would recommend . . . .*   2 4 6
21 *If I were in your position, I would . . . .*   3
22 *I would . . . , if I were in your position.*   17
23 *You would be well advised to/be wise to . . . .*   0 3
24 *My reaction would be . . . .*   1 37

Practice

a ▶ What does she say?

b You are chatting to a friend. Suddenly you notice he may miss the last bus home.
    ▶ What do you say?
    i *Oh! It's five to twelve! You'd better leave now!*
    ii *Oh! It's five to twelve! I would advise leaving now!*
    iii *Oh! It's five to twelve! I think you ought to leave now!*
    ▶ What else could you say?

c ▶ When would you say this?
I reckon you should sell it, before it breaks down for ever!
    i to a friend at his home, who wants advice about selling his car
    ii to a new business client, in his car, about selling it
    iii to your husband, in the garden, about the petrol-driven lawnmower

Key a 1–5 **b** i most appropriate, iii also possible (ii too formal) 7, 11, 13 (1–4 equally possible)
c i and iii (situation ii too formal for these words)

82 Advising someone not to do something

1 *I don't think you should . . . .*   0 3

You are near the front of a queue outside a London cinema. A tourist approaches you. You know he has no chance of getting in to see the film. He asks you:

    Is this the queue for ' Star Wars III '?
2 *Yes, but **I wouldn't wait** **if I were you**, you won't get in, and the
film's already started.*   17
3 *If I were you, I wouldn't . . . .*   0 3

in other situations

4 *I don't think you ought to ....*	0	3

 You are on a beach at the foot of a cliff with your boyfriend. He thinks it is easy to climb straight up the cliff from the shore, but you don't think it's safe.

You walk up the path, if you like. I'm climbing!

5 *You'd better not, it looks really dangerous!*		0	3
6 *Don't go that way/Go the other way.* [or any suitable imperative]			30
7 *I don't reckon you should ....*		0	3
8 *Take my advice and ....* 9 *Just ....* 10 *Don't just ....*			37
11 *(If I were you,) I'd think twice about ....*	4	6	8
12 *(If I were you,) I'd think twice before ....*			4
13 *It's up to you but I wouldn't ....*		0	3

in other situations

14 *I wouldn't ... if I were in your shoes.*		16
15 *If I were in your shoes I wouldn't ....* 16 *Why don't you ... ?*	0	3
17 *The way I see it, you should/shouldn't ....*	0	3

F You have just been introduced to an important business client. During the conversation, he says he is dining out this evening.

I think I shall try the 'Golden Duck' restaurant.

18 *I wouldn't recommend the 'Golden Duck' actually. It doesn't have*			
a very good reputation. Have you tried the 'Silver Trout'?	2	4	6
19 *I wouldn't advise ....*	2	4	6
20 *You would be well advised to/not to ....*		0	3
21 *If you follow my advice, you'll ....*			3
22 *My (own) advice would be ....*		1	37
23 *I would advise against ....*		0	4–6

in other situations

24 *If I were in your position, I wouldn't ....*	0	3
25 *I wouldn't ... if I were in your position.*		17
26 *My reaction would be ....*	1	37

Practice

a ▶ What does he say?

b Your friend has been given a very old motorbike. You think the brakes don't work. He wants to try it out immediately.

▶ What do you say?

i *I would advise against riding it without testing the brakes first.*

ii *Don't ride it without testing the brakes first.*

iii *I wouldn't ride it without testing the brakes first, if I were you.*

▶ What else could you say?

c ▶ When would you say this?

You would be well advised not to become involved.

i talking at home to your best friend, Jill, about a quarrel between two of her friends

ii talking to a friend, in a pub, about a strike at work

iii talking to your assistant, in a meeting, about a dispute at work

Key **a** 1–4, 13   **b** ii and iii, 1–16   **c** iii (too formal for i and ii)

83 Warning someone

| **1** *Look out!* | 0 |

In a café, a waitress, carrying a tray full of food, is not looking where she is going and is about to empty the tray over you.

2 *Be careful! You'll drop the tray!*	0
3 *Watch out!*	0
4 *Watch out for ....*	6
5 *Mind you don't ....*	3

in other situations

6 *Make sure you don't ....* **7** *Make sure you ....*	3
8 *Be ready for ....*	6
9 *Be careful of ....*	4 6
10 *Fire!/Gas!/The milk!/Your cigarette!*	
[or other suitable nouns/phrases carrying danger]	31

I You are in the garden having tea with your girlfriend. A large bee is about to land on her neck.

11 *Whatever you do, don't move!*	37
12 *Mind out!*	0
13 *Mind ....*	6

138

F In a formal meeting at your office, a member of the board has just suggested cutting the work force by 25%, and has asked for immediate approval.

14 ***In no circumstances must we/should we/ought we to*** *come to a hasty decision on this.*	3
15 ***I would be extremely careful of . . . if I were you.***	16
16 ***I would be extremely careful to/not to . . . if I were you.***	17
17 ***On no account should we . . . .***	3

Practice

a ▶ What does he say?

b A friend is about to mend a fuse while the electricity is still switched on.
   ▶ What do you say?
   i *Whatever you do, don't touch the wires!*
   ii *Be careful! The electricity's still on!*
   iii *In no circumstances should you mend the fuse without turning off the electricity.*
   ▶ What else could you say?

c ▶ When would you say this?
   Mind out!
   i You arrive late at a board meeting. You speak to a colleague whose papers are in your way.
   ii You are learning to ski with a friend. You go completely out of control and head straight towards him.
   iii You are running to catch a bus. An old lady doesn't see you and steps between you and the bus.

Key **a** 1, 3, 4 **b** i and ii (iii too formal), 5–7 **c** ii (words too informal for i and iii)

84 Suggesting

1 *Shall we . . . ?*   3

You are driving along a country road when you see a girl standing by her moped which has broken down. You stop and try to help.

It's no good. It won't start.
2 *You could leave it here and come with me to the nearest town.*   3
3 *We might as well . . . .*   **4** *Would it be an idea to . . . ?*   3

in other situations

5 *We might . . . .*   3
6 *Do you think it would be an idea to . . . ?*   3

I It's the weekend and you and your friend are bored. It's sunny.

I feel like doing something different today.
7 *I know! Let's go to the seaside!*   3
8 *Let's . . . .*   3
9 *Let's . . . (then,) shall we?*   17
10 *What about . . . , (then)?*   **11** *How about . . . , (then)?*   4–6
12 *I tell you what: we'll . . . .*   3
13 *We could always . . . , (then).*   3
14 *Fancy . . . , (then)?*   4 6
15 *Why don't we . . . , (then)?*   3

in other situations

16 *Why not . . . , (then)?*   **17** *Surely he could . . . , (then)?*   3
18 *Come for a swim/Go to the pictures.*
[or other suitable imperative sentence]   30
19 *. . . , then.*   37

F You are talking in your office to an important businessman whom you have just met and who may place a very large order with your firm. So far you have only talked socially. You want to start talking business.

20 *Well, Mr Grant, perhaps you'd care to outline your requirements, (then)?*   3
21 *May/Might I suggest . . . , (then)?*   4 6 7
22 *If I may/might make a suggestion: . . . .*   33 35
23 *Would you care to . . . , (then)?*   3

Practice

a ▶ What does he say?

b ▶ When would you say this?
   Fancy a cup of tea?
   i   to an important new business client halfway through a meeting
   ii to a friend who has been walking round London all afternoon with you
   iii to an elderly man who has fallen over in the street outside your house and
       looks shaken. You do not know him.

c You have been out with your friend, Pete, to a party. You are returning with
   him to his house. He discovers he has lost his key and can't get in. You suggest
   opening a window.
   ▶ What do you say?

d You are in a meeting at work. An important business client is present. You think
   you have the answer to the problem of rapidly falling|sales.
   ▶ What do you say?
   i   *I know! Let's cut profit margins by 5%!*
   ii *Why don't we consider commissioning a more recent market survey?*
   iii *If I may make a suggestion, there appears to be another way of interpreting the
       figures.*
   ▶ What else could you say?

Key **a** 1, (2 with change of pronoun to 'we'), 3, 4, 6 (8, 9, 11, 13–15 also possible if they know
each other well) **b** ii (i and iii not informal enough) **c** 7–13, 15, 16, 18, 19; 1, 2, 4–6 equally possible **d** ii and iii (i too informal), 21, 22, 25–28 most appropriate, 4–6, (2 with change of pronoun to
'we') also possible

85 Requesting

1 *Could you . . . , please?*   0 17

You come back to your parked car to find that there is not enough space for you to get out. The man in the car behind yours is taking up more space than he needs.

---

2 *Excuse me.* **Do you think you could** *move back a little,* **please?**   0 17
Oh, sorry! Yes, of course!
3 *Could I ask you to . . . ?*   0 3
4 *Would/Could you . . . , please?*   0 17
5 *Would you mind . . . , (please)?*   0 4 5
6 *(Oh dear,) I'm not sure I can get out/I seem to be boxed in.*
[or other similar statement showing the other person that you want
him to do something for you]   27
7 *Do you mind . . . , (please)?*   4 5
8 *Can I get out of there? Will there be room for me to get out?*
[or other similar question showing the other person that you want him to do
something for you]   28

---

in other situations

---

9 *If you could . . . I'd be (very) grateful.*   17
10 *I'd be (very) grateful if you'd . . . .*   3

I You are mending a fuse. A friend is watching you. You need a penknife and don't
want to let go of the fuse.

---

11 *Got a penknife?*   6
Yes. Just a minute.
12 *Any chance of . . . ?*   4–6
13 *You couldn't . . . , ⁿcould you?*   17
14 *Can you . . . ?*   3
15 *. . . , please?*   34
16 *You haven't got . . . , ⁿhave you?*   16
17 *Do me a favour and . . . .*   37
18 *. . . , ⁿ will you ⁿwould you/ⁿcould you/ⁿcan you, (please)?*   37
19 *Blast, where did I put that penknife?/Ooh, is that my*
penknife over there? [or other similar question showing the other
person that you want him to do something for you]   28
20 *Damn. Lost my penknife!/Oh, that's where my penknife got to!*
[or other similar statement showing the other person that you want
him to do something for you]   27

21   *Mind . . . ?*   4   5
22   *Don't. . . , will you?*   17

F   You are expecting a very important visitor from Canada. You are ringing him to find
out exactly when he will arrive. He answers:

I don't think I can say definitely yet.
23   Oh, I see. **Do you think it would be possible** to let us know as soon as you decide,
Mr Denver? We can make arrangements to meet you at the airport, then.   0   1
24   *Would it be possible for you to . . . .*   25   *Could you possibly . . . ?* 0   3
26   *Would there be any possibility of . . . ?*   4–6
27   *We should be most grateful if . . . .*   12
28   *Would you be so kind as to . . . ?*   3

29   *We should be most grateful.*   0
30   *I hope you don't mind my asking, but . . . .*   34   35
31   *I'm sorry to trouble you, but . . . .*   34   35

Practice

a   ▶   What does the customer say?

b   You have just bought a camera and want to ask the assistant how you can
pay—if, for example, he will take a cheque.
▶   What do you say?

c   ▶   When would you say this?
Got a light?
   i   in a restaurant after a meal, to a business client you know very well after he's
given you a cigar
   ii   to a stranger in the foyer of a West End theatre
   iii   to a friend as you're waiting for a bus

d   You are telephoning an important business client, whom you have never met
before, to see if you can change the date of a meeting.
▶   What do you say?
   i   *Any chance of meeting on Thursday instead?*
   ii   *Would it be possible to meet on Thursday instead?*
   iii   *Blast! The only day I can make it is Thursday!*

Key   a 1–5 most appropriate, 13–16, 18, 21, 25 also possible   **b** 1 and 2 (with pronoun change to 'I')
3–5, 6 (or other similar statement), most appropriate, 13, 14, 20 (or other similar statement) also
possible   **c** i and iii (ii too formal)   **d** ii (i and iii not formal enough)

1 *Well done! Now . . . !*   33–35 37 38

You are teaching your boss's wife, to whom you have just been introduced, how to play tennis. She has never served before.

> I didn't realize it was so difficult. I don't think I'll ever learn!

2 *No!* **You're doing fine!**   **3** *You're doing very well.*   0
4 *That's fine/good/lovely/all right.*   0

in other situations

5 *I wish I could do as well.*   0
6 *That's better than I could do.*   0
7 *Don't worry, I'm sure you'll do better this time.*   0

I You are on a cycling tour with your friend, Dave. You are going up a steep hill and Dave is finding it difficult. It's getting late and you don't want to stop.

8 *You can do it!*   **9** *Come on!*   **10** *Go on!*   0
11 *Stick to it!*   **12** *Keep it up!*   **13** *Keep at it!*   0
14 *Don't give up (now)!*   **15** *Nearly there!*   0

in other situations

16 *Great!/Terrific!/Lovely!*   **17** *I'm right behind you!*   0

F You are representing your international company at a meeting in England. You have been told to encourage expansion in the English subsidiary firm.

> Perhaps we could hear the view of our colleague?

18 *Yes, indeed.* **You have our whole-hearted support.**   0
19 *You have our backing . . . .*   0 1
20 *We feel you should go ahead.*   0

in other situations

21 *First class!*   **22** *That's most encouraging!*   0
23 *There's no reason to feel/be discouraged.*   0
24 *There's nothing to feel/be discouraged about.*   0

Practice

a ▶ What does he say?

b You are at the races. Two horses are neck and neck near the finishing post. Your horse is called 'Slowcoach'.
▶ What do you say?

c You are teaching your friend, Paul, how to ski. He is having a lot of problems.
▶ What do you say?
i *You can do it!* ii *That's all right!* iii *That's most encouraging!*

d ▶ When would you say this?
You have my whole-hearted support.
i in a café to a friend who is considering taking driving lessons
ii during a 'working lunch' in a pub to a friend and colleague who is proposing changes at work
iii in a board meeting at work to the chairman who is asking officially for a vote of confidence

Key **a** 8–14 **b** 8–15 **c** i and ii (iii too formal) **d** iii (possibly ii)

87 Persuading

1 *Won't you . . . , please?* 0 17

A man is trying unsuccessfully to get out of a car park. He can't raise the barrier. You are late and don't want to wait all day. He keeps refusing your help.

It's all right, I've nearly done it. Ow! My hand!
2 *Please let me try. I think I know how it works.* 0 3
3 *Why don't you . . . ?* **4** *Do . . . .* 0 3

    5 *I really think you'd do well to . . . .*   0 3

    6 *Are you really sure you can't/couldn't . . . ?*   0 3

I You and your friend, Trisha, have decided to go swimming in the sea on a rather cold day. You have gone in first but Trisha has put her toe in the water three times, and then pulled it out again quickly on each occasion.

    Oooh! It's far too cold!

    7 *Oh, **come on** Trish! It's not as bad as that!*   0

    8 *Go on!*   9 *Don't be like that!*   10 *↗Please!*   0

    11 *Not even for me/for my sake?*   12 *Just for me!*   0

    13 *Just this once!*   0

    14 *You're not going to let me down, are you?*   0

F In a committee meeting at work the feeling is that your company should merge with a larger one. You disagree and have tried several times, unsuccessfully, to alter the decision. You decide to try one last time. The chairman speaks.

    Well, we've discussed it fully now, I think.

    15 *But **surely the best course of action would be to** wait until we have a report on the P2 project.*   3

    16 *Surely the most sensible thing would be to . . . .*   3

    17 *I really think it would be a pity if we didn't . . . .*   0 3

    18 *How can I persuade you to . . . ?*   0 3

    19 *But surely it's in our own interests to . . . .*   0 3

    20 *Could you/Couldn't you be persuaded . . . ?*   0 1 7

    21 *Can't I persuade you . . . ?*   0 1 7

    22 *Are you quite sure you won't reconsider . . . ?*   0 |4 6

    23 *Are you quite sure you've taken everything into account?*   0

    24 *Can I/Could I/Couldn't I persuade you . . . ?*   0 1 7

Practice

a ▶ What does the customer say?

b Your friend, Ted, wants to go to the cinema. You want to go to the theatre.
▶ What do you say?
Ted: *It's a very good film you know, better than your play!*
You: . . . .
Ted: *But we went to the theatre last week!*
You: . . . .
Ted: *I still think you'd enjoy the film more!*
You: . . . .
Ted: *Oh, all right then. Hey, look! Last performance Friday 17th. But it's the 18th today!*

c You have interviewed a Mr Reynolds for a job with your firm as sales manager and offered him the job. He phones you two days later to say that on balance he has decided to accept another job. You want him very much and would like to see him again.
▶ What do you say?
Mr Reynolds: *Well . . . they've made an offer I really can't refuse.*
You: . . . .
Mr Reynolds: *Well . . . I don't really think I can change my mind at this stage.*
You: . . . .
Mr Reynolds: *All right, maybe we could meet for a final discussion on Friday.*

Key a 2, 4, 6 most appropriate, 10 also possible **b** 7–13 most appropriate, 4 also possible **c** 15–24, 2–6 also possible

88 Complaining

| 1 | *I want to complain about . . . .* | 4–6 |

You have booked a room at a hotel and find when you arrive that the hotel clerk says there is no room for you.

	I'm sorry, sir, we have no record of your booking.	
2	*(Well,) this is most unsatisfactory. I booked the room myself a week ago. I want to speak to the manager, please.*	0
3	*(I'm afraid) . . . it just isn't good enough.*	15
4	*. . . just won't do!* 5 *. . . really is the limit!*	15
6	*What can you do/are you going to do about . . . ?*	4–6
7	*Can you do anything about . . . ?*	4–6
8	*I'm sorry to say this, but . . . .*	33
9	*Something must be/will have to be done . . . .*	0 1
10	*Something must be/will have to be done about . . . .*	4–6

11	*(I'm afraid) I've got a complaint about . . . .*	4–6
12	*(I'm afraid) I have a complaint to make.*	0
13	*Would you mind not . . . .*	4
14	*Would you please not . . . .*	3

I Your friend, Ron, has agreed to come with you and two other friends to London. Suddenly he changes his mind and says he wants to go to the seaside. He has done this sort of thing three times in the last week.

It'll be nice on the beach today. I think I'll go swimming.

15	*You can't possibly do that. We all agreed last night we'd go to London!*	0	3
16	*(Really!) I've just about had enough.*	0	
17	*(Really!) I've just about had enough of . . . .*	4–6	
18	*(Look here!) You can't go around . . . .*	4	
19	*(Honestly!) You're always . . . .*	4	
20	*(Really!) I'm fed up with . . . .*	4–6	
21	*(Hey!) For goodness sake!* 22 *Do you ↘mind?*	0	
23	*(Look,) I wish you'd/you wouldn't . . . .*	0	3

24	*(Look,) I wish you would/wouldn't . . . .*	0	3
25	*You've got to do something about . . . .*	4–6	

F You have had problem after problem at your hotel. Finally you see the manager in his office to make a formal complaint.

Come in. Now, what seems to be the trouble, sir?

26	*I wish to complain in the strongest terms about the service in this hotel.*	4–6	
27	*I'm not at all satisfied . . . .*	0	3
28	*I'm not at all satisfied with . . . .*	4–6	

29	*I really do/must object to . . . .*	4–6
30	*I take great exception to . . . .*	4–6

Practice

a ▶ What does he actually say?

b Your friend, Peter, has spent nearly three hours trying to choose a present for his wife. As a result you are both in danger of missing your plane home.
▶ What do you say?
i *Look, I wish you'd make up your mind! If you don't, we'll miss the plane!*
ii *I wish to complain in the strongest terms about your inability to come to a decision. Our plane leaves in half an hour!*
iii *I'm sorry to say this, but if we spend any longer here, we'll miss our plane!*
▶ What else could you say?

c You are chairing a board meeting about falling profits.
▶ What do you say?

i *I'm not at all satisfied.*
ii *It just won't do.*
iii *I'm fed up with it.*
▶ What else could you say?

d You are with a friend in a pub discussing problems at work.
▶ What do you say?
i *I wish to complain in the strongest terms about it.*
ii *It just won't do.*
iii *I'm fed up with it.*
▶ What else could you say?

Key a 1–8, 14, 15 **b** i and iii (ii too formal), 13, 19 most appropriate, 5 also possible **c** i and ii (iii too informal), 28 most appropriate, 2–4, 8 also possible **d** ii and iii (i too formal), 14, 15; 3, 5, 8 also possible

89 Threatening

1 *If ..., I'll ....* [use *shall/will* in the second part of the sentence] 13

A bus conductor tells you rudely to get off the bus because it is full. You object to his manner.

That's the lot! No more! Come on you! Off!	
2 *If I were you, I'd be a little more polite **or** I'll have to report you to London Transport!*	19
3 *If I were you, I wouldn't ... or ....*	19
4 *If I were you I wouldn't, or ....*	33
5 *I would/I wouldn't ... if I were you, or ....*	19
6 *I would/I wouldn't if I were you, or ....*	33
7 *Unless ..., I'll ....* [use *shall/will* in the second part of the sentence]	13

149

I You see a group of young boys throwing stones at cars as they pass by.

8 ***Do that (again) and*** *I'll call the police!*	12
9 ***...and ....*** [use *shall/will* after *and*]	13
10 ***Don't ... or ....***	19
11 ***Just you try!*** 12 ***Watch it!***	0
13 ***Just you ....*** [use *shall/will* in the second part of the sentence]	3
14 ***Don't you dare!*** 15 ***Just you dare!***	0
16 ***Try ... and ....***	18
17 ***I'll ....***	3
18 ***Just don't ..., that's all!***	17

F A company owes your firm several thousand pounds, and repeated requests for payments have been ignored. You ring the manager to speak to him personally.

19 ***If you don't*** *settle your account within ten days* ***I shall be forced to*** *put the matter in the hands of our solicitors.*	0 19
20 ***If you cannot ... I shall be obliged to ....***	19
21 ***You'd be very/most unwise to/not to ....***	0 3
22 ***You'd be well advised to/not to ....***	0 3
23 ***Far be it from me to resort to threats, but (I'm afraid) ....***	33
24 ***If you don't/Unless you ... (I'm afraid) you leave me with little alternative but to ....***	19
25 ***(I'm afraid) if ... you leave me with little alternative but to ....***	19
26 ***I don't really want to say this, but if ..., we shall ....***	12

Practice

a ▶ What does he say?

b It's 3 o'clock in the morning and you are trying to get to sleep. Twice you have telephoned your new next door neighbour to complain about the noise of a party being held there, but the noise is still just as bad. You telephone again, but get very little cooperation.
▶ What do you say?

c You are on holiday by the seaside with your friend. He is doing a handstand on the sand. You say: *Like me to give you a push?*
▶ What does he say?
  i *You'd be most unwise to do that!*
  ii *Just you dare!*
  iii *I wouldn't if I were you!*
▶ What else could he say?

d Your firm's production schedules have been held up several times because your supplier has delivered late. You are telephoning the manager of the firm concerned.

▶ What do you say?
i *Well, Mr Blythe, if your next consignment doesn't arrive within three days, you leave me with little alternative but to cancel our contract.*
ii *Well, Mr Blythe, just don't send us any more late consignments, that's all!*
iii *If I were you I wouldn't send us any more late consignments, Mr Blythe, or we may have to look elsewhere for a supplier.*

Key **a** 1–3, 5, 7 most appropriate, 19 also possible **b** 1–3, 5, 7 most appropriate, 19–26 also possible **c** ii and iii (i too formal), 8–17 most appropriate, 1–6 also possible **d** i and iii (ii too informal)

90 Saying you are willing to do something

1 *Certainly.*	0

You are opening a temporary bank account and the clerk requires examples of your signature.

Would you sign this card three times, please? There, there and there.

2 *(Yes,) of course.*	0

in other situations

3 *(No,) of course not.*				0
4 *(Yes,) I don't see why not.* [could sound reluctant or grudging]				0
5 *I'd be (only too) happy to . . . .*			0	3
6 *(No/Yes,) I don't mind . . . .*	0	4–6	8	10
7 *(No/Yes,) I don't mind . . . in the least/in the slightest/at all.*			0	16
8 *I'm (quite) prepared to . . . .*			0	3
9 *(Yes,) I'll . . . .*				3
10 *I'll . . . if you like.*				17

I You are having lunch with your friend, Jeremy. He finds he has run out of money.

You couldn't lend me a couple of quid till tomorrow, could you?

11 *Sure.*	**12** *Right you are.*	**13** *OK.*		0
14 *Yeah.*	**15** *Mmm.*	**16** *No problem.*		0

in other situations

17 *Why not.*	0

F You are visiting an English subsidiary of your firm. At the end of a meeting, the director addresses you.

> We were wondering if you might give an after-dinner speech at our firm's annual Christmas party?

18	*I should be delighted.*	0 1
19	*I should be most happy/most pleased . . . .*	0 1
20	*By all means.*	0

---

in other situations

21	*I see no objection (whatsoever).*	} [could sound reluctant	0
22	*I see no objection (whatsoever) to . . . .*	or grudging]	4–6
23	*(I think) we could undertake . . . .*		1 6
24	*I'm (perfectly/quite) willing . . . .*		0 1
25	*Naturally.* [when you don't think the other person needs to ask, because you would have done it anyway]		0

Practice

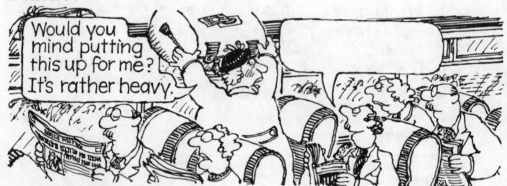

> Would you mind putting this up for me? It's rather heavy.

a ▶ What does he say?
  i *I'm perfectly willing to do so.*
  ii *Certainly.*
  iii *I should be delighted.*
  ▶ What else could he say?

b ▶ When would you say this?
  I should be delighted.
  i The bank manager's secretary asks you if you mind waiting five minutes to see the manager, as he's been delayed.
  ii Your best friend asks you if you'll give him a lift to work, as his car has broken down.
  iii Just before a meeting begins, your employer introduces you to an important business client and asks if you'll act as his guide on a visit to London.
  ▶ What else could you say?

c You are on holiday touring Scotland with your friend, Terry. He asks you if you would change places on the coach with him.
  Terry: *Could we change places for a bit? My legs are too long for this seat.*
  ▶ What do you say?

Key **a** ii (i and iii too formal), 2, 3, 5, 9 most appropriate, 11–16 also possible   **b** iii (i and ii too informal), 19, 20 most appropriate, 1, 2, 5 also possible   **c** 11–16 most appropriate, 1, 2, 6, 7, 9 also possible

91 Saying you are willing to do something under certain conditions

1 *Yes, if . . . .*   12

You are in a travel agent's in London. You want to fly from London to Istanbul.

I'm afraid the direct flight is fully booked, but there is room on
the flight that goes via Rome. Is that all right?

2 *Certainly, as long as there's no difference in the air fare.*		12
3 *Certainly, if/provided . . . .*		12
4 *Yes, as long as/provided . . . .*		12
5 *Certainly, but . . . .* 6 *Yes, but . . . .*	33–35	37
7 *Yes, but that (rather) depends/depends on . . . .*	4–6 8	10
8 *I don't mind, as long as/if/provided . . . .*		12
9 *I don't see why not, as long as/if/provided . . . .*		12
10 *I don't mind, but . . . .* 11 *I don't see why not, but . . . .*	33–35	37
12 *Yes, though . . . .*		14
13 *I'll . . . , as long as/if/provided . . . .* 14 *I'll . . . , but . . . .*		19
15 *Of course, as long as/if/provided . . . .*		12
16 *Of course, but . . . .*	33–35	37
17 *I'd be happy to, as long as/if/provided . . . .*		12
18 *I'm quite prepared to, as long as/if/provided . . . .*		12
19 *I'd be happy to, but . . . .*	33–35	37
20 *I'm quite prepared to, but . . . .*	33–35	37

I Your friend, Pete, asks a favour.

Oh, by the way, would you mind if I borrowed your cassette this evening?

21 *Right you are, but take good care of it!*	33–35	37
22 *Right you are, as long as/if/provided . . . .*		12
23 *OK, as long as/if/provided . . . .*		12
24 *Yeah, as long as/if/provided . . . .*		12
25 *Mmm, as long as/if/provided . . . .*		12
26 *No problem, as long as/if/provided . . . .*		12
27 *Why not, as long as/if/provided . . . .*		12
28 *Sure, as long as/if/provided . . . .*		12
29 *OK, but . . . .* 30 *Yeah, but . . . .*	33–35	37
31 *Mmm, but . . . .* 32 *No problem, but . . . .*	33–35	37
33 *Why not, but . . . .* 34 *Sure, but . . . .*	33–35	37
35 *I suppose so, as long as/if/provided . . . .* } [could sound		12
36 *I suppose so, but . . . .* } reluctant or grudging]	33–35	37

153

F The manager of the hotel you have booked into asks you a favour.

> I wonder if you would be prepared to change rooms with another guest, sir? We appear to have made an error.

37 *I see no objection (whatsoever), provided that the room is of the same standard as my present one.* 12

38 *I see no objection (whatsoever), as long as/if/with the proviso that/on condition that/on the assumption that/on the understanding that ....* 12

39 *I'm (perfectly/quite) willing, as long as/if/provided/with the proviso that/on condition that/on the assumption that/on the understanding that ....* 12

40 *I'm (perfectly/quite) willing to, as long as/if/provided/with the proviso that/on condition that/on the assumption that/on the understanding that ....* 12

41 *Very well, as long as/if/provided/with the proviso that/on condition that/on the assumption that/on the understanding that ....* [fairly reluctant] 12

42 *By all means, as long as/if/provided/with the proviso that/on condition that/on the assumption that/on the understanding that ....* 12

43 *I see no objection (whatsoever), but ....* 33–35 37
44 *I'm (perfectly/quite) willing, but ....* 33–35 37
45 *I'm (perfectly/quite) willing to, but ....* 33–35 37
46 *Very well, but ....* [fairly reluctant] 47 *By all means, but ....* 33–35 37

---

in other situations

---

48 *I should be delighted/(most) happy/(most) pleased, as long as/if/provided/with the proviso that/on condition that/on the assumption that/on the understanding that ....* 12

49 *I should be delighted to/(most) happy to/(most) pleased to, as long as/if/provided/with the proviso that/on condition that/on the assumption that/on the understanding that ....* 12

50 *Naturally, so long as/if/provided/with the proviso that/on condition that/on the assumption that/on the understanding that ....* [when you don't think the other person needs to ask, because you would have done it anyway] 12

51 *I should be delighted/(most) happy/(most) pleased, but ....* 33–35 37
52 *I should be delighted to/(most) happy to/(most) pleased to, but ....* 33–35 37
53 *Naturally, but ....* [when you don't think the other person needs to ask, because you would have done it anyway] 33–35 37

Practice

Would you mind climbing to get it?

...hold the ladder.

a ▶ What does he actually say?

b ▶ When would you say this?
Sure, but don't lend it to anyone else!
  i   in answer to your boss, in a business meeting, handing him your pen
  ii in answer to a friend, at home, handing him a book you've just bought
  iii in answer to a client, whom you know very well, at a party in your house,
      after a few drinks, handing him a cassette of your favourite music

c You have arranged to go to the theatre with your friend, Chris. She rings to say
that she can only get very expensive tickets.
Chris: *Do you still want to go?*
  ▶ What do you say?
  i   *Yes, as long as you think it's a good play.*
  ii *Mmm, if you think it's a good play.*
  iii *Very well, with the proviso that it's a good play.*

d In an important business meeting a colleague suggests that you are not willing
to see your department reorganized.
Colleague: *I understand you were totally against the whole idea of reorganization.*
You: *Not at all . . . .*
  ▶ What do you actually say?

Key **a** 1–6 most appropriate, 21–23, 25, 28–31, 42, 47 also possible **b** ii and iii (i too formal)
c i and ii (iii too formal) **d** 37–39, 43, 44, 48, 51

92 Saying you are unwilling to do something

| 1 *I didn't really want to . . . .* | | 0 | 3 |

A traffic warden asks you to park in a very small space. You do not think there is
enough room.

You can park over there.
2	*I'd rather not, actually. I'll drive on to the car park. There's more room there.*	0	
3	*I don't really want to . . . .*	0	3
4	*I don't think I can/could . . . , actually.*	0	17
5	*I'm not sure I can/could . . . , actually.*	0	17
6	*It'd be a little awkward/difficult, actually.*	0	
7	*Well, I think I'd rather/rather not/prefer to/prefer not to . . . .*	0	3

155

8 *I wish I could, but* . . . . 9 *I'd like to be able to, but*	33–35	37
10 *I'm afraid I can't/couldn't possibly*		
[rather strong; smile as you say it]	0	3

I   A friend, Tim, hopes you are going in his direction and asks you a favour.

Any chance of a lift to the station?		
11 *I'd like to, but I'm not going that way today, sorry.*	33–35	37
12 *It's not that I don't want to, but/it's just that*	33–35	37
13 *Well, I er,*	33–35	37
14 *I don't (really) fancy* . . . . }		4–6
15 *I'm not (too) keen on* . . . . } [smile as you say it]		4–6

F   At a formal meeting you are discussing an offer that has been made to take over your firm.

Well, gentlemen, what reaction do you have to the Simpson offer?			
16 *Well, I'd be rather reluctant to accept it unless we are guaranteed fuller representation on the new board.*		0	3
17 *I'm not (totally/entirely) convinced we should*		0	3
18 *I'm not really willing/wouldn't really be willing*		0	1
19 *I'm not willing to/wouldn't be willing to* . . . . [very firm]		0	3
20 *(Well,) to be frank, I don't think*		0	7
21 *(Well,) on the whole, I don't think*			7
22 *I have (certain) (serious) reservations about*	4–6	8	10

23 *I'm not (too) sure that we would find ourselves able to*	0	3

Practice

a ▶ What does the customer say?

b   The manager of a first-class hotel you are staying at asks you to change rooms, as there has been a double booking. You particularly want the room you originally booked.
Manager: *Would you object to Room 17, sir? It's very comfortable.*
▶ What do you say?

156

i   *Well, I don't really want to change rooms. I asked for that room particularly.*
   ii *Well, I don't really fancy being chucked out of my room!*
   iii *Well, I'd be rather reluctant to move at this stage.*

c ▶ When would you say this?
   I have serious reservations about the whole matter.
   i   Your friend, Tessa, has asked you if you mind looking after her particularly
       fierce dog while she goes away for the day.
   ii The director of a subsidiary company in England is drawing up plans for
       expansion to be financed by your major company.
   iii You are in a post office and want to send a parcel home. You think the
       parcel is well wrapped, but the post office clerk is a little reluctant to
       accept it. He suggests you go away and wrap the parcel up again.

Key   a 1–7, 10   **b** i and iii   **c** ii

93 Refusing to do something

1 *I'm sorry, I can't . . . .*		0 3

Someone you would like to get to know better invites you out to the cinema.
Unfortunately you have already arranged to go out.

	It's really a very good film.	
2	*I'm sorry, it's not possible, maybe another evening?*	0 1
3	*I'm sorry, I'm not . . . .*	4
4	*I'm sorry, I can't/couldn't (possibly) . . . .*	0 3
5	*I'm afraid I can't/couldn't (possibly) . . . .*	0 3
6	*I'm afraid not.*	0
7	*I'd rather not, (actually) . . . .*	0 3
8	*I'm sorry, I don't think I can/could . . . .*	0 3

---

in other situations

---

9 *Unfortunately, ...* 10 *. . . , actually.*	33
11 *Actually, ...*	33

I Your friend, Bill, comes round to see you and asks for your help.

	You couldn't lend me your camera for a week, could you? Mine's broken and I'm off on holiday tomorrow.	
12	*Sorry, mine's being repaired.*	0 33
13	*Would if I could, but . . . .*	33
14	*(Only) wish I could, but . . . .*	33
15	*(Sorry,) out of the question.* [rather strong; to close friends only]	0

16	*Sorry, don't reckon I can/could . . . .*	0	3
17	*Can't really see how I can/could . . . .*	0	3
18	*Sorry, that's/it's (simply/just) not on.* [rather strong; only		0
19	*No, I (certainly) won't!* if you're angry]		0
20	*Not likely!* 21 *No way!* [rather strong; to		0
22	*You must be joking!* close friends only]		0
23	*Pull the other one!*		0

F An unreliable customer has rung you with an order from his firm. However, payment for the previous order you supplied is long overdue.

We were hoping to place this large order with you.

24	*(Well,) I'm sorry to say it's not possible to meet any more orders until the account for your previous order has been settled. It's in fact three months overdue.*	0	1
25	*(Well,) I'm afraid it's not possible . . . .*	0	1
26	*I'm afraid/I'm sorry to say it's (quite) impossible . . . .*	0	1
27	*I'm afraid/I'm sorry to say there is/there can be no question of . . . .*	4–6	
28	*I'm afraid/I'm sorry to say we cannot see our way clear to . . . .*	4–6	
29	*. . . is (quite) out of the question I'm afraid/I'm sorry to say.*	15	
30	*I'm afraid/I'm sorry to say . . .'s really not possible.*	16	

| 31 | *I've given this matter a great deal of thought but/and . . . .* | 33 | |
| 32 | *I regret to say that we find ourselves unable to . . . .* | 0 | 3 |

Practice

There are no first class seats available on that flight, I'm afraid. Would you mind travelling second class?

a ▶ What does he say?

b A taxi-driver charges you a high price for driving you to Heathrow Airport. You did not agree the fare before you left. He says: *That's £20, please.*
▶ What do you say?

c ▶ When would you say this:
It's quite out of the question, I'm sorry to say.
 i to a shop assistant who is just closing the shop and asks you to come back the next day
 ii to a friend you are seeing off on holiday who asks you to carry the heaviest of his two bags to the station

iii   to your boss in an interview when he asks you to reconsider your resignation

d   The friends you are staying with ask you to baby-sit for them. You have already arranged to go out.
▶   What do you say?

Key   a 5, 7, 10, 11; 29 equally possible   **b** 3–5, 8, 12, 18   **c** iii   **d** 12–14, 16, 17 most appropriate, 1–11 also possible

94   Starting a conversation with a stranger

1 *Excuse me, . . . ?*	33–35

At a party you see someone you think you recognize, but are not quite sure.

2 *I hope you don't mind my/me asking, but* haven't we met somewhere before?	34	35
3 *Excuse my/me asking, but . . . ?* 4 *Excuse me, but . . . ?*	34	35

in other situations

5 *Sorry, (but) I couldn't help overhearing . . . .*	6	7
6 *(I'm) sorry to trouble you, but . . . .*	33–35	
7 *Lovely/Nice* etc *day, (isn't it)!*	0	
8 *Lovely/Nice* etc *weather, (isn't it)!*	0	
9 *Terrible/Horrible* etc *day, (isn't it)!*	0	
10 *Warm/Hot/Windy/Cold/Freezing, isn't it!*	0	

I   At your friend, Nicola's, party to celebrate her engagement, you see someone you would like to meet. Everybody is dancing, laughing or chatting.

11 *Hello! Are you a friend of Nicola's?*	0
12 *Hi! Great party/music/band* etc *(isn't it)!*	0
13 *Sorry, but . . . ?*	34 35

F   In a first-class compartment in a train you think you recognize a famous person.

14 *I (do) beg your pardon, but* aren't you Lord Hagbourne? As a matter of fact I am!	34	35
15 *Forgive me (for asking), but . . . ?*	34	35
16 *Do excuse me, but . . . ?*	34	35

Practice

a ▶ What does he actually say?
　　▶ What else could he say?

b You are waiting outside an interview room, to be interviewed for a temporary office job in England. You are keen to make a good impression. A young lady comes along the corridor.
　　▶ What do you say?
　　i　*Hi! You Mr Morgan's secretary, then?*
　　ii　*Excuse me asking, but are you Mr Morgan's secretary?*
　　iii　*Do excuse me, but are you Mr Morgan's secretary?*
　　▶ What else could you say?

c You are in a dentist's waiting room. The only other patient is a little girl who looks very miserable. You know the dentist is a good one, and start a conversation with the girl by telling her so.
　　▶ What do you say?

d Travelling in the first-class compartment of a train, you think you recognize the man who, you have heard, may be taking over your firm. You want to start a conversation with him.
　　▶ What do you say?

Key　a 1–4, 9, 10　**b** ii and iii (i too informal), 1–4　**c** 11, 12　**d** 14–16 most appropriate, 1–4 also possible

95 Introducing yourself

1 *How do you do? My name's* Peter Reynolds.

Peter Reynolds is on a trip to England to meet other sales managers of his company from all over the world. Before official proceedings begin, he goes up to someone he thinks he recognizes as the recently appointed sales manager for East Asia.

2 ***Excuse me, my name's*** *Peter Reynolds.* 6
   Oh. How do you do!
3 ***Excuse me./How do you do? I don't think we've met before.***
   My name's **...** [your first name and surname, e g *Peter Reynolds*]. 6
4 ***Excuse me./How do you do? I don't think we've met before.***
   I'm **...** [your first name and surname]. 6

in other situations (speaking on the telephone)

5  ***Hello?/Good morning/afternoon/evening. This is ...***
   [your first name and surname] ***speaking.*** 16

6 ***Hello?/Good morning/afternoon/evening. My***
   name's **...** [your first name and surname]. 6

7 ***Hello?/Good morning/afternoon/evening.*** **...** [your first name
   and surname] ***speaking/here.*** 16

I At a New Year's Party where everyone is dancing, laughing and chatting, Peter Reynolds sees someone he thinks he recognizes.

8 ***Hello!*** *You must be Jilly Merchant.* ***I'm*** *Peter (Reynolds).* 6
9 ***Hi! I'm*** **...** [your first name, or first name and surname, e g *Pete* or *Pete Reynolds*]. 6

in other situations

10 ***Hello? (This is)*** **...** [your first name, or first name and surname]. 6

F Peter Reynolds is giving a talk at his firm's annual international sales conference. He has only recently joined the company and many in the audience do not know him.

11 ***May I introduce myself:*** *Peter Reynolds, sales manager, Northern Europe.* 6
12 ***First let me introduce myself:*** **...** [your first name and surname, e g
    Peter Reynolds, your job e g *marketing manager, Dunn Exports Ltd*]. 6
13 ***Allow me to introduce myself:*** **...** [your first name and surname, your job]. 6

Practice

a ▶ What does the man with the briefcase say?

161

b Dave Seldon has gone to a disco with his friend, Bill. At the disco Bill is just about to introduce Dave to a girl he knows when he is suddenly called away. Dave decides to introduce himself.

▶ What does he say?

i *Hello, I'm Dave. I'm a friend of Bill's.*

ii *Allow me to introduce myself. I'm Dave Seldon, a friend of Bill's.*

iii *How do you do? I'm Dave Seldon, a friend of Bill's.*

▶ What else could he say?

c Sally Mason is going to phone a close friend, Terry Nichols, to arrange a time to meet for lunch.

▶ What does she say?

i *Hello? Mr Nichols? My name's Mason.*

ii *Hello? Terry? Sally Mason here.*

iii *Hello? Terry? This is Sally.*

Key **a** 1 (3 and 4 with 'How do you do', but not 'Excuse me') most appropriate, 11, 13 also possible **b** i most appropriate, iii also possible (ii too formal), 9 most appropriate, 1 (3 and 4 with 'How do you do', but not 'Excuse me') also possible **c** iii most appropriate, ii also possible (i too formal)

96 Introducing someone

1 **This is** *John Davis.*	6

You are visiting an English branch of your company with a colleague from your own country. At a reception after working hours you introduce him to an English colleague.

2 *Oh,* **Paul,** **I'd like you to meet** *Stephen Parker.* How do you do?	6
3 **Have you met Michael Sims?** [or other first name and surname]	0
4 **Do you know Peter Reynolds?** [or other first name and surname]	0

in other situations

5 **By the way, do you know each other?** *David Bowie—* **Paul McCartney.** [or other first name and surname]	0

I You are in a pub with your friend, Jenny, when your brother Pete comes in. He doesn't know Jenny.

6 *Pete,* **meet** *Jenny.*	6
7 **Oh, look, here's Pete! Pete—Jenny, Jenny—Pete.** [or other, sometimes abbreviated, first names]	0

8 *Oh,/Look,/Oh Look, here's Pete. Pete, meet Jenny.*
[or other, sometimes abbreviated, first names]   0

F You are visiting an English firm, Watson Electronics, for the second time, as a sales representative of your company. You have brought another representative, Mr Harris, with you, to meet the Director of Watson Electronics.

---

9 *Good morning, Mr Watson!* **May I introduce** *Mr Harris, our*
   new representative. He'll be taking over from me in April.   6
10 *Let me introduce (our director/our marketing manager)*
   [or other title] *Mr Granger/Miss James/David Hawkins*
   [or similarly expressed name].   0
11 *Allow me to introduce (our director/our marketing*
   manager) [or other title] *Mr Granger/Miss James/*
   David Hawkins [or other similarly expressed name]. [very formal].   0
12 *I'd like to introduce (our director/our marketing manager)*
   [or other title] *Mr Granger/Miss James/David Hawkins*
   [or other similarly expressed name].   0

---

in other situations

13 *It is with great pleasure that I introduce (to you) Mr*
   Malcolm Horsely/Mr Peter Burgess/Mrs Jane Taplow
   [or other similarly expressed name], *Director of Cavendish*
   Enterprises/Distribution Manager of Rosco Supermarkets
   [or other title]. [used to introduce a speaker/lecturer etc]   0

Practice

a ▶ What does he actually say?

b You are staying with your English friend, Dave, for a few weeks. You are both lying in the park, when a girl who is learning English at the same language school as you approaches. You know her well, and introduce her to your English friend.
   ▶ What do you say?
   i *Hello! Dave, let me introduce my fellow student, Chantal. We're both studying at the same language school.*
   ii *Oh, look! Here's Chantal! We're both at the same language school.*
   iii *Hello, Chantal! Chantal—Dave, Dave—Chantal. We're both at the same language school.*
   ▶ What else could you say?

163

c ▶ When would you say this?

Allow me to introduce Mr Schendel, a colleague from Vienna.
  i   to your good friend, Pete, at a party in his house
  ii to the director of an English subsidiary company you are visiting, at a sales
      meeting you have both been invited to attend
  iii to your English friend, Tony, when your colleague and friend Herbert
      Schendel meets him for the first time

Key **a** 3, 4   **b** ii and iii (i too formal) 6, 8 most appropriate, 1–14 also possible   **c** ii (too formal for i
or iii)

97 Answering an introduction

1 *How do you do?*   0

You are at a party given by a business colleague in England, but you don't know
many people. Your colleague introduces you to a young man.

Do you know Peter Reynolds?
2 *No, I don't think so. How do you do?*   0
3 *(No,) I don't think I do. How do you do?/Pleased to meet*
   *****you./I've been looking forward to meeting you (for some***
   *****time)./I've been wanting to meet you (for some time).***   0
4 *No, I don't (actually). How do you do?/Pleased to meet*
   *****you./I've been looking forward to meeting you (for some***
   *****time)./I've been wanting to meet you (for some time).***   0

---

in other situations

---

5 *Yes, (I think) I have/(I think) I do.*   0
6 *Yes,/I think we have, (haven't we?)/we do, (don't we?)*   0
7 *(No,) I don't think I have. How do you do?/Pleased to meet*
   *****you./I've been looking forward to meeting you (for some***
   *****time)./I've been wanting to meet you (for some time).***   0
8 *(No,) I don't think we have, (have we?)/we do, (do we?) How do you do?/*
   *****Pleased to meet you./I've been looking forward to meeting you***
   *****(for some time)./I've been wanting to meet you (for some time).***   0
9 *No, I haven't/we haven't/we don't, (actually). How do you do?/Pleased*
   *****to meet you./I've been looking forward to meeting you (for***
   *****some time)./I've been wanting to meet you (for some time).***   0
10 *Yes, we've already met, (actually).*   **11 *Pleased to meet you.***   0
12 *I've been looking forward to meeting you (for some time).*   0
13 *I've been wanting to meet you (for some time).*   0

I It's a lovely day. You're going to the seaside with your good friend, Bill, and a friend of Bill's, Tessa, who you've never met before. Bill introduces you and Tessa to each other.

> Ramon—Tessa, Tessa—Ramon.

14 ***Hi, Tessa!***   0
   Hi, Ramon!
15 ***Hello, (Tessa)!*** [or other first name]   0
16 ***Nice/Good to meet you, (Tessa)!*** [or other first name]   0

F You are attending your company's sales exhibition in England. A colleague introduces a potentially very important customer to you.

> Ah, Pietro, I'd like to introduce Mr Basil Richards of Durobrit Enterprises.
> Mr Richards, this is Mr Pietro Morelli, Director of our Rome branch.

17 ***I'm delighted to meet you, Mr Richards.***   0
18 ***(How do you do?) I'm delighted to meet you, Mr Richards/***
   Dr Blunt/Miss Price [or other similarly expressed name].   0
19 ***(How do you do?) I'm delighted to make your acquaintance,***
   Mr Richards/Dr Blunt/Miss Price [or other similarly expressed name].   0
20 ***(No,) I don't believe I've had/(No,) I haven't yet had the pleasure.***   0

Practice

This is Gabriella Petrocelli, from Florence — Gabriella, this is Tony Newson, our new designer.

a ▶ What does she say?

b ▶ When would you say this?
   Hi, Pete!
   i   at a football match when your best friend introduces one of his friends to you
   ii in a meeting when your boss introduces a prospective client to you
   iii at the house of an old friend you haven't seen for years when he introduces
       his small son of five years old to you

c You are on a business trip with your boss to England where your company has its headquarters. Your boss has just introduced you to *his* new English boss.
   Your boss: *Lena, this is Mr Clarke.*
   ▶ What do you say?
   i   *Hi, Mr Clarke.*
   ii *How do you do, Mr Clarke.*
   iii *Delighted to make your acquaintance, Mr Clarke.*

Key **a** 1, 11–16   **b** i and iii (too informal for ii)   **c** ii and iii (i too informal)

98 Attracting someone's attention

1 *Excuse me!* 0

On a bus you notice that a young lady who is getting off has left her purse on the seat.

2 *Sorry, but isn't that your purse?* 33–35
Oh, thanks very much.

in other situations

3 *Sorry to trouble/bother you, but . . . .* 33–35

I Your friend, Jim, has been visiting you. When he leaves, you notice he's forgotten his umbrella. You run after him.

4 *Hey, Jim! You've forgotton your umbrella!* 0
5 *(Oy!/Hey!) Jim!/Sally!* [or other first name] 0
6 *Oy!/Hey! (Jim!/Sally!)* [or other first name]
[could sound rude, but can be used when attracting someone's attention to warn them about something] 0
7 *Oy!/Hey! You!* 0
8 *Oy!/Hey! You, there!* } [only when you're very angry—sounds rude] 0

in other situations

9 *'Scuse me (butting in), but . . . .* 33–35
10 *Sorry (to butt in), but . . . .* 33–35
11 *Look!/Listen!/Watch!* [or other imperative] 30

F You are about to address a sales meeting of your company at a conference.

12 *May I have your attention (for a moment), please!* 0
13 *(Er, ah, hmm,)* [throat noise to attract attention] *I wonder if we could begin/make a start* etc. 0

in other situations

14 *(Er/Excuse me,) Could I just mention that . . . .* 7

166

Practice

a ▶ What does the customer say?

b ▶ When would you say this?
Could I just mention that your taxi's waiting outside?
  i   to your boss in a business meeting   ii   to your best friend at a party
  iii to a business friend you know well during the firm's annual Christmas
      Party

You are on holiday in Scotland, bird-watching with your friend, Angus.
c Suddenly, you see a very rare bird. Angus hasn't noticed it.
  ▶ What do you say?
  i   *Sorry to trouble you, but isn't that a golden eagle over there?*
  ii *Look! A golden eagle!*
  iii *Angus!* (and point at the golden eagle)
  ▶ What else could you say?

Key **a** 1–3, 13   **b** i (too formal for ii or iii)   **c** ii and iii (i too formal) 4

99 Greeting someone

1 *Morning!*   0

You see a colleague you haven't seen for some time.

2 *John! Good to see you (again)!*   0
It's good to see you!
3 *(How/Very) nice to see you (again)!*   0

---

in other situations

4 *Afternoon!* [from 12 noon or after lunch to the end of the working day]   0
5 *Evening!* [after work or from about 6 pm onwards]   0
6 *Dear Mr/Mrs/Miss/Ms/Michael Crowther,*
[or other title or first name, plus surname; when writing]   0

167

I You see your friend, Trevor, in the street.

Hello!
7 *Hi (Trevor)! How are you?*   0
A bit older than when you saw me last. Otherwise, fine. How are you?
8 *Hi there, (Trevor/Judy)!* [or other first name]   0
9 *Hello (there, Trevor/Judy)!* [or other first name]   0

in other situations

10 *Long time no see!* [when its some time since you last met the
other person]   0
11 *(Ah, Lynda/Steve)* [or other first name] *Just the person I
wanted to see.*   0
12 *Just the person/lady/man* etc *I was looking for.*   0
13 *The⁷very person/girl/chap* etc *I was after.*   0
14 *Dear all,*   0
15 *Hi everybody!*   0
16 *Dear/My dear Chris/Mandy,* etc [or other first name]   0
17 *Dearest/My dearest Chris/Mandy,* etc   [when   0
[or other first name]   writing]
18 *Darling/My darling Chris/Mandy,* etc
[or other first name] [love letters]   0

F You walk into a sales conference. Some top-level managers you do not know
well are there.

19 *Good morning,* gentlemen!   0
Good morning!

in other situations

20 *Good afternoon!* [from 12 noon or after lunch to the end of the
working day]   0
21 *Good evening!* [after work or from 6 pm onwards]   0
22 *Dear Sir,*   0
23 *Dear Madam,*   0
24 *Dear Sir or Madam,* [if you don't know exactly who   [when writing]
will deal with your letter in e g a government department]
25 *Sir,*   [usually sounds cold/angry]   0
26 *Madam,*   0

Practice

a   You see these people at these times. You don't know any of them very well.
It's the first time you've seen them today.
   i   Mr Jones—3 pm
   ii   Miss Jay—11 am
   iii Mrs Higgins—8.30 pm
   iv   Mrs Laker—9 pm
   v   Mr Simpson—4 pm
   ▶ What do you say to each one?

b   One afternoon, a sales representative sees these people

who	where
i chairman of the board	the boardroom
ii best friend	a coffee shop
iii colleague he doesn't know well	the office

▶   How does he greet each one?

c   A young diplomat meets a foreign Ambassador for the second time and says:
Hi there! Long time no see!
▶   What does the Ambassador think?
i   *Nice young man, isn't he?*
ii   *Really, he needn't be so polite.*
iii   *Who does he think he is? The Prime Minister?*

d   You're writing letters/postcards

to	about
i five colleagues at work	the great holiday you're having
ii a bank manager	borrowing some money
iii your wife/husband	how you're missing her/him

▶   How would you begin each letter/postcard?

Key   a i and v, Afternoon, ii Morning, iii and iv Evening   **b** i 20   **b** ii 7–13   **b** iii 4   **c** iii   **d** i Dear all,/Hi everybody!   **d** ii Dear Sir,   **d** iii 16–18 + appropriate name

00   Asking how someone is

1 *How are you?*	0

You meet a business acquaintance from another firm. You rarely see him.

2 *Ah, Mr Blake. Are you well?*	0
As well as can be expected, thank you. And you?	
3 *How are you keeping?*	0

in other situations

4 *Are you better?* [after someone has been ill]	0

You meet someone who was in your class at a language school last year.

5   *It's great to see you again! So—how's life?*   0
     Fine, thanks.
6   *How goes it with ⟍you?*   7   *How goes it?*   0
8   *How's life treating ⟍you?*   9   *How are things with ⟍you?*   0
10 *In good shape, are you?*   0
11 *How's things?* [very informal]   0
12 *What are ⟍you up to/you up to these days/* ⎫ [when you want to
     nowadays?   ⎬ catch up with the   0
13 *What's new?*   ⎪ other person's news]   0
14 *What's the latest?*   ⎭   0

F You have just greeted a fairly important customer at the airport.

15 *I trust you're keeping well?*   0
     Very well indeed, thank you.

in other situations

16 *I hope all goes well with you?*   0

Practice

a   You meet someone you do not know well. You think: *Is she well and happy?*
   ▶ What do you say?

b   You are about to begin some delicate and difficult negotiations with someone
   you do not particularly like or trust. Before starting, you ask politely after his
   health.
   ▶ What do you say?
   i   *How's life?*
   ii   *In good shape, are you?*
   iii *I hope you're keeping well?*

c ▶ Who is saying something inappropriate? What should he or she say?

Key   a 1–3   **b** iii   **c** Sally, 5–14 most appropriate, 1 and 3 also possible

170

Saying how you are

1 *Very well, (thank you).* 0

You meet a teacher from your language school in the cinema foyer.

Hello! How are you?
2 *I'm fine, (thank you). How are you?* 0
3 *All right, (thank you).* 0
4 *Quite well, (thank you).* [when you're not feeling 100% well or cheerful] 0

I A friend asks how you are. You're feeling very happy.

Hi there! How are you?
5 *Oh, (I'm) on top of the world, (thanks).* 0
6 *(I'm) full of the joys of spring!* **7** *Fine, (thanks).* 0
8 *So-so, (thanks).* 0
9 *OK, (thanks).* 0
10 *Mustn't grumble.* 0
11 *Can't complain.* 0
12 *Fair to middling, (thanks).* [when you're not feeling 0
13 *Not so/too bad, (thanks).* 100% well or cheerful] 0
14 *Pretty fair, (thanks).* 0
15 *Bearing up, (bearing up).* 0
16 *Surviving, (thanks).* 0
17 *Still alive—just.* [when you're not feeling at all well] 0

F The sales manager of a firm hoping to obtain your custom rings you up. You have met once, briefly. Before getting down to business, he asks after your health.

And how are you keeping?
18 *I'm extremely well, (thank you).* 0
19 *I'm in excellent health, (thank you).* 0
20 *I'm very well indeed, (thank you).* 0

Practice

a Mr Peters and Mr Dent meet. They don't know each other very well.
Mr Peters: *How are you?*
Mr Dent: . . . .
Mr Peters: *Oh, good.*
▶ What does Mr Dent say?

b ▶ What do Simon, Jill and David reply?
Chris: *Hello, everyone. Well, how are you all?*
Simon: . . . .
Jill: . . . .
David: . . . .

c Your boss comes into your office just after you've heard you've overspent your annual budget by a huge amount. He doesn't know.
Boss: *How are you? Well?*
You think: *Well is the last thing I feel. But I mustn't let him know that.*
▶ What do you actually say?

Key a 1–4 most appropriate, 18–20 also possible **b** Simon 17, Jill 8–15 most appropriate, 4 also possible, David 5–7 most appropriate, 1–3 also possible **c** 1–3

102 Giving someone your general good wishes

1 *All the best!*	0

A colleague is leaving your firm for another job.

2 *Every success in your new job!*	6
Thank you very much. It'll be a challenge, anyway.	
3 *Every success with*	6
4 *All the very best.*	0
5 *All the (very) best in*	6
6 *All the (very) best with*	6
7 *(The very/The) best of luck.*	0
8 *(The very/The) best of luck in*	6
9 *(The very/The) best of luck with*	6
10 *I hope everything goes well.*	0
11 *I hope everything goes well with/in*	6

12	*(I hope you) have a good time.*	0
13	*(I hope you) have a good/pleasant/enjoyable* etc *holiday/trip/journey* etc.	0
14	*(Please) give my best wishes to Don Black/Jim Smith* [or other name].	0
15	*(Please) give Don Black/Jim Smith* [or other name]. *my best wishes.*	0
16	*(Please) remember me to Don Black/Jim Smith* [or other name]	0
17	*With (very) best wishes,*	0
18	*With warmest wishes,*	0

[when you want someone to pass your good wishes on to a third person] (14–16)

[when writing] (17–18)

I Two friends are off to a party. You're off to the cinema.

19	*Enjoy yourselves!*	0
	Thanks. You too!	
20	*Have a good/nice* etc *time/party* etc.	0
21	*Have fun!*	

22	*Good luck.*	0
23	*Good luck with . . . .*	6
24	*Good luck in . . . .*	6
25	*Hope things go well/all right/OK with . . . .*	6
26	*Regards to Annie/Mike.* [or other name]	0
27	*Say hello to Annie/Mike* [or other name] *(for me).*	0
28	*Give my love to Annie/Mike.* [or other name]	0

[when the other person is facing a challenge] (22–25)

[when you want someone to pass your good wishes on to a third person] (26–28)

F A colleague you do not know well is leaving the firm to set up his own company. He has come to take his leave.

29	*I'd like to wish you every success in* *your new venture.*	4	6
	Thank you. If you are ever in need of a job, please don't hesitate to contact me.		
30	*May I wish you every success with . . . .*		6
31	*I'd like to wish you/May I wish you every success.*		0
32	*I wish you success.*		0
33	*I wish you success in . . . .*	4	6
34	*I wish you success with . . . .*		6

35	*Please give my regards to John Carter/Mr Jones.* [or other name]	0
36	*Would you give John Carter/Mr Jones* [or other name] *my best wishes/kind regards?*	0
37	*Please convey my very best wishes/kindest regards to John Carter/Mr Jones.* [or other name] [very formal]	0
38	*With kindest regards,* [when writing]	0

[when you want someone to pass your good wishes on to a third person] (35–37)

Practice

a ▶ What is Ms Thomson saying?

b A colleague of yours is going to see someone (Paul Dixon) whom you know quite well (but not very well).
▶ What do you say?

c You want a friend to pass on good wishes to two other friends (Tim and Rosie).
▶ What do you say?

d You're talking to your friend, Pete.
You: *. . . your driving test tomorrow.*
Pete: *Thanks. Bet I don't pass, though.*
You: *Course you will!*
▶ What do you say?

e A managing director is talking to a promising young employee who has decided to change jobs.
Managing Director: *. . . your chosen career.*
Employee: *Thank you. And thank you too for all you've done for me in the past.*
▶ What does the Managing Director say?

Key **a** 7–16, 22–25, 35, 36 all possible, according to how well the businesswomen know each other **b** 14–16 **c** 26–28 most appropriate, 14–16 also possible **d** 23–25 most appropriate, 5, 6, 8, 9, 11 also possible **e** 29, 30, 33, 34 most appropriate, 2, 3, 5, 6, 8, 9, 11 also possible

103 Responding to general good wishes

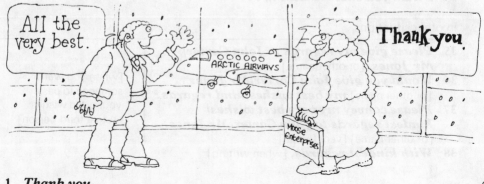

1 *Thank you.*

0

174

You are about to negotiate a tricky deal. A colleague speaks to you about it.

Best of luck with the TT deal.
2 ***Thank you very much.***   0

in other situations

3 ***(Very) many thanks.***   0

I You're going on a trip to the US, and a colleague, Joe, is going to the UK.

Have a good time, then.
4 ***Thanks, Joe. You too!***   0

in other situations

5 ***Cheers.*** [very informal]   0

Practice

a   You're going to England for the summer. An acquaintance says: *I hope you have a good time.*
▶ What do you say?

b   A friend and colleague says to you on a Friday night: *Have a good weekend.*
▶ What's your reply?

Key   **a** 1 and 2   **b** 4 and 5 most appropriate, 1 and 2 also possible

104 Giving someone good wishes on a special occasion

1 ***(A) merry Christmas (to you)!***   0

It's several days before Christmas. You're leaving your office.

2 ***Have a good Christmas!***   0
Thank you. Same to you.

175

in other situations

3 *(Have a) happy birthday/anniversary/Easter!*
4 *A merry Christmas and a happy New Year!*
5 *A merry Christmas/Xmas and a happy 1995!* } [when 0
6 *The season's greetings.* } writing] 0

I It's your girlfriend's or boyfriend's birthday.

7 *Many happy returns (of the day)!* 0
Thanks.
8 *Happy birthday!* 0

in other situations

9 *Happy anniversary!* **10** *Happy Christmas!* 0
11 *Happy Easter!* **12** *Happy New Year!* 0

F You are the chairman of the board visiting your company's subsidiary in England. You walk into a junior secretary's office just as someone is wishing her a happy birthday.

13 *Er, may I wish you/I'd like to wish you many happy
returns of the day,* Miss Curtis. 0
Oh, thank you very much.
14 *May I wish you/I'd like to wish you a happy birthday.* 0
15 *Please accept my best wishes on the occasion of* .... } [when 6
16 *I should like to offer you my best/warmest wishes on the* } writing] 6
occasion of ....

Practice

a It's 25 December.
▶ What do you say to everybody you know?

b ▶ What do you say to these people on these occasions?

	person	date/occasion
i	a friendly neighbour	his birthday
ii	a neighbour you won't see on Christmas Day	19 December
iii	your English aunt of whom you're very fond	her birthday
iv	a very old gentleman whom you hardly know	his birthday

c ▶ What should he write?

d One of the ex-employees of your firm is 100 years old next week. You write to him.

▶ What do you say?

Key **a** 1 and 2 most appropriate, 4 also possible **b** i 7 and 8 **b** ii 1 and 2 most appropriate, 4 also possible **b** iii 7 and 8 most appropriate, 3 also possible **b** iv 13 and 14 **c** 1, 4–6 **d** 15 and 16

105 Responding to good wishes on a special occasion

1 *(Thank you. And) a happy New Year to you too!*	0
2 *(Thank you. And) the same to you!*	0
3 *(Thank you.) You too!*	0

in other situations

4 *(Thank you.) And a merry Christmas/happy Easter to you!*	0

Practice

a ▶ What does he say?

Key 2, 3 (4, but not Easter!)

106 Proposing a toast

1 *Here's to . . . .*   5 6

I You're at a pub with some friends. Jason has just bought a round of drinks. You raise your glass.

2 *Cheers!*   0
Cheers!

F You are talking to a diplomat at an Embassy reception. Cocktails are brought round. You raise your glass.

3 *Your very good health,* Mr Pilkington.   0
Thank you. And yours.

in other situations

4 *I should like to propose a toast to our host/hostess/hosts/
the bride* etc: *his/her/their very good health.*
[for very formal toasts on public occasions]   0

Practice

a ▶ What does he say?

b ▶ Who is saying something inappropriate? What should he or she say?

c ▶ Who is saying something inappropriate? What should he say?

Key **a** 1 most appropriate, 2 also possible **b** Rita, too formal, 1, 2 **c** Mr Christie, too informal, 3

107 Inviting someone

1 *Would you like to . . . ?*	1

You're saying goodbye to someone you've met briefly at a conference.

2	*And if ever you're in Scunthorpe, **please do** look me up.*	0 3
3	*I'd very much like you to . . . .*	0 3
4	*You will . . . . won't you?*	0 17
5	*Do . . . .*	0 3

179

    6   *Shall we ... ?*   7   *Won't you ... ?*   3

I You're going to a disco with some friends. On the way there, you run into another friend, Sally.

    8   *Hey, Sally, we're going to the Hammersmith Palais.* **D'you fancy**
        coming along?   4 6
    9   *What about ... ?*   4–6
  10   *Come and ....*   3
  11   *Why don't you ... ?*   12   *Like to ... ?*   13   *You must ....*   0 3

F At the end of a summer school in England, you invite the Director of Studies (whom you hardly know) to a farewell dinner with some of the students.

  14   **We should be very pleased if you could** *come and have dinner*
       with us this evening.   0 3
  15   **We should be delighted if you were able to/could ....**   0 3
  16   **Would you care to ... ?**   0 3
  17   **Perhaps you'd care to ... ?** } [could sound tentative]   0 3

  18   **The Directors of AA Export/Michael & Edith Clegg** etc
       request the pleasure of your company at a reception/dinner
       etc *(to mark the occasion of/in honour of/to celebrate* etc
       remarkable sales results/our 25th wedding anniversary etc).   0
  19   **The Directors of AA Export/Michael & Edith Clegg** etc
       request the pleasure of the company of Mr John Davis/Miss
       Jean Smith etc **at a reception/dinner** etc *(to mark the occasion*
       of/in honour of/to celebrate etc *remarkable sales results/*
       our 25th wedding anniversary etc).   0
  20   **The Directors of AA Export/Michael & Edith Clegg** etc
       take/have pleasure in inviting you/Mr John Davis/Miss Jean
       Smith etc **to a reception/dinner** etc *(to mark the occasion of/in*
       honour of/to celebrate etc *remarkable sales results/our 25th*
       wedding anniversary etc).   0
  21   **The Directors of AA Export/Michael & Edith Clegg** etc
       invite you/Mr John Davis/Miss Jean Smith etc **to a reception/**
       dinner etc *(to mark the occasion of/in honour of/to celebrate* etc
       remarkable sales results/our 25th wedding anniversary etc).   0
  22   **You are cordially invited to attend a reception/dinner** etc
       (to mark the occasion of/in honour of/to celebrate etc
       remarkable sales results/our 25th wedding anniversary etc).   0

Practice

a Here is your diary. Today is Monday. Invite these people to these things.

MONDAY Mr. Smith (new chairman of board) – Dinner.

TUESDAY Sally – Tennis.

WEDNESDAY John & Olivia – disco.

▶ What do you say?

b Two scientists are talking.
Jones: *. . . and I'll be at the New York Conference. I hear you'll be giving a paper?*
Williams: *Yes. . . . .*
Jones: *Thank you. I'd like to hear your views.*
▶ What does Williams say?

c The managing director of your firm, KZ Electronics, asks you: *Could you draft an invitation card, please, from me, for a reception to celebrate the opening of our new branch in Tokyo? Thanks.*
▶ What do you write?

d i Invite a business client you have just met to join you in doing something interesting in London.
  ii Invite Pia, a friend you've met on your package tour of England, to do something nice this evening.

Key **a** i 14 and 15 with changes of pronoun to 'I'; 16, 17 also possible; 1, 3 also possible **a** ii 8–12 most appropriate; 1, 4, 6 also possible **a** iii 8, 9, 11–13 most appropriate; 1, 4–7 also possible **b** 14 and 15 with changes of pronoun to 'I'; 16, 17 most appropriate; 2–5, 7 also possible **c** 18–22 **d** i 14 and 15 with changes of pronoun to 'I'; 16, 17 (1, 3–6 equally possible) **d** ii 8–13 most appropriate; 1–6 also possible

108 Accepting an invitation

1 *(Thank you.) I'd like to (very much).*

0 3

Someone you have recently met invites you to see Shakespeare's 'A Midsummer Night's Dream'.

	It's an open-air production in Regent's Park. Would you like to come along?	
2	*I would, very much. (Thank you).*	0
3	*That would be very nice.*	0
4	*It would be very nice to . . . .*	0 3
5	*That sounds a (very) nice idea.* 6 *With pleasure.*	0
7	*I'd like nothing better.* [very enthusiastic]	0
8	*I'd like nothing better than to . . . .* [very enthusiastic]	3

in other situations

9	*Yes, I will/do* etc. [depends on the main verb in the invitation]	0

I A friend puts his head round your door at lunchtime.

	Let me buy you a pint and a sandwich down 'The Blue Lion'.	
10	*You're on! (Thanks very much/a lot).*	0
11	*Ra·ther!* 12 *All right (then)!*	0
13	*I'll take you up on that.* 14 *I won't say no!*	0
15	*Great/Lovely/Smashing!* etc.	0

in other situations

16	*You certainly can!* 17 *OK!* 18 *You bet!*	0
19	*I'd love to . . . .*	0 3

F After a day of hard negotiations on a multi-million pound deal, the senior negotiator on the other side invites you and your colleagues out for the evening.

	Would you care to join me for dinner at my club?	
20	*We'd very much like to . . . .*	0 3
21	*We'd be delighted to . . . .*	0 3
22	*That's really very/most kind of you.*	0
23	*What a delightful/splendid* etc *idea. (Thank you.)*	0
24	*That would give us great/the greatest of pleasure.* [very formal]	0
25	*It would give us great/the greatest of pleasure to . . . .* [very formal]	0 3

in other situations

26	*With the greatest of pleasure.*	0
27	*Mr/Mrs/Ms/Miss Evelyn Parkinson/Steven Piper/Mr & Mrs Luke Smith* etc *wishes/wish to thank Mr/Mrs/Ms/Miss Hilary Jacobs/Miranda Johnson/Mr & Mrs Ernest Jones* etc *for his/her/their kind invitation to a garden party/ dinner dance* etc *on August 24th/December 23rd* etc *and has/have/takes/take great pleasure in accepting.* [written reply to a very formal invitation]	0

Practice

a Someone you don't know too well invites you to watch the annual Oxford vs Cambridge Boat Race.
You think: *Good idea.*
▶ What do you say?

b You are formally invited to a dinner party on 18 July by Miss Fay Mills.
▶ Accept, formally and in writing.

c You like climbing mountains. A colleague you have hardly ever spoken to invites you to go in his car and spend a weekend in the Scottish Highlands. You decide to accept.
▶ What do you say?

d Your friend, Tessa, says: *Fancy sharing a Greek villa with us this summer?*
You'd like to.
▶ What do you say?

Key **a** 1–6, 9 **b** 27 **c** 20–26 (20, 21, 24, 25 with appropriate change of pronoun) most appropriate, 1–9 also possible **d** 10–15, 17–19 most appropriate, 1–9 also possible

109 Declining an invitation

1 *Thank you (very much), but . . . .* 33

Several people at your language school plan to go on a fifteen-mile walk one Sunday morning. The organizer (whom you only know by sight) comes up to you.

Would you like to join us? We'll be starting early, at half past six or so.
2 *Well, er, **that's very kind of you, but** I don't usually get up till ten on Sundays.* 33
3 *Thank you (very much) for asking me, but . . . .* 33
4 *I'm (very/terribly* etc*) sorry, I don't think I can.* ⎫ [followed by 0
5 *I'm (very/terribly* etc*) sorry, I can't.* ⎭ a reason or excuse] 0
6 *I'd like to, but . . . .*   7 *I wish I could, but . . . .* 33
8 *I'm afraid I've already promised to . . . . (But thank you very much all the same.)* 3

I Some friends invite you to go with them on a picnic in the countryside.

> Why don't you come with us? There'll be strawberries and champagne and . . . .

9 *I'd love to, but I've got an exam that afternoon.*   33

10 *Oh, what a shame—I'm going to be somewhere else./I won't be here* etc. [or other reason or excuse]   27

11 *Sorry, I can't. (But thanks anyway).*   0

F At an archeological conference, several delegates who are interested in Roman history invite you on an outing.

> We're planning to examine some sixth century sites in Hertfordshire. Would you care to join us?

12 *Much as I should like to, I'm afraid I'm already booked up for that day—looking at Celtic settlements in Scotland, actually.*   33

13 *Much to my regret, ...*   33

14 *That's (very/extremely etc) kind of you, but . . . .*   33

15 *Sadly . . . . (However, thank you for inviting me.)*   33

16 *Unfortunately, ... (However, thank you for thinking of me.)*   33

17 *Mr/Mrs/Ms/Miss Leslie Cooper/Susan Lacey/Mr & Mrs Mark Cooper* etc *thanks/thank Mr & Mrs Charles Dartington/ the management of GTL Cars Ltd* etc *for their kind invitation, but regrets/regret that owing to a prior engagement, he/ she/they will be unable to attend.* [written reply to a very formal invitation]   0

Practice

a Three people invite her out on three days. She can't go.
▶ What does she say for each day?

b Your friend, Lynne, invites you for a ride on the Ghost Train at the local fair. You don't like the idea.
▶ How do you decline the invitation?

c You have received a formal invitation from the Supakon Advertising Agency to a buffet supper. But you will be in Addis Ababa that evening.
▶ How do you decline, in writing?

d Sally: *Hey, Cuthbert, fancy coming to our fancy dress party? It'll be a real laugh. Say you'll come!*

Cuthbert: *Sadly, on that particular evening I shall be in the process of revising for an examination. However, thank you for inviting me.*

▶ What might Sally think?

i *Pity he can't come. But why is he being so formal?*

ii *What a rude answer.*

iii *Poor old Cuthbert, he's got brain damage from too much revision! He can't give a normal answer to a friendly invitation now.*

Key **a** 9–11 most appropriate, 1–8 also possible (for all 3 invitations) **b** 11 ; 4, 5, 8 equally possible
c 17 **d** i and iii (the answer is not rude, but too formal for the situation)

110 Offering something

1	*Will you have . . . ?*	6

You and a colleague are waiting for a table at a restaurant.

2	*While we're waiting,* **can I offer you** *a drink?* Thanks very much.	6
3	*Won't you have . . . ?* 4 *Would you like . . . ?*	6
5	*What would you say to . . . ?*	6
6	*Why don't you have . . . ?*	6
7	*What can I get you?*	0

in other situations

8	*What will you have?*	0
9	*(Please) help yourself to . . . .* 10 *Please take . . . .*	6

I It's your birthday, and you're handing round chocolates to your friends.

11	*Like one?* I'd love one. Great, they've got liqueur fillings. My favourites.	6
12	*Have . . . .*	6
13	*Chocolate?/Glass of wine?/Cheese sandwich?* [or other noun]	31

in other situations

14	*Grab yourself . . . .*	6
15	*What's it to be?* ⎱ 16 *What's yours?* ⎰ [usually for drinks]	0 0

F You're holding a buffet lunch for a group of visiting businessmen. You address one of them.

17 ***Would you care for** some lobster salad?*   6
   I'm a vegetarian, as a matter of fact. And these nut cutlets look excellent.
18 ***Could I/I wonder if I might give/pass/get/offer** etc **you** . . . ?*   6
19 ***Allow me to give/pass** etc **you** . . . .*   6
20 ***Do have** . . . .*   6

Practice

a At a tea party, you see someone with an empty plate, looking rather/hungry.
   There are lots of cucumber sandwiches and jam tarts on the table.
   ▶ What do you say?

b ▶ Who is saying something inappropriate?
   ▶ What would be more appropriate?

c At a civic reception an elderly gentleman (whom you've spoken to once,
   briefly) is looking with interest at a dish of caviar at the other end of the table.
   You think: *I bet he's after the caviar.*
   ▶ What do you actually say?

Key **a** 1–4, 6, 7, 8–10 most appropriate, 17–20 also possible   **b** Phil, 11–13 most appropriate, 1, 4, 6 also
possible   **c** 17–20 most appropriate, 1–4 also possible

III Accepting an offer of something

1 ***Thank you.***   0

On a plane flight, you tell the air hostess you feel unwell.

Would you like a travel sickness pill?

2	*Yes, please. Quickly!*	0
3	*Thanks very much/a lot.*	0
4	*I'd like . . . very much, (please).*	16
5	*That would be very nice/a great help* etc.	0
6	*Thank you, I would.*	0

in other situations

7	*Thank you, I will* etc. [depends on the verb in the offer]	0
8	*I can think of nothing nicer/better* etc.	0

I You're sunbathing on the beach. A friend is about to go and buy some ice-cream.

Fancy a raspberry ripple?

9	*Ooh, please. A couple, if you can get them.*	0
10	*Lovely/Great/Smashing!* etc.	0
11	*I'd love . . . !*	6
12	*You bet!*	0

F You are a member of an inter-governmental commission visiting the U.K. A Member of Parliament gives you dinner at his home. After dinner, he offers you a drink.

Would you care for some brandy?

13	*That'd be delightful.*	0
14	*Thank you so much.*	0

in other situations

15	*With pleasure.* 16 *With the greatest of pleasure.*	0

Practice

a You are travelling to London on a full train. You have a very bad cough. Another passenger offers you a packet and says: *Would you like a cough sweet?*
▶ What do you say?

b At a formal dinner, an elderly lady you do not know says to you: *Would you care for some caviar?*
You think: *Great.*
▶ What do you say?

c Your friend, Bill, says: *I've just finished this book—Agatha Christie's* Death on the Nile. *It's a terrific murder story. Like to borrow it?*
▶ What do you say?

Key a 1–7 **b** 13, 14 most appropriate, 1–7 also possible **c** 9–12 most appropriate, 1–7 also possible

112 Declining an offer of something

1 No, thank you.   0

You go to Sunday lunch with an English family for the first time. Your hostess offers you a second helping of food.

Will you have a little more sponge pudding?
2 *Not for me, thank you. Especially after that nice steak and kidney pie.*   0
3 *I'm not sure I can/could, (thank you).*   0
4 *No, I (really) won't, thank you.*   0
5 *No, thank you very much.*   0
6 *(No,) thank you, I couldn't/won't etc.*   0

I   You're having a pub lunch with some colleagues. You've just finished your drink.

Same again?
7 *No, thanks, (really,) (I won't).*   0
8 *Not for me, thanks.*   9 *I won't, thanks.*   0
10 *Thanks all the same, but I won't/couldn't etc.*   0
11 *If it's all the same to you, I won't.*   0
12 *Not this time, thanks.*   0

F   You are invited to a formal dinner with the Cultural Attaché at the British Embassy. The dinner is over.

Will you have a cigar?
13 *That's very kind, but I won't, (thank you).*   0

Practice

a   A stranger comes up to you in Trafalgar Square and offers you a free ticket to a concert by the Pink Rats Rock Band. You don't like the Pink Rats.
▶   What do you say?

b ▶ What does Peter say?

c Before a dinner party, your host, an important business client you have recently met, offers you sherry. After your second glass, he offers you some more.
▶ What do you say?

Key **a** 1, 4, 5 (7–9 equally possible) **b** 7–9, 11 **c** 13 most appropriate, 1, 2, 4–6 also possible

113 Giving something to someone

1 *I'd like to give you ....*	6

You hand over a document to a colleague.

2 *Here's a copy of the department's quarterly report.*	6
Thank you, but my waste-paper bin's full.	
3 *Can I give you ... ?* 4 *This is the/your ....*	6
5 *Here are the/your ....*	6
6 *Here you are.*	0
7 *A/The ... for you.* 8 *The ... you asked for.*	16
9 *Your copy of the minutes./The Smithson report.* [or similar phrase]	31

---

in other situations

10 *... is/are for you.*	[usually for pleasant	15
11 *I'd like you to/I want you to have ....*	and/or important items]	6

I You and your friend, Phil, are doing some repairs to your car.

Can you pass me that big spanner?
12 *Sure. Here.* 0

in other situations

13	**Want . . . ?** ⎫ [said while handing whatever is	6
14	**Need . . . ?** ⎭ required to the other person]	6

F You are giving a present to an employee of your English subsidiary firm, who is retiring. All the other employees have gathered for the little ceremony.

15 ***I have great pleasure in presenting you with*** *this small token of the firm's gratitude for forty years' outstanding service.*   6
    Thank you very much. That's really very kind.

16 ***Allow me to present you with . . . .***   17 ***Please accept . . . .***   6

in other situations (when writing)

18	***I attach . . . .***	6
19	***I enclose . . . .***	6
20	***Please find attached . . . .***	6
21	***Please find enclosed . . . .***	6
22	***Encl.*** [= 'there is one enclosure'] ⎫ [written under	0
23	***Encls.*** [= 'there is more than one enclosure'] ⎭ the signature]	0

Practice

..... my room key ....

a ▶ What does he say?

b ▶ Who might say this and when?
Here.
   i An air hostess giving a passenger a newspaper to read.
   ii A girl giving her boyfriend the drying-up cloth.

c You write a letter asking an English publisher to send you some English books. With the letter you send an International Money Order.
   ▶ What do you write at the end of the letter?

Key **a** 1–4, 6–9 **b** ii (too informal for i) **c** 18–22

1 ***Thank you.***   0

You are changing platforms on the London Underground with a very heavy suitcase. Someone sees you struggling with it.

     Can I help you with your suitcase?
2 *Oh, that's very kind of you.* ***Thank you very much.***   0
3 ***Thank you very much for ....***   4 6
4 ***Many thanks.***   5   ***Thank you very much indeed.***   0
6 ***Many thanks for ....***   7   ***Thank you very much indeed for ....***   4 6

---

in other situations

---

8 ***Much appreciated.*** ⎫   0
9 ***(I'm) much obliged.*** ⎬ [after a favour is completed]   0

I   Your secretary has just brought in a photocopy you asked for.

10 ***Thanks,*** *Lynda.*   11   ***Thanks very much.***   12   ***Thanks a lot.***   0
13 ***Thanks very much for ....***   14   ***Thanks a lot for ....***   4 6

---

in other situations

---

15 ***That is/was really nice of you ....*** ⎫   0 1
16 ***Thanks a million.***   ⎬ [strong]   0
17 ***Thanks a million for ....***   ⎭   4 6
18 ***Cheers.*** ⎫   0
19 ***Great.*** ⎬ [very informal]   0

F   You recently asked the Trade Attaché at the British Embassy to help you find an importer for your goods into the U.K.

     I've found a firm in Harwich who are interested in handling your
     company's product.
20 *Oh, that's excellent.* ***I'm (really) very grateful (to you).***   0
21 ***I'm (really) very grateful to you for ....***   4 6
22 ***I (really) do appreciate ... (very much).***   4–6
23 ***I'm extremely/immensely/most*** *etc* ***grateful (to you).*** ⎫   0
24 ***I'm extremely/immensely/most*** *etc* ***grateful to you for ....*** ⎪   4 6
25 ***That is/was very/extremely*** *etc* ***good of you.*** ⎬ [strong]   0
26 ***Thank you so very much for ....*** ⎪   4 6
27 ***I'm (very) much/extremely obliged (to you).*** ⎪   0
28 ***I'm (very) much/extremely obliged to you for ....*** ⎭   4 6

29 *I really can't thank you enough.*
30 *I really can't thank you enough for . . . .* } [very strong]

0
4 6

---

in other situations

31 *I should like to say how (very/deeply etc) grateful I am.*
32 *I should like to say how (very/deeply etc) grateful*
I am for . . . .
33 *I should like to express my gratitude/appreciation.*
34 *I should like to express my gratitude/appreciation for . . . .*
35 *It is/was very/extremely etc good of you to . . . .* [strong]

}
[very
formal]

0

6
0
6
1

Practice

a   You leave your change behind in a shop. The shop assistant runs after you
and gives it to you.
  ▶   What do you say?

b   You bring back a souvenir (a small plastic model of the Houses of Parliament)
from a trip to London and give it to a friend. He says: *I'm immensely*
grateful to you.
  ▶   Is this appropriate or inappropriate?
  ▶   What else could he say?

c   The two men have never met.
  ▶   What does the old gentleman say to the younger man?

Key   **a** 1–9 most appropriate, 10–17 also possible   **b** inappropriate, 10–14 most appropriate, 1–8
also possible   **c** 20–30 most appropriate, 1–15 also possible

15 Responding to thanks

1 *Not at all.*   0

You have just explained to a colleague how a new photocopier works.

I see. Thank you for explaining.
2 *It's a pleasure.*   **3 *My pleasure.***   0
4 *(Please) don't mention it.*   **5 *(It's) no trouble at all.***   0

---

in other situations

6 *Thank you.* [if you *also* have some small thing to say 'thank you' for]
7 *Thank ↘you.* [if you think it's *you* who should be saying 'thank you',
         not the other person]   0

I You have just lent a friend five pounds to get home with.

You've saved my bacon. Thanks.
**8 *That's all right. I don't charge much interest by the way—ten per
cent or so!***   0
9 *That's OK.*   **10 *Any time.*** [very informal]   0
11 [Nod and smile]   0

F You have just driven an important business client, whom you have never met
before, to the airport.

Thank you very much for the lift.
12 *I was glad to be of (some) service.*   0
13 *I'm glad to have been of (some) service.*   0
14 *Delighted I was able to help.*   0

---

in other situations

15 *Delighted to have been of assistance.* [very formal]   0
16 *It was the least I could do.* [when the other person has either been
in great trouble, or was very helpful to you on an earlier occasion]   0
17 *You would have done the same in my place/position, I'm sure.*   0

Practice

a ▶ What does the driver say?

b At a conference you have lent a copy of a scientific journal to another delegate because he has lost his own copy, and told you that he could not possibly give his conference speech without referring to it. You do not know him well.
Delegate: *I'm most grateful to you for lending it to me. Thank you.*
▶ What do you say?

c A colleague you know very well says: *Thanks for mending my typewriter.*
▶ What do you say?

Key **a** 1–5 most appropriate, 8–10 also possible   **b** 12–17 (1–4 equally possible)   **c** 8–11 most appropriate, 1–5 also possible

116 Complimenting

1 What . . . !	6

You compliment someone on their appearance.

2 That's a (very) nice/smart coat (you're wearing).	6
Thank you.	
3 Those are (very) nice/smart . . . (you're wearing).	6
4 . . . suit/suits you (very well).	15
5 You look (very) nice/smart.	0
6 What (a) nice/smart	6
7 . . . look/looks (very) nice/smart etc.	15

8 *You're looking (rather/very etc) smart/dapper etc.* 0
[men's clothes/appearance]
9 *You're looking (extremely/very) smart/glamorous etc.* 0
[women's clothes/appearance]

in other situations

10 *(I must say) ... is/are (really) very good.* 15
11 *... is/are really/quite/absolutely etc delicious/beautiful etc.* } [food] 15
12 *Congratulations on ... — it's/they are very good/excellent etc.* } 16

I You compliment a friend on her appearance.

13 *I like the hair style!* 6
Thanks. Skinheads are back in fashion, you know!
14 *I love/adore etc ... !* 6
15 *Cor!/Wow! etc.* 0
16 *(Mm!) You look great/terrific/fantastic etc.* 0
17 *You're looking good!* 0
18 *... is/are really terrific/super/smashing/lovely/fantastic etc.* 15
19 *What a/What super/smashing/terrific etc ... !* 6

F An important business partner and his wife have invited you to dinner at their London home, and served you a rather grand meal.

20 *If I may say so, these truffles are delicious/excellent.* 16
I'm so glad. They're from our own little farm in the Périgord, aren't they, darling?
21 *If I may say so, ... is (most/quite) delicious/excellent.* 16
22 *I must congratulate you on ....* 6
23 *I really must express my admiration for ....* } [food] 6
24 *My compliments on ....* 6
25 *You really have surpassed yourself with ....* 6

in other situations

26 *May I say how elegant/enchanting |etc you look?* } [women's clothes/appearance] 0
27 *If I may say so, ... is/are quite charming/ enchanting.* 16

Practice

Mr Fairfax   Mrs Bracknell   Mr Worthing   Mr Bunbury

a ▶ What does Mr Fairfax say to each of them?

b You are a guest at the house of someone you've just met and are beginning to get to know. This is what you have for dinner:

>   *Lobster soup*
>   *Veal cutlets cooked in white wine*
>   *Syllabub*

You compliment your hostess on all three courses.

▶ What do you say?

c ▶ Is the compliment appropriate?
  ▶ What else could he say?

d You want to tell your girlfriend you like her eyeshadow, her nail varnish and her earrings.

▶ What do you say?

e How do you compliment these people on this food?

	person	food
i	your manager's wife (you hardly know her)	cheese soufflé
ii	friend	banana custard
iii	friend	prawn curry
iv	your director's wife (you've met her for the first time)	yorkshire pudding

Key a 1, 2, 3–9, 26, 27 **b** 10–12; 20–22, 24 also possible **c** No, 26, 27 **d** 13–19 most appropriate, 3–5, 7, 9 also possible **e** i 20–25 most appropriate, 10–12 also possible **e** ii 13–15, 18, 19 most appropriate, 10–12 also possible **e** iii 13–15, 18, 19 most appropriate, 10–12 also possible **e** iv 20–25 most appropriate, 10–12 also possible

II7 Congratulating

1 *Congratulations!*

0

A colleague from your English subsidiary firm has just obtained a big contract.

2 **Congratulations on** *winning the LG contract.* 4 6
Thank you. We just succeeded in bribing the right people, I suppose.

I Your friend, Mandy, has just passed an important exam.

3 **Well done,** *Mandy!* 0
Thanks. It was a fluke more than anything.
4 **Nice one, (Mandy)!** 0
5 **Good old Mandy!** 0
6 **Fantastic!/Terrific!** etc. 0

in other situations

7 **It was great to hear** 6 7
8 **It was great to hear about** 5 6

F An English colleague you do not know well has just been given a more important post than his present one.

9 **I must congratulate you on** *your promotion.* 4 6
Thank you very much. I don't suppose the fact that the chairman's niece is my wife has anything to do with it.
10 **I must congratulate you.** 0
11 **Let me/May I congratulate you.** 0
12 **Let me/May I congratulate you on** 4 6
13 **Please accept my warmest/heartiest congratulations.** 0
14 **Please accept my warmest/heartiest congratulations on** 4 6
15 **I'd like to congratulate you.** 0
16 **I'd like to congratulate you on** 4 6
17 **Allow me to offer my (warmest/heartiest) congratulations.** } [very formal] 0
18 **Allow me to offer my (warmest/heartiest) congratulations on** 4 6

in other situations

19 **I'd like to be the first to congratulate you.** 0
20 **I'd like to be the first to congratulate you on** 4 6

Practice

a ▶ What are they saying?

b You have just won a donkey race at the seaside and a friend says: *Nice one!*
▶ What do you think?
i Don't be so pompous.
ii Don't be so cheeky.
iii Nice of him to congratulate me.

c A business acquaintance you do not know well has made a very successful speech at a big convention. You think: *Good for you!*
▶ What do you actually say?

Key **a** 1, 2, (3, 5, 6 equally possible) **b** iii, ii also possible **c** 9–16 most appropriate, 1, 2 also possible

118 Responding to compliments or congratulations

1 *Thank you.* 0

You have just translated a letter from your own language into English. A colleague sees it.

You know, if you don't mind my saying so, your written English is very good indeed.
2 *It's (very) nice of you to say so.* *It's not up to native-speaker standards yet, though!* 0
3 *Thank you (very much) for saying so.* 0

in other situations

4 *(Oh good,) I'm glad you think so.* ⎫ [when the other person is enjoying 0
5 *(Oh good,) I'm glad you like . . . .* ⎭ what he has complimented
you on, e g good food/drink] 4 6
6 *You . . . very well yourself, (as a matter of fact).*
[when the other person also deserves to be complimented] 17
7 *(Oh,) . . . is/are nothing special actually/really.* ⎫ [and other 15
8 *(Oh,) . . . is/are very old/dull etc actually/really.* ⎬ modest 15
9 *(Oh,) I have a lot to learn yet.* ⎭ responses] 0

I You are dancing. Your partner moves with real style.

Hey, you're a terrific dancer!
10 *Oh, thanks!* 0
11 *(Oh,) not really.* 0
12 *(Oh, there's) nothing to it, actually.* ⎬ [and other modest responses] 0
13 *Flattery'll get you nowhere!* [light-hearted response] 0

F You invite a business acquaintance to your country villa for informal weekend talks. He says:

> What a magnificent view! And the air—it's so fresh and cool! You certainly have a wonderful place here.

14 *It's (very) good of you to say so.*   0

15 *How (very/extremely) nice/kind/good* etc *of you to say so.*   0

Practice

a ▶ What does Mrs Mills say?

b ▶ When would you say this?
Nothing to it really.
  i   when your boss in a large company praises a report you have written
  ii   when a friend compliments you on having lost a lot of weight in a short time
  iii   when a stranger at a seaside resort says he admires your ability to swim 100 metres underwater

c   Chairman of the board: *I must congratulate you on your handling of the recent negotiations with our suppliers.*
You: . . . .
Chairman of the board: *Well, you did an extremely good job, in my view.*
  ▶ What do you say?

Key   **a** 1–3, 7, 8 (14, 15 equally possible)   **b** ii (too informal for i or ii)   **c** 14, 15 most appropriate (1–3 also possible)

119   Saying sorry

1 *(Oh,) I'm sorry . . . !*   0   1   7

You are driving your car in England. You forget you have to drive on the left. The driver of another car has to brake hard to avoid hitting you.

That wasn't very clever, was it?

2	*I'm very sorry.*	0	1	7
3	*I'm/I really am so/very/terribly/awfully sorry ....*	0	1	7
4	*I'm/I really am so/very/terribly/awfully sorry for ....*	4	6	
5	*I'm/I really am so/very/terribly/awfully sorry about ....*	4	6	
6	*I'm sorry, it/that was (entirely) my fault.*	0		

in other situations

7	*Excuse me.*	[mostly used (1) *before* or *while* you	0	
8	*Excuse me for ....*	are doing things which you think may	4	6
9	*Pardon me.*	offend people, or, (2) *after* sneezing	0	
10	*Pardon me for ....*	coughing, hiccuping, burping, etc]	4	6

I While dancing, you tread on your partner's toe.

11	*Ooops! Sorry!* That's OK. I'm beginning to get used to it!	0	1	7
12	*Sorry for ....* 16 *Sorry about ....*	4	6	
13	*(Oh,) my fault.*	0		
14	*(Oh,) my fault for ....*	4	6	
15	*How stupid/silly/clumsy etc of me ....*	0	1	

in other situations

16	*I feel bad about ....*	4	6

F You have a severe disagreement about an investment plan with a senior colleague, and use some rather strong language. You speak to him afterwards.

17	*Please accept my apologies for* what I said just now. Not at all. May I say I quite understand your feelings about the RTZ investments.	4	6	
18	*Please accept my apologies.*	0		
19	*It/That was very hasty/foolish/careless etc of me, I'm afraid.*	0		
20	*(Please) forgive me.*	0		
21	*(Please) forgive me for ....*	4	6	
22	*I'm extremely sorry ....*	0	1	7
23	*I'm extremely sorry for ....*	4	6	
24	*I can't tell you how sorry I am.*	0		
25	*I can't tell you how sorry I am for ....*	4	6	
26	*I (really) do/must apologize.*	0		
27	*I (really) do/must apologize for ....*	4	6	
28	*I (really) do/must apologize about ....*	4	6	
29	*May I offer you my profoundest/sincerest apologies.*	[very formal and strong]	0	
30	*May I offer you my profoundest/sincerest apologies for ....*		4	6

31 *I (do) beg your pardon.*	[mostly used for smaller 'offences', eg	0
32 *I (do) beg your pardon for ....*	bumping into someone, or contradicting	
	someone and then being proved wrong]	0

Practice

a ▶ What does he say?

b You are in a small car with four friends. You suddenly sneeze.
   ▶ What do you say?

c You are playing a game of football on the lawn with the children of
   some friends. You kick a small boy of seven by mistake.
   You say: *Oh, please accept my apologies.*
   ▶ What does he think?
   i *What a lot of big words. Can't he just say he's sorry?*
   ii *It hurts a bit, but that's all right.*
   iii *You can't play football and you can't speak English properly either.*
   ▶ What else could you say?

d ▶ Who is saying something inappropriate?

Key a 1–6 most appropriate, 11, 16, 21 also possible   **b** 11, 13 most appropriate, 1, 10 also possible
c i or iii, 11, 13 (1 equally possible)   **d** Mr Smith

1 *That's quite all right.* 0

You are a guest at someone's house. You knock several plates and glasses on to the floor by mistake.

Oh, I'm terribly sorry.
2 *Not at all. Now we have an excuse for buying some nice new ones.* 0
3 *Please ˅don't be.* 4 *Please don't worry.* 0
5 *It (really) doesn't matter at all.* 0
6 *(Please) think nothing ˅of it.* 0
7 *(Please) don't give it another thought.* 0

I | A friend promises to ring you up one evening, but doesn't. You see him next day.

Sorry I didn't ring you last night. I was watching Truffaut's 'Day for Night' on telly.
8 *That's OK. Actually, when the Truffaut film came on I took the phone off the hook anyway!* 0
9 *That's all right.* 10 *Forget it.* 11 *Not to worry.* 0

in other situations

12 *What ˅for?/Whatever ˅for?* [very informal] 0
13 *Please don't feel bad about it.* [in reply to very strong apologies] 0
14 *Let's forget it.* [when you feel rather hurt/offended, but don't want to show it] 0

F | At a trade exhibition, a junior colleague is talking to you about your firm's confidential NBU project. He suddenly realizes a representative of a competing firm has been standing behind him, listening, and has now walked away.

I must apologize for being so careless. I really didn't think there was anyone there.
15 *There's no reason to apologize. I've decided, anyway, that we should drop the NBU project.* 0
16 *There's no reason to apologize for . . . .* 4 6
17 *That's/It's perfectly all right.* 0
18 *That's/It's really not necessary.* 0
19 *Apologies are really quite unnecessary.* 0
20 *It's really of no importance.* 0

---

in other situations

21 *Of course/certainly* etc. 0

Practice

a ▶ What does the man reply?

b Your firm's Wages Department rings you up and says: *I'm afraid we have to tell you that your pay cheque has been mislaid. It may be some days before we can find it. We do apologize for any inconvenience this may cause you.*
You think: *They really are incompetent. But I won't show my feelings.*
▶ How do you accept their apology?

c A friend who's spending the weekend in your house says: *Oh, I'm sorry, I've finished off the last of your coffee.*
▶ What do you say?
  i *Not to worry. I can soon get some more.*
  ii *Forget it. There's plenty more in the cupboard.*
  iii *Apologies are quite unnecessary. I shall send James out to get us some more.*
▶ What else could you say?

Key **a** 1, 2, 5 (8, 9, 17 equally possible) **b** 17 (1, 2, 5, 9 equally possible) **c** i or ii (iii too formal), 8, 9 most appropriate, 1, 5 also possible

121 Showing sympathy

1 *I'm (very) sorry to hear . . . .*   6 7

Someone in a station buffet with you finds his briefcase has been stolen.

And the worst of it is, it contained the complete manuscript for my book. The only copy.

2 *(Oh dear,) I ˅am sorry (to hear that).*   0
3 *(Oh dear,) I'm (most) awfully/dreadfully etc sorry . . . .*   0 1 7

4 *(Oh dear,) I'm (most) awfully/dreadfully etc sorry about . . . .*	5	6
5 *(Oh) that's/what (terribly/extremely) etc bad luck.*		0
6 *That ˅is a pity/shame etc.*		0
7 *How upsetting/annoying etc.*		0
8 *How terrible/awful etc (for you).*		0
9 *You must be very upset/annoyed etc.*		0
10 *You must be very upset/annoyed etc about . . . .*		4–6

I On the first day of the Christmas holiday, you ring up a friend, Jill, to invite her to a party that evening. She tells you she has flu.

11 *Oh, Jill, that's awful. I'm ever so sorry.* Well, at least I'll have got over it for the New Year—I hope! In time to throw a party myself. And you're number one on the guest list!	0
12 *(Oh,) how/that's dreadful/rotten/awful/ghastly etc. (I'm ever so sorry.)*	0
13 *Oh no! (I'm ever so sorry.)*	0
14 *Oh dear. (I'm ever so sorry.)*	0
15 *Poor old you/John.* [or whatever the person's name is] *(I'm ever so sorry.)*	0
16 *(Oh,) hard luck.*	0
17 *(Oh,) what a shame . . . .*	0 7
18 *. . . is a crying shame, (it really is).*	15

in other situations

19 *I know how it feels.* [if you've had the same unpleasant experience]	0
20 *Bless you!* [only after someone has sneezed]	0

F A business acquaintance has just heard that he is to be made redundant.

21 *I'm extremely sorry to hear that.* Well, I can't help feeling I'm escaping from a sinking ship.	6	7
22 *I am/was deeply sorry to hear/learn etc*	6	7
23 *I am/was deeply sorry to hear/learn etc about . . . .*	5	6
24 *I am/was most upset/deeply sorry etc to hear/learn etc*	6	7
25 *I am/was most upset/deeply sorry etc to hear/learn etc about . . . .*	5	6
26 *I am/was most upset/deeply sorry etc to hear/learn etc of . . . .*		6
27 *What a terrible situation for you.*		0
28 *I do sympathize, (I assure you).*		0

in other situations (when writing)

29 *You have my deepest sympathy (at this difficult/tragic time).*			0
30 *You have my (sincere) condolences (at this time of bereavement).*	[usually when someone has died]		0
31 *Please accept my (heartfelt) condolences.*			0
32 *I was (most) distressed to learn about/of/ that . . . .*	5	6	7

Practice

He was knocked down by a car. He was in hospital for six weeks.

a ▶ What does she say?

b You are talking to your friend, Paul.
▶ What do you say?

Paul: *You know I was meant to be going on holiday tomorrow to Mexico? Well, yesterday I found my passport had run out and it was too late to renew it.*
You: . . . .
Paul: *And then the travel agent told me that the hotel I was booked into hadn't been built yet.*
You: . . . .
Paul: *And now I've heard the air traffic controllers at Heathrow are on strike.*
You: . . . . *Look, I'm planning to go to Skegness tomorrow. Why don't you come with me?*

c You have just heard that someone you knew and liked greatly has died.
▶ What do you write to their nearest relation or relations?

d Someone in your firm you only know slightly says: *I had invested all my life's savings in that one company. And I've just heard that they've gone bankrupt.*
You think: *That's terrible.*
▶ What do you say?

Key **a** 1–10 (11–15, 17, 18 equally possible) **b** 11 (12, but not 'ghastly', which is too strong), 13–19 most appropriate, 1, 2, 5–10 also possible **c** 29–32 **d** 21 (1–10 equally possible)

122 Leaving someone politely for a short time

Excuse me.

1 *Excuse me.*

0

On a guided tour of Edinburgh, you are walking down the street talking to your guide. Suddenly you notice something in a shop window.

2	*Excuse me, I must just* see how much those Scottish kilts cost. They're cheap.	3
3	*Excuse me a moment/minute.*	0
4	*Excuse me, I'll be back in a moment/minute.*	0
5	*Excuse me, I shan't be a moment/minute.*	0

I You are talking to your friend, John, at a party. You suddenly experience the need to go to the toilet. You wait for a suitable pause in the conversation.

6	*'Scuse me John. Back in a sec.* Right you are. I'll go and get us both another drink.	0
7	*'Scuse me.* 8 *('Scuse me.) Back in a mo.*	0
9	*Hang on a mo/sec.* 10 *'Scuse me. Won't be a mo/sec.*	0
11	*('Scuse me.) I'll be right back.*	0

in other situations

12	*Don't wait for me.* ⎱ [when you and the other person are on	0
13	*I'll catch you up.* ⎰ your way somewhere together]	0

F You are holding an important meeting in your office. Your secretary comes in.

I'm sorry to interrupt, sir, but the director of Buzz Electronics has just arrived. He would like to speak to you rather urgently.

14	*Thank you.* **Would you excuse me (for a moment), please,** *gentlemen? Mr Carstairs, perhaps you could take over?*	0
15	*I'm afraid I must/have to leave you for a moment/a minute or two/a short while.*	0
16	*Will you excuse me (for a moment), please?*	0
17	*I wonder if you'd excuse me (for a moment/a minute)* etc.	0

Practice

a   You have advertised for someone to share a flat with you while you are in England. An applicant comes to see you. While you are talking the doorbell rings.

▶ What do you say to him?

b   You are about to start delicate negotiations with a British governmental delegation. An aide enters the room and informs you in a whisper that there is a telephone call for you from your Foreign Ministry.

▶ What do you say to the members of the delegation?

   i   *I'm afraid I have to leave you for a moment.*

   ii   *Will you excuse me, please?*

  iii   *I'll be right back.*

  iv   *Excuse me, I shan't be a moment.*

▶ What else could you say?

c ▶ What does she say to the others?

Key a 1–5 most appropriate, 6–11, 14, 16 also possible **b** i, ii, iv (iii too informal), 14, 17 most appropriate, 1, 3, 5 also possible **c** 6–11

123 Ending a conversation

1 *(Well,) I'm afraid I must go now.*   0

Somebody you have met by chance in the lounge of your hotel is talking to you.

The country's in a terrible state. Low growth rate. High unemployment. High taxes. I mean, take the British tax system for example. The basic rate . . .

2 *Goodness! I've just remembered. I've promised to meet a friend in five minutes. **I'm afraid I really must go.** I'm so sorry. 'Bye.*   0

3 *(I hope you don't mind, but) I really have to go/have to be going/must be going now.*   0

4 *(It's been very nice/interesting etc talking to you, but) I'm afraid I oughtn't to/shouldn't/mustn't/can't stay any longer.*   0

5 *I'm (awfully) sorry, but I'm meeting someone in five minutes/I've got to make a phone call etc.* [or other reason or excuse for leaving]   0

6  *(Someone's just come in/Someone wants to speak to me/I'm in a meeting, I'm afraid/I'm on another line just at the moment etc)—can/could/may I/I wonder if I could ring/call you back (later/in a few minutes etc)?*   0

I One afternoon, you go out to get some money from the bank. You stop to have a chat with your friend, Dora, in the street. She says:

So you had a nice time in Brighton?

7 *Yes, it was super . . . . Oh, Dora, just look at the time! Twenty past three. The banks shut at half past. **(Sorry,) I've got to dash (now).** 'Bye.*   0

8 ***(Sorry,) I've got to/I must rush/fly/go (now).***   0

9 ***(Sorry,) I must be off (now).***   0

10 ***(Right,) I'm off (now).*** [only if it's known/expected that you have to go]   0

in other situations

11 ***(Sorry,) I must/I'd better be moving/getting along/be getting on my way.*** [when you are not in a great hurry, or do not want to *seem* to be in a great hurry]   0

12 ***Well, better be going, I suppose.*** [when you are reluctant, or want to *seem* to be reluctant, to go]   0

F You are discussing your firm's performance on the stock market with your external accountant. He says:

. . . and we think your preferential shares are undervalued at present.

13 *Thank you. That's very useful to know. Now, I have to attend a shareholders' meeting in a few minutes, so **I'm afraid we shall have to leave it there.***   0

14 *I hope you'll/Please forgive/excuse me, but . . . .*   33

15 *I must apologize, but I'm afraid . . . .*   33

Practice

Miss Clarke, you really must visit the London Dungeon. It's absolutely...

a ▶ What does she say?

b

you're talking to	about	*and you want to end the conversation because. . .*
i a very important new client	the finer points of a big contract	a still more important client has arrived to see you
ii a stranger	the weather	the subject isn't terribly interesting
iii a friend	life in general	it's four in the morning
iv a close colleague	your weekend plans	your bus is about to leave

▶ What do you say in each case?

Key **a** 1–5 most appropriate, 7, 8, 11 also possible   **b** i 13–16 most appropriate, 1–5 also possible **b** ii 1–5 most appropriate, 7–9, 11, 12 also possible   **b** iii (8 with 'go') 9–12 most appropriate, 1–3 also possible   **b** iv 7–9 most appropriate, 1–3 also possible

124 Saying goodbye

1 *Goodbye!*	0

You are seeing a colleague off at the airport.

2 *Goodbye then.* Goodbye.	0

in other situations

3 *I'll look forward to seeing you soon/next week,* etc. *Goodbye for now.*	0
4 *Goodnight, (then).*	0
5 *Yours, Judith Davies/Michael Clarke* [your name]. [to end a letter]	0

I You're saying goodbye to a friend.

6 *Bye!* Bye.	0
7 *Bye-bye!* 8 *Bye for now!*	0
9 *See you (soon/later/tomorrow/around)!*	0
10 *I'll be seeing you!* 11 *Cheerio!* 12 *Cheers!*	0
13 [just wave your hand]	0

14 *Mind how you go. Bye!* 15 *Look after yourself. Bye!*	0
16 *Take care. Bye!*	0
17 *Look forward to seeing you soon/next week* etc. *Bye!*	0
18 *Love, Judy/Mike* etc. [your name]	0
19 *Lots of love, Judy/Mike* etc. [your name]	0
20 *With all my love, Judy/Mike* etc. [your name] } [to end a letter]	0
21 *Love and kisses, Judy/Mike* etc. [your name]	
[very informal and affectionate]	0

F   After completing successful negotiations with a customer, you see him off at the airport. As you say goodbye, you shake hands with him.

22 *(I look forward to seeing you again soon.) Goodbye.*	0

23 *Yours sincerely, Judith Wood/Michael Stone/* }	
L. A. Grundy etc. [your name] } [to end a letter]	0
24 *Yours faithfully, Judith Wood/Michael Stone/*	
L. A. Grundy etc. [your name]	0

Practice

a ▶ What does the student say?

b ▶ When would you say this?
Good night.
  i   At 6 p m. (you won't see the other person till next day)
  ii   At 10 p m. (you won't see the other person till next day)
  iii   At 10 p m. (you'll see the other person again at 11 p m)

c ▶ Who is saying something inappropriate? What should he say?

210

d ▶ What's the last thing you say to a close colleague at the end of the working day?

e You are writing letters:

to	about
i your boyfriend/girlfriend	your feelings for him/her
ii an English employer you have not met	when you will arrive in England
iii the same teacher who taught you last year at a language school	coming back to the school this year

▶ What do you write at the end of each letter?

Key a 1 **b** ii (i also possible when darkness has fallen) **c** Mr Curtis, 1, 22 **d** 6–13 most appropriate, 1, 2, 4 also possible **e** i 18–21 **e** ii 23, 24 **e** iii 5 most appropriate, 23, 24 also possible

125 Asking someone to say something again

| 1 *Pardon?* | 0 |

You are driving from Dover to Birmingham via London. You get lost and ask a policeman the way.

. . . and follow the A40 till you reach the North Circular.	
2 *I'm sorry, I didn't catch the last word. The North . . . ?*	6
3 *I'm sorry?*	0
4 *I'm sorry, I didn't hear . . . .*	6
5 *I'm sorry, what was that word/his name etc again?*	0
6 *I'm sorry, what did you say?/what was that?*	0
7 *What was/were the etc first/last etc word/words/sentence/ sentences etc again please?*	0
8 *Would you/Could you repeat what you said/that name/the last word etc, please?*	0
9 *Sorry? The North Circle?/The North Cycle? etc* [i e you try to repeat what you *think* you heard]	0

in other situations

10 *I'm sorry, when/who/where/what* etc *did you say?*   0
11 *I'm sorry, I didn't hear what you said.* [when you want the
speaker to repeat most or all of what he said]   0
12 *I'm sorry, I couldn't hear what you said.* [when a noise drowns
out the other person's words]   0

I You're phoning your boyfriend. Suddenly the line begins to crackle.

. . . will you bzzcrrr marry bzzzcrrzz me?
13 *What was that (again)?*   0
I said, will you marry me?
14 *Sorry?*   **15** *Come again?*   0
16 *(Sorry,) what did you say?*   0
17 *What?*   0
18 *You what?*   0
19 *Eh?*   [very informal indeed—only to close friends]   0
20 *Mmm?*   0
21 *(Sorry,) I didn't get any of that.*   0
[when you haven't heard/understood anything]

---

in other situations

22 *When?/Where?/Who?* etc.   0

F You are attending a seminar entitled 'Export Shipping'. The seminar leader gives a
brief introduction. You are making notes.

Where there are few direct sailings to the country in question,
goods are often trans-shipped, as it is called.
23 *I'm sorry, would you mind repeating* that word again, *(please)?*   6
24 *I'm sorry, could you/could I ask you to repeat that word/
sentence/explanation* etc, *(please)?*   16

---

in other situations

25 *I beg your pardon?*   0

Practice

Qzzchlbwrm

a ▶ What does she say?

212

b You are speaking to a government economist at an international forum on the world economic situation.

Economist: *Of course, the unfortunate thing about Keynes's multiplier theory is that it also works in reverse.*

You think: *If he could say all that a second time, I'm sure I'd understand.*

► What do you say?

c Janet: *Hey, there was this terrific thing on telly last night, what was it called, oh yeah, ' The Reasons . . . '* (telephone rings)

Mick: *Could I ask you to repeat that?*

Sally: *What was the programme called again?*

Janet: *' The Reasons Why People Get Married'.*

► Who is saying something inappropriate? What should they say?

Key **a** 1–6, 8–12 most appropriate, 13, 14, 16, 25 also possible   **b** 23–25 most appropriate, 1, 3, 8, 9, also possible   **c** Mick (too formal), 13–17, 20–22

126 Checking that you have understood

1	*Does that mean . . . ?*		7

It's 10 a m. You are just going to park your car in a public car park. A colleague who is with you sees a sign about payment.

	It says: ' 2 hour maximum stay '.		
2	*So we have to be gone by twelve?*	33	35
	That's right.		
3	*If I understand/I've understood etc right, ...*	33	35
4	*So is the basic/general idea that . . . ?*		7
5	*So am I right in saying . . . ?*		7
6	*I'm sorry if I'm being/I seem a little slow/stupid, but I'm not sure I understand. Does this mean/Does that mean/Do you mean . . . ?*		7
7	*(I'm sorry,) I'm not sure I understand. Does this mean/Does that mean/Do you mean . . . ?*		7

A friend is talking about the arrangements for a celebration.

> Right, before we go to the Chow Ching for a Chinese meal, we'll drop in at the Coach and Horses—after meeting up at Gary's place first, of course.

You mean first we meet at Gary's, then we go for a drink, then we eat. Right? 7

> You've got it, you've got it!

9 *(Sorry,) I'm not quite with you/with that/with what you've just said* etc. *You mean/Does it mean . . . ?* 4–7

10 *In other words . . . . (Right)?* 33–36

---

in other situations

11 *That means . . . . (Right?)* [can be used when you're interpreting the speaker's words, or drawing a conclusion that he hasn't drawn] 33 35

12 *If I've got it right, then . . . .* 33 35

13 *If I've got the picture, then . . . .* 33 35

14 *(So) what it/that* etc *boils down to is . . . . (Yeah/Right?)* 7

15 *(So) what you mean/he* etc *means is . . . . (Right?)* 7

16 *(So) what you're/he's* etc *really saying is . . . . (Right?)* [could sound as if you think the other person has expressed himself badly or unclearly] 7

You are trying to persuade your marketing director, Mr Grosvenor, to let you go and sound out a potential new market.

> Mm. I think we need to do a proper desk survey first. Besides, the expense of sending you out there would be substantial. And aren't you anyway fully occupied with tying up the POB contract?

17 *Would I be right in supposing you don't want me to go?* 7 14

18 *Would I be correct in saying . . . ?* 6 7 14

19 *If I understand you/that* etc *correctly, ...* 33 35

20 *This/That seems to be tantamount to saying . . . .* 7

21 *The implication seems to be . . . .* 7

22 *So, if I take your meaning rightly, ...* 33 35

23 *If I've followed you/If I follow you rightly, then . . . .* 33 35

24 *Just to be quite clear/certain about this/that/what's just been said/decided* etc: *. . . .* 33–35

25 *Can I get one thing/this clear? . . . .* [could sound as though you think the other person has expressed himself badly or unclearly] 33–35

Practice

a ▶ What does he say?

b You and a friend are transit passengers at an airport. You hear this announcement: *All transit passengers are requested to proceed to Lounge 3.*
You want to be sure you have understood.
▶ What do you say to your friend?

c ▶ When would you say this?
The implication seems to be . . .
   i when you think a colleague is suggesting you have acted dishonestly
   ii when you are checking with a friend the meaning of 'Chelsea for the Cup', written on a wall
   iii when your director is dropping hints about your needing to spend less of your budget

Key **a** 1, 2, 6, 7 most appropriate, 8, 10, 11 (24 first two alternatives) also possible **b** 10, 11, 15 most appropriate, 1, 2, 7 also possible **c** i, (iii if you don't have a close relationship with him), (ii too formal)

127 Checking that someone has understood you

1	*Do you see what I mean?*	0

Someone has asked you to explain pedestrian crossings in the U.K. to them.

2	*If you're a pedestrian waiting to step on to the zebra crossing, it's up to the driver to decide whether to stop or not. But if you've already started to cross, the driver is compelled by law to stop.* **I hope that's clear?**	0
	Yes, absolutely.	
3	*That's clear, ⸍is it/⸍isn't it?* ⎫ [could sound brusque or sharp]	0
4	*Do you understand . . . ?* ⎭	6
5	*. . . , if you see what I mean.*	33
6	*Does that seem to make sense?*	0

in other situations

7	*Do you know what I mean?*	0

I You are proudly explaining the rules of cricket, as you understand them, to a companion on a package tour.

8 *There are twenty-two players. Eleven of them come on to the field. The*
   other eleven then come on one by one, and the eleven already on try
   and send them off one by one. Then they change round and do it all
   again. **Are you with me?**   0
   Ye—es. Er, and just how long does all this go on?
   It's been known to last five days.
9 **D'you see?**   10 **Right?**   11 **OK?**   12 **Yeah?**   0
13 **Get it?**   14 **Got it?**   0

---

in other situations

15 **Know what I mean?** ⎫ [when you're checking if the   0
16 **Know what I'm getting at?** ⎬ other person has understood an   0
17 **Know what I'm driving at?** ⎭ opinion or argument, not facts] 0
18 **(Has the) penny dropped?** ⎫ [when a close   0
19 **Are you there yet?** ⎬ friend is slow   0
20 **(Have you) got the message yet?** ⎭ to understand]   0

F As managing director you are explaining to someone in your firm the importance of meeting production deadlines.

21 *If we do not meet these deadlines, our customers will lose faith in us.*
   The next stages in the process are: loss of orders; redundancies;
   bankruptcy. **I trust I make myself clear?**   0
   All too clear.
22 **Am I making/Do I make myself clear?**   0
23 **Is that reasonably clear?**   0
24 **I don't know if I am making/I'm not sure if I make myself clear.**   0
25 **. . . , if you follow/understand me.**   33
26 **. . . , if you follow/understand** ⎫ [when you're checking if the   33
   my meaning. ⎬ other person has understood an
27 **. . . , if you take my point.** ⎭ opinion or argument, not facts]   33
28 **Have I made myself clear?** ⎫ [after you've explained   0
29 **If there's anything you haven't** ⎬ something at length]
   understood, please say so. ⎭   0

Practice

DIARY
Meeting with Lacey 10AM
Meeting with Jones 11
Meeting with Smith 12
Lunch with White 1PM
Meeting with Green 2PM
Meeting with Brown 3PM
Meeting with Black 4.30

... and the meeting with Lacey will now be at 4.30.

a ▶ What does he say next?

b   A good friend has just explained to you how to make a phone call from a public call box. She then says: *Do I make myself clear?*

▶ What do you think?

i   *Yes. Now I know.*   ii   *Yes, but why is she so unfriendly?*

iii   *Yes, but she sounds a bit like a grand lady talking to a servant.*

▶ What should she have said?

c   You are talking to an official about the terms of a big development loan your government is about to make to his government. You say: *We would however stipulate that it be repaid within a three-year period.*

You think: *Do you understand?*

▶ What do you say?

Key   **a** 2, 3, 6 most appropriate, 8–11, 22–25 also possible   **b** ii or iii, 8–14   **c** 21, 22, 24, 27, 28 most appropriate, 2, 3 also possible

128 Saying something again

1   *I said, ...*   33–38

You're telling a taxi driver where you want to go.

137B Winterton Gardens, please.
Where?

2   ***Winterton Gardens, a hundred and thirty-seven B./One three seven B Winterton Gardens./Winterton Gardens, one three seven B.*** [ie you repeat the information in a simpler, clearer way, if possible]   27–32

---

in other situations

---

3   *I was just saying/* ⎫   [when you are repeating something you do   7
        remarking etc . . . . ⎬   not think was very important *or* when
4   *I was just asking/* ⎪   you are repeating it to someone who
        wondering etc . . . . ⎭   did not hear what you said the first time]   8–11

I   You go for a walk in the countryside with some friends, Paul and Sue. You reach the top of a hill before them.

Hey, the view from here's terrific.
Can't hear you. Hang on a sec. . . . Now. What did you say?

5   ***What I said was,*** *it's a terrific view.*   33–38

6 ***Are you deaf? I said . . . .*** [very informal; only to very close friends]   33–38

F You are discussing politics with your neighbour at a big formal dinner. The noise of other conversations round you is very loud.

> *I feel the Government should attempt to control imports of mineral water. It's flooding the market.*
> I beg your pardon?

7 ***I was (just/merely) expressing the view*** *that we should dam up the flood of mineral water imports. Or we'll be swept away.*   7

8 ***I was (just/merely) making the suggestion/putting forward the opinion/proposing*** *etc . . . .*   7

9 ***I was (just/merely) pointing out/stating*** *etc* ***the fact*** *. . . .*   7
10 ***I was (just/merely) enquiring/wondering*** *etc . . . .*   8–11

Practice

a ▶ What does he say?

b You are at a marketing conference, which is being held in a large hall. During a discussion, you stand up to make a suggestion, but some people at the far end of the hall cannot hear you. You repeat your suggestion.
     ▶ What do you say?
     i   *I said, would it not be a good idea to set up a working party to look at the problem?*
     ii   *Are you deaf? I said let's get a load of people with nothing better to do to look at this.*
     iii   *I was proposing that a working party be set up to examine this in detail.*

c You have just received a telegram with some good news. You rush to tell a friend.
Mike! I've won fifty thousand pounds on the pools!
Mike (staring absent-mindedly out of the window) : *Uh?*
     ▶ What do you say?

Key   **a** 1, 2, (3 'saying', but not 'remarking'), 4 most appropriate, 5 also possible   **b** i or iii (ii too informal)   **c** 5, 6 most appropriate, 1, 2 also possible

1 *What I mean is, ...*   33–37

You are explaining what happens when you import a live animal into the U.K.

> *Well, it goes into quarantine for six months.*
> Goes into what?

2 *In other words, it is kept in isolation until the authorities are*
certain that it is carrying no diseases.   33–37
3 *Basically, ...*   33–37
4 *What I meant was/mean is, ...*   33–35 37
5 *To put it/Let me put it another way: . . . .*   33–37
6 *That's to say, ...*   33–37

---

in other situations

7 *. . . , or rather, ...* [when you want to correct what you've just said]   33–37
8 *. . . , or better, ...* [when you want to suggest a *stylistically* better
way of saying what you've just said]   33–37
9 *. . . , i. e.* [= ' that is to say : '] *. . . .* ⎫   33–37
10 *. . . , viz* [= ' in more detail : '], *. . . .* ⎭ [usually written] 33–37

I You are talking to your girlfriend.

> *You know er, you are, er, poetry in motion, er, the most wonderful*
> *person in the world, er, a dream come true.*
> Uh?

11 *Er, what I'm trying to say is, I love you.*   33 35 37
I bet you say that to all the girls.
12 *What I'm getting at/driving at is, ...*   33 35 37
13 *All I'm trying to say is, ...*⎫ [when you don't think you're   33 35 37
14 *All I mean is. . . . .*   ⎭ saying anything very important] 33 35 37

F You are discussing terms with a customer who is buying a large quantity of
your product.

15 *We can't, however, offer you more than our normal 10% reduction*
on the trade price. Perhaps I should make that clearer by
saying that if we give you any more than that, we'd actually be
running at a loss.   7
16 *If I can rephrase that/rephrase what I've just said: . . . .*   34 35 37

17 *Perhaps it would be more accurate to say/if I said . . . .*
[when you want both to repeat and to correct what you've just said]   7

Practice

a ▶ The tourist means he doesn't like it. So what does he say next?

b ▶ Who is saying something inappropriate?
Jackie: *I don't think there's life anywhere else in the universe. There can't be.*
Don: *I'm not so sure.*
Phil: *You mean there are millions of little green men out there watching us all the time?*
Don: *If I can rephrase what I've just said, it is theoretically possible that there is
     life on other planets.*
▶ What should he say?

c Representatives of two governments are holding a meeting to discuss trade
between them.
First representative: *. . . so it may be necessary to increase our import tariffs on all
your products.*
Second representative: *I'm sorry, I don't quite understand.*
First representative thinks: *I'd better say it very simply then. Our people will have
to pay more for the goods they buy from you.*
▶ What does he say?

Key **a** 1, 4–6; 11–14 also possible   **b** Don (when he answers Phil), 11–14 most appropriate, 1, 4,
5 also possible   **c** 15, 16

130 Giving an example

1 *. . . , for example.*   33–35   37   38

You are talking about London theatres.

2 *There are some good pub theatres. The Bush,* **for instance.**   33–35 37 38

---

in other situations

3 *Take . . . ,* **for instance/for example.**   16
4 *. . . ,* **such as . . . .**   38
5 *. . . ,* **e. g.** [= ' for example '] **, ...** [usually written]   33 34 37 38

I You are discussing politics with a friend.

Let's face it, all the nationalized concerns are a complete disaster.
Not one of them makes a profit.
6 *Nonsense.* **Look at** *the Post Office, or British Gas. They're making a fortune.*   4–6
7 *(I mean,)* **what about . . . ?**   **8** **Take . . . .**   4–6

---

in other situations

9 *Like . . . ,* **(for example/instance).**   16

F You are giving a talk to a group of businessmen.

10 *Trade between our two countries has increased very rapidly in recent*
years. **Let me take an example:** *last year we exported a hundred*
million dollars' worth of raw materials to your country. This year so
far we have already exported twice that.   33 38
11 **To illustrate this point/what I mean** *etc,* **let us look at/**
examine/consider *etc . . . .*   4   6
12 **To give you an example of this/what I mean, take** *. . . .*   4–6
13 **An example of this/that would be** *. . . .*   4–6
14 **Let me/Allow me to cite an example/an instance/some/a**
few *etc* **examples/instances:** *. . . .*   33 38
15 **To exemplify what I mean/this point** *etc,* **let us look**
at/examine *etc . . . .*   4   6

Practice

a ▶ What does the traveller say?

b A lecturer is giving a rather formal lecture on William Shakespeare to a group of
literature students. These are his notes: *No author expressed better than W.S.*
problem 'is life worth living?' e g Hamlet's speech 'To be or not to be'.
▶ What does he actually say?

c ▶ Who is saying something inappropriate?
▶ What else would be appropriate?

Key **a** 1–4 most appropriate, 7, 9 also possible   **b** 10–15 most appropriate, 1, 2 also possible
c Steve, 6, 8, 9 most appropriate, 1–3 also possible

131 Showing you are listening

1 *⌃Really!/⌃Really?*	0

An acquaintance is telling you about his new ciné camera.

And it's got an f.1.9 9–30 mm lens. And a 220° shutter as well.

2 *I ⌃see.* **3** *Oh ⌃yes.* **4** *⌃Mmm/A ⌃ha.*	0
5 *How ⌃interesting!* **6** *I know what you mean.*	0
7 *Has it?/Does it?* etc. [or other echo question]	32
8 *Do you use low-light film?/Has it got sound?* etc.	
[or other question to show you are interested]	0
9 [Nod and smile/Raise eyebrows]	

in other situations

10 *⌃Oh!/⌃Oh?* ⎫ [surprised]	0
11 *⌃Well, ⌄well!* ⎭	0

A friend is passing on some gossip.

She wanted to, but of course he said no.
12 Tell me ⌃⌄more. 0
She got her own way in the end.

---

in other situations

13 ⌄No! 0
14 ⌃Fancy ⌄that! ⎫|[surprised] 0
15 ⌃Well I⌄ never! ⎭ 0
16 Well ⌃I'll be ⌄ blowed. ⎫ [to close friends, when you are surprised] 0
17 ⌃Well I'm ⌄blessed/⌄blowed. ⎭ 0

A member of the foreign diplomatic corps in your capital city is talking to you.
You don't know him.

It's my view, of course, that the international community should
boycott the conference.
18 In⌃⌄deed? 0
Yes, and if that has no effect, impose a trade embargo on the
participating countries.

Practice

It was built in 1652!

a ▶ What does she say?

b ▶ How would you show you were listening to these people talking about these things?

	who	*what*
i	a colleague you know well	how he nearly caught the biggest fish of all time
ii	director of another firm	how he intends to put your firm out of business

Key a 1–5 (7 with 'Was it?') (8, with other question, e g 'Do you know who built it?') 9–11 (13–18 equally possible) **b** i 13–17 most appropriate, 1–7 (8, with other question), 9–11 also possible **b** ii 18 most appropriate, 1–5, 7, (8, with other question), (9, raising eyebrows, not nodding or smiling) 10, 11 also possible

132 Taking up a point

1 *It's interesting you should say so, because*   12

A tourist on your tour is talking to you. You don't know her well.

We were staying at the Grand Hotel, and one evening the most
awful draught began blowing under our bedroom door.

2 *Mm. **That reminds me of** the time we were camping at Skegness
and our tent blew away.*   4–6
3 *It's strange/surprising* etc *you should say so/that, because*   12
4 *Talking of ..., ...*   5 *On the subject of ..., ...*   22

---

in other situations

6 *About ..., ...*   22
7 *(But) to go back to what you/he/she* etc
were/was saying about ..., ...   [when you want to go   22
8 *Somebody/You mentioned ... just now.*   back to an *earlier* point]
Well, ...   18
9 *Sorry to interrupt, but did I hear/overhear you/someone* etc
say ... ? [when you want to join in a conversation by taking up a point]   6   7

I   Your friend, Ginny, is talking to you.

Do you know, last night I dreamt the world was coming to an end.

10 *Funny/strange/odd you should say so/that. I dreamt exactly
the same thing. But we're all still here!*   0
11 *What a coincidence! ....*   0

---

in other situations

12 *Sorry to butt in, but did I hear you/someone* etc *say ... ?*
[when you want to join in a conversation by taking up a point]   7
13 *Hang on, can we stick with that point about ... ?*
[when you want|to stop someone from changing the subject]   4–6

F   You are at an important business meeting. A few minutes ago export credits were
mentioned. The discussion has now moved away from that subject.

---

14 *If I may just go back (for a moment) to what Mr Mills was
saying about export credits: I think we need to secure these credits
before we make any further plans.*   22

15 *To take up your/that/Mr Smith's/Mrs White's* etc *(last)*
   point/remark etc *(about . . . , . . .).*   22

16 *If I might refer back to . . . , ...*   22

Practice

a ▶ What does Mr Hill say?

b You are talking with a representative of a firm who have a contract to supply
   you with goods. They have failed to meet the terms of the contract.
   Representative: *I can only apologize for any shortcomings on our part over the last
   year. But looking forward to next year for a moment, prospects seem good. For
   example, ...*
   ▶ What do you say?
   i *Yes, but if I may just go back to the question of your record so far, ...*
   ii *Yes, but to take up your last remark about shortcomings, er, unfortunately we
      cannot see any alternative but to invoke the penalty clause in the contract.*
   iii *Hang on, can we stick with that point about your* past *performance. Never
      mind about next year.*

c You are chatting to your friend, Andrew.
   Andrew: *I'm going to buy a new colour T.V.*
   You think: *So am I!*
   Andrew: *Oh good! We can go and choose them together!*
   ▶ What do you actually say?

Key **a** 1, 3; 10, 11 also possible **b** i or ii (iii probably too informal) **c** 10, 11

133 Giving yourself time to think

1 *(Er,) let me see, ...*   33–38

A colleague at work asks you a question.

Do you know where Adam Uppe works?	
2 *In the, (er,) what's it called,* the Electronic Data Processing Section.	38
3 *. . . , what is/are he/she/they called, . . . ?*	38
4 *. . . , oh, ...* 5 *. . . , er, ...* 6 *. . . , um, ...*	33–38
7 *. . . , (oh,/er,/um,) what was he/she/it called/what were they*	
called, . . . ?	38
8 *. . . , (oh,/er,/um,) what's his/her/its name/what are their*	
names, . . . ?	38
9 *. . . , (oh,/er,/um,) what d'you call him/her/it/them, . . . ?*	38
10 *. . . , (oh,/er,/um,) let me think/let me see, ...*	33–38
11 *. . . , just a moment, ...*	33–38

in other situations

12 *. . . , just let me get this right, ...*	⎫ [when you want several	33–38
13 *. . . , just let me think about*	⎬ seconds at least to	
this/that a moment:	⎭ think about a problem]	33–38
14 *Well, er, ...*		33–38
15 *. . . , you see, ...*	⎫ [when you want to engage the other person's	33–38
16 *. . . , you know, ...*	⎭ sympathy, as well as give yourself time to think]	33–38
17 *. . . , how shall I put it . . . ?*	⎫	33–38
18 *. . . , now what's/what was the word/*	⎬ [when you are trying to think	
phrase/expression etc *(again) . . . ?*	of the right word or phrase]	
19 *. . . sort of . . . .*	⎭	33–38.

I A friend asks you a question.

What's the new London Underground line called?	
20 *The Jumble Line, no, oh, it's on the tip of my tongue—the*	
Jubilee Line, that's it. The Jubilee Line.	38
21 *. . . , hang on a sec, ...*	33–38
22 *. . . , I've nearly got it, er, ...*	38

F You are being interviewed by a selection board.

How would you describe yourself?	
23 *May I think about that for a moment?*	0
Certainly.	

in other situations

24 *(Now) how can I/should I put this/it . . . ?*	33–38
25 *(Now) how can I best say this/it . . . ?*	33–38

Practice

a ▶ What does he say?

b Someone more senior than you at work asks: *What aspect of our after-sales service do you think needs improvement?*
You (wanting time to think): *Er, hang on a sec.*
▶ What might your senior colleague think?
  i *Of course. He needs time to answer that one.*
  ii *He obviously thinks I'm his best friend. I'm not.*
  iii *He doesn't think I deserve respect, eh? I'll teach him a lesson.*
▶ What else could you say?

c Your friend, Bill, asks you: *What's the date today?*
You (getting out your diary to have a look): *. . . . , it's the 10th.*
▶ What do you say?

Key a 1, 4–6, 10 (with 'see') most appropriate, 21 also possible **b** ii (possibly iii), 23 most appropriate, 1, 4–6, 10, 14 also possible **c** 21, 22 most appropriate, 1, 4–6, 10, 11 also possible

134 Changing the subject

1 *(Just) to change the subject (for a moment), ...*   33–35 37

An assistant in a tourist agency is talking to you.

And here's a brochure about the history of the town.
2 *Thank you very much. (Oh,) by the way, can I get a bus to the centre from here?*   33–35 37
3 *(Oh,) incidentally, ...*   **4** *(Oh,) while I remember, ...*   33–35 37
5 *(Oh,) before I forget, ...*   33–35 37

6 *(Oh,) I know what I meant to say/tell you . . . .*   33 35 37

7 *(Oh,) I know what I meant to ask you . . . .*   34 35

---

in other situations

8 *. . . , but that's (just/purely)*
    by the way.   [*after* you've   33–35 37
                           changed the subject
9 *. . . , but that's (perhaps)*   for a moment]
    beside the point.   33–35 37

I   A friend's talking to you about an exam he's just taken.

But with luck, I'll have passed.

10 *I'll keep my fingers crossed. (Ooh,) I knew there was something
I meant to tell you. We've got an invitation from Jason and
Debbie, for next Sunday, to celebrate the end of the exams.*   33 35 37

---

in other situations

11 *(Hey/Ooh/Oh,) I nearly forgot!* . . . [just before you end the
conversation or leave etc]   33–35 37

F   You are chairing a business meeting. A discussion about a takeover bid has just
ended.

12 *If we could move on now to* the question of the Twinkis contract.   6

13 *I think we ought to move on to/Could we move on now to . . . .*   6

14 *On an entirely different matter, now, ...*   33–35

15 *The next item on the agenda is . . . .* [when the meeting is
working specifically to a written agenda]   6

Practice

MR WESTGATE   MISS DAVIS

a ▶ What does Mr Westgate actually say?

b Who would you say this to, after a conversation about other things?
Hey, I nearly forgot! . . .
  i   to an air hostess, about getting a drink of cold water
  ii to a friend, about another friend's birthday party
  iii to your director at work, about the chances of an increase in salary

c You have called a meeting to discuss the advertising campaign for a new
product. You say: *. . . so that settles the question of the slogan.*
You then think: *Right, now let's talk about advertising time on T.V.*
  ▶ What do you actually say?

Key **a** 1–5, 7 most appropriate   **b** i or ii (too informal for iii)   **c** 12–13

1 *In other words, ...* 33–37

You're talking with someone about how best to travel from London to Scotland.
You want to do it cheaply.

   The train's too expensive. Perhaps I could go by bus. Or, cheaper
still, hitch-hike. On the other hand, the most convenient way
would be to hire a car. But then that's expensive, too.

2 *Mm. **Basically it comes down to** whether you hitch-hike or go
by bus.*   4–6 8 10

3 *(So) basically, ...*   33–37

4 *(So) the basic question is, ...*   34

5 *(So) what I'm/you're/we're saying is, ...*   33 35–37

---

in other situations

---

6 *The point I'm making/I'm trying to make is, ...*
   [often when others haven't followed your argument]   33–35 37

I Your friend, Chris, invites you to a game of darts in a pub. He tells you how to
throw a dart.

   Put your foot on that line. That's it. Now decide where you want
the dart to land on the board. OK. Now practise the movement
of throwing, like that, yes . . . three or four times . . . and
now . . . throw!

7 *So what it boils down to is, shutting your eyes and letting the
dart go? Because that's what I did!*   4–6 8 10
                                                 33 34 37 38

8 *So what it comes down to is, ...*   4–6 8 10
                                                 33 34 37 38

9 *(To put it) in a nutshell, (then) . . . .*   33 34 37 38

F At a departmental meeting, you are explaining the management's reaction to a
project recently proposed by your department.

---

10 *They were not satisfied with our justification of the project, nor with
the timing, nor indeed with the costings. **In short,** we shall have to
re-examine every aspect of it from scratch.*   33–38

11 *In a word, (then,) . . . .*   33–38

Practice

a ▶ What does Dr Carey actually say?

b ▶ Who is saying something inappropriate?
   ▶ What should he say?

c You are just finishing a long speech to some colleagues about the future of your company. You think: *Basically, things look terrific for the next 20 years.*
   ▶ How do you actually finish your speech?

Key **a** 1, 5 **b** Paul, 7–9 most appropriate, 1 also possible **c** 13, 14 most appropriate, 1, 3, 5 also possible

136 Finding out about pronunciation

1 **How do you pronounce this word?**
  'Business'.
  Thank you.
2 **How do you pronounce this name/expression** etc?
3 **'Ex⌐plain'—isthat the right/correct pronunciation?**
4 **What is the right/correct way to pronounce this
  word/name** etc?
5 **Do you say '⌐describe' or 'des⌐cribe'?**
6 **Where is the stress in this word/name** etc?
7 **Will you tell/correct me if I pronounce something wrongly,
  please?**
8 **What intonation should I use if I want to express
  pleasure/sympathy/annoyance** etc?

137 Finding out about spelling

1 **How do you spell** 'accommodation'?
  A-C-C-O-M-M-O-D-A-T-I-O-N.
  Thank you.
2 **Is this/that the right/correct spelling of** 'accommodation'?
3 **Do you spell** 'offering' **with** one or two r's?
4 **Do the Americans spell this word in the same
  way as the British?**
5 **I'm not sure if I've spelt this word/name/expression** etc
  right/correctly. Can you check it for me, (please)?
6 I've written a/this note/letter/memo etc. **Will you check my
  spelling, please?**

138 Finding out about correctness

1   *Is it correct to say, 'I have had lunch with her yesterday'?*
    No—you should say, 'I had lunch'.
    Oh, I see. Thank you.
2   *I wrote/said, 'I went shopping this morning'. Was/is that right/correct?*
3   *Can I say, 'I went to shop this afternoon'?*
4   *I asked the taxi to 'halt'. Was/Is that the right/correct word?*
5   *Is this sentence correct: 'I go home for Christmas'?*
6   *Which is correct: 'They worked' or 'They did work'?*
7   *When do we/you use 'had had'? Can you give me an example?*
8   *Will you tell/teach me how to use 'although', (please)?*
9   *Will you tell/correct me if I make a mistake, (please)?*

139 Finding out about meaning

1   *What does 'Sale' mean?*
    Oh, it's when they reduce the prices of things in the shops.
2   *I don't understand this word/expression/sentence. Can you help me?*
3   *Mr Smith talked about a 'gallery'. What does this mean?*
4   *Does 'bright' mean 'shiny' or 'clever'?*
5   *What is the opposite of 'polite'?*
6   *Does 'sharp' sometimes mean 'quick-thinking'?*
7   *What is another word for 'rich'?*
8   *What other words are there for 'ill'?*
9   *What is another way of saying 'Go away'?*
10 *Do 'take part' and 'participate' mean the same thing?*

11 *What's the difference between* a '*club*' *and* a '*society*'?
12 *Is there a difference in meaning between* '*purse*' *and* '*handbag*'?
13 *What is a/the word for* '*running very fast*'?
14 *What is a/the word for/to describe something that* is very hard?
15 *What is a/the word to describe/for someone who* is very intelligent?
16 *What is a/the word to describe someone who* doesn't eat meat?
17 *What is a/the word to describe the thing/things* you use to
tie up your shoes?
18 *What do you call someone who* thinks only of himself?
19 *What do you call* a plant *that* grows in a garden but you didn't plant it?
20 *What happens if I use* '*stout*' *instead of* '*fat*' *about someone*?
21 *Does it make sense if I say* '*He's over the moon about his
promotion*'?
22 *Do/Can you use* '*mean*' *to mean* '*unkind*'?
23 *When would you use the word* '*pal*'?
24 *When would you use the expression* '*highly confidential*'?
25 *Does* '*fair*' *have more than one meaning*?

40 Finding out about appropriateness

1 *Is it appropriate to say* '*How d'you do?*' *if* I meet someone for the
first time?
Usually, yes, that's quite all right.
2 *What should I say/ask if/when* I want to attract someone's
attention?
3 *What should I say if* I want to thank someone *neutrally/
informally/formally*?
4 *If I want* a stranger to help me, *what should I say/ask*?
5 In German, when friends drink together, *we say* '*Prosit!*' *How do
you say that in English*?
6 *Should/Can I use* '*Hello*' *if/when* I meet someone for the first time?
7 *If I'm leaving a friend's house, should I say* '*Goodbye*' *or
*'*Bye-bye*'?
8 *Is* '*kid*' *an informal sort of word*?
9 *Is* '*child*' *a neutral sort of word*?
10 *Is* '*infant*' *a formal sort of word*?
11 *Would it be too informal/formal to say/write* '*My dear sir*' *if
I was talking/writing to* a company director?
12 *When is it appropriate to say,* '*I'm much obliged*'?
13 *If I say,* '*Thank you ↘very much*' *is it more polite than* '*Thank
you very ↘much*'?

233

Extra practice material

Section A

These exercises help you to practise things you will often find yourself having to do when you refer to the main part of this book: such things as choosing the right function, or deciding whether a situation is formal or informal. The exercises practise the various functions in the book together.

You will find the key to these exercises on p 237.

A1   Would you be likely to use *informal* language in these situations?
Answer *yes* or *no*.

you are talking to:	*about:*	*when/where:*
i a government official	losing your passport	the passport office
ii a close friend	a TV comedy	at home
iii a senior executive	the problems in your department	at a meeting
iv a friend	losing your passport	in a pub
v a colleague	a football match	in your car

A2   Would you be likely to use *formal* language in these situations?
Answer *yes* or *no*.

you are talking to:	*about:*	*when/where:*
i a diplomat	his country breaking international law	at a congress
ii a girlfriend	her cooking	at her flat
iii someone you know well	a party	at a restaurant
iv the managing director	your salary	in his office
v someone you don't know well	your company's future	at a conference

A3   Would you be more likely to use *formal* or *informal* language in these situations? Answer *formal* or *informal*.

you are talking to:	*about:*	*when/where:*
i a young teenager	a Christmas present	on Christmas Day
ii your employer	your resignation	in his office
iii a neighbour	the weather	in his garden
iv your best friend	your salary	in a pub
v a speaker lecturing at a big international conference	a matter you disagree with him about	during the debate after his lecture

A4   Which functions do these expressions belong to? Choose from the list of functions below. Answer 1, 2 etc.

Expressions:
  i *Well, basically we seem to be saying the same thing.*
  ii *This is how you do it: ....*
  iii *I'm sorry to hear that.*
  iv *I'd prefer not to say anything about it.*
  v *I don't know how.*
  vi *If I were you, I wouldn't.*
  vii *Does that mean ... ?*
  viii *Let me see ....*

Functions:
1 Showing sympathy
2 Advising someone not to do something
3 Saying you are not able to do something
4 Telling someone how to do something
5 Giving yourself time to think
6 Saying you have reached agreement
7 Checking that you have understood
8 Avoiding giving an opinion

A5   Which functions would you be likely to use in these situations? Choose from the list of functions below. Answer 1, 2 etc.

Situation:
  i You think your secretary might forget to post a letter.
  ii You're thinking of all the horrible things that would happen if you missed your flight back home.
  iii You've just been with your friend, Sally, to a rock concert.
  iv You think your train goes at ten, but your friend, John, says it goes at eleven. You want to check that he's certain.
  v Your friend, Sarah, tells you she's failed an exam.
  vi You are trying to decide which is a nicer place, London or New York.
  vii Your car won't start. A friend thinks it's because the lights are on. You don't think that matters.
  viii You tell your friend, Sue, that Shakespeare was Australian. She says he was English. You suddenly remember that he was English after all.

Functions:
1 Asking if someone is sure about something
2 Asking how someone feels after something happens
3 Saying something is not important
4 Reminding
5 Saying you are wrong and someone else is right
6 Talking about what might happen
7 Comparing
8 Showing sympathy

A6   Which functions do these (*informal*) expressions belong to? Choose from the list of functions below. Answer 1, 2 etc.

Expressions:
  i *I'd plump for ... every time.*

ii *I don't reckon I'll ....*
iii *How's life?*
iv *Smashing!*
v *'Scuse me! I'll be right back.*
vi *Well, I never!*
vii *Come off it!*
viii *No, ...*

Functions:
1 Expressing surprise
2 Saying what you prefer
3 Correcting someone
4 Saying you are pleased
5 Disagreeing
6 Saying you do not intend to do something
7 Leaving someone politely for a short time
8 Asking how someone is

A7 Which functions do these (*formal*) expressions belong to? Choose from the list of functions below. Answer 1, 2 etc.

Expressions:
i *The next item on the agenda is ....*
ii *That's perfectly all right.*
iii *That's really most kind.*
iv *I'm afraid we couldn't allow that.*
v *I feel obliged to ....*
vi *If I could explain: ....*
vii *I can't say I find ... fascinating.*
viii *I take great exception to ....*

Functions:
1 Giving reasons
2 Changing the subject
3 Saying you are displeased or angry
4 Accepting an apology
5 Saying what you think you ought to do
6 Accepting an invitation
7 Saying you are not interested
8 Refusing permission

A8 What are the functions in these dialogues? Choose from any function in the list on p xviii. Answer e g
Saying you are relieved.

i *The policeman didn't see you jump that red light.*
   Thank heavens for that.
ii *Do you enjoy skiing?*
   I adore it.
iii *What are your views on nuclear energy?*
   I can't say I have any views on the subject.
iv *I think life is wonderful, I really do.*
   Agreed, but it has greater and lesser degrees of wonderfulness, I feel.
v *Are you for or against sacking Jones?*
   I'm totally against it.

vi *That's an expensive car. How are you going to pay for it?*
  ***I'm hoping** my father will lend me some money.*
vii *Can you remember what Chris's address is?*
  *Sorry, **my mind's gone a complete blank.***
viii ***Here's to** your future, Candy.*
  Thanks.

Section B

**Please read the following notes before working on the practice material
for the first time.**

■ These exercises are to give you some more practice in using the expressions in
the main part of the book. But they are different from the exercises in the main
part because
1 you can practise expressions from different functions in one exercise,
  and
2 you can, if you want to, work together with a partner.

■ In each Part of Section B, you will find, first of all, a list of function
numbers—for example, Functions 1 2 3 4. These are references to the types of
the functions practised in this Part. (If you want to remind yourself of the names
of the functions, look up the List of Functions on p xvii.) Under the function
numbers, you will see either a table, or some pictures, or an uncompleted text, or
an incorrect text.

■ Then you will find *Pairwork* and/or *Self-study*.

 Pairwork means 'Practise the dialogue below with a partner'.

 Self-study means 'Practise saying the sentences to yourself if you have no partner'
or 'Practise writing these sentences'.

 Pairwork or self-study means 'Practise the exercise with a partner, or by yourself
if you have no partner'.

Then, under each of those, you will find examples of what you have to say or write. By looking at the table, pictures or text above them, you will be able to make a lot more sentences of the same kind.

■ Begin by practising the (*neutral*) expression in the example. When you are doing that successfully, try to use *other* neutral expressions from the same function. (The function number is given after each example, if you want to remind yourself just what those neutral expressions are.) But please be careful! You may have to use a different grammatical structure from the one given in the example. Use the Structural Code List on p 262 to help you. Also, you will not always be able to use *all* the expressions given. Some of them will not fit. If you are in any doubt, ask your teacher or someone who speaks English well.

■ After that, if you wish, and if your English is sufficiently advanced, you can go on to practise informal or formal language by following the instructions after the sign ●. Besides substituting informal or formal functional expressions, you may sometimes need to make the *other* language in the exercise more informal or more formal.

■ There are no keys to these Exercises so, if you are not sure about an answer, ask your teacher or someone who speaks English well.

■ **Note to teachers** Many of the exercises can be extended to obtain further practice if desired. With exercise B1, for example, students can think up more countries and languages and talk about them in the same way; with exercise B2 they can write out similar diary entries of their own and talk about them; with exercise B3 they can discuss the map much more extensively; and so on.

B1 Functions 1 2 3 4

Look at this table of countries and the languages spoken in some of them.

Country	Language(s)
Albania	?
Canada	English, French
China	Chinese
Benin	?
Jordan	Arabic
Mexico	Spanish, English
Mongolia	?
Sweden	Swedish

Talk or write about all the countries and languages in the table, like this:

 Exercise a

Could you tell me *what language they speak in Albania?* (Function 1)
I don't know. (Function 4)

Could you tell me *what languages they speak in Canada?* (Function 1)
Yes, English and French.

Exercise b

D'you know *what language they speak in Albania?* (Function 2)
No, I don't. (Function 4)

238

D'you know *what languages they speak in Canada?* (Function 2)
Yes, English and French.

Exercise c

(Only talk about Canada, China, Jordan and Mexico)
I gather *they speak English and French in Canada.* (Function 3)
I know. (Function 3)

 Exercise a

(Only talk or write about Canada, China, Jordan and Mexico)
I gather *they speak English and French in Canada.* (Function 3)

Exercise b

(Only talk or write about Albania, Benin and Mongolia)
I don't know *what language they speak in Albania.* (Function 4)

● Now imagine you are talking about the same things with:

  i a good friend who's travelled around a lot
 ii a former Foreign Service diplomat, whom you've just met

B2 Functions 6 7 8

Look at this diary of a visitor to the U.K.

Talk or write about all the dates in the diary, like this:

 Exercise

Do you remember *what you did on the 1st?* (Function 6)

*Yes. **I remember** visiting KN Products.* (Function 7)

Do you remember *what you did on the 2nd?* (Function 6)
No, **I've forgotten.** (Function 8)

 Exercise

I remember *visiting KN Products on the 1st.* (Function 7)
I've forgotten *what I did on the 2nd.* (Function 8)

● Now practise talking about the same things with:

i a colleague you get on with very well
ii your managing director, whom you don't know very well

B3 Functions 9 10 11 12

Look at this map of part of the London Underground. Imagine you are at Green
Park station.

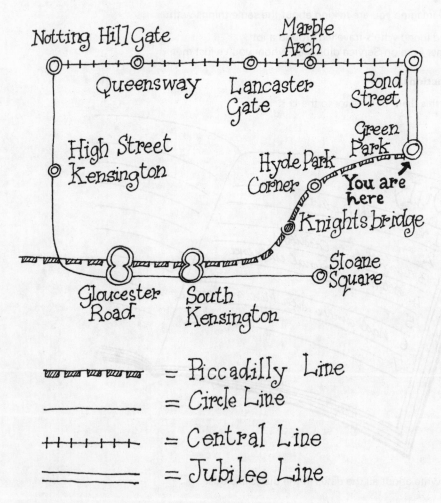

Look at these statements (some are correct, some are not).

Lancaster Gate *is on the Central Line.* **Knightsbridge** *is four stops from here.*

Sloane Square *and* South Kensington *are next to each other.* Queensway *is between* Lancaster Gate *and* Marble Arch. Bond Street *is on the Central Line and the Piccadilly Line.* South Kensington *isn't on the same line as* High Street Kensington. Gloucester Road *isn't on the same line as* Notting Hill Gate. Sloane Square *is six stops from here.*

Talk or write about the statements about the Underground, like this:

 Exercise

Lancaster Gate *is on the Central Line.* **Is that right?** (Function 9)
Yes, that's right (Function 10)

Knightsbridge *is four stops from here.* **Is that right?** (Function 9)
No, that's not right. (Function 11) **In fact,** *it's two stops from here.* (Function 12)

 Exercise

Lancaster Gate *is on the Central Line.* **Yes, that's right.** (Function 10)
Knightsbridge *is four stops from here.* **That's not right.** (Function 11)
In fact, *it's two stops from here.* (Function 12)

● Now practise talking about the same things with:

i an elderly person with a very formal manner
ii a teenager who lives in the same house as you

B4 Functions 14 15 16 17

Look at this list of things three companies plan to do in the future. Someone who knows the companies well has written remarks against each item.

	SMITHS LTD.	KINGS LTD.	BAKERS LTD.
Sell more goods	yes	yes	yes?
Expand overseas	yes?	?	no
Borrow more money	?	yes?	yes
Employ more people	no	no	?

Talk or write about each company in turn, like this:

 Exercise

D'you think Smiths'll sell more goods?
I'm sure *they will.* (Function 14)
D'you think they'll expand overseas?
Probably. (Function 15)

D'you think they'll borrow more money?
I'm not sure. (Function 16)

D'you think they'll employ more people?
No, **I don't think** *they will.* (Function 17)

Exercise

I'm sure Smiths'll sell more goods. (Function 14)
I think they'll expand overseas. (Function 15)
I'm not sure if they'll borrow more money. (Function 16)
I don't think they'll employ more people. (Function 17)

● Now practise talking about the same things with:

i a senior consultant in a business meeting
ii your secretary (with whom you're friendly)

B5 Functions 19 20 21 22 23 25 26

Look at this conversation between three secretaries in an office.

Susie:	*Oh Debbie, Mandy, I must tell you! I've been offered another job! (Phone rings) I'll tell you about it in a moment. (She picks up the phone) Hello ....*
Mandy:	[*Curious*—where?]
Debbie:	*Mm. Somewhere exciting, perhaps.*
Susie:	*Yes ..., yes .... Bye. (She puts down the phone) The job's in New York, with the United Nations.*
Mandy:	*Well, well.* [*How feels?*]
Susie:	[*Look forward*]
Debbie:	*New York! Well.* [*Hope*—like it]
Susie:	[*Hope*—be fun] [*Hope*—come and see me] *Just one problem, though.* [*Worry*—leave friends behind]
Mandy:	*Oh, you'll soon make friends there. The job is the important thing. I wish I had your luck.* [*Worry*—about work]
Susie:	*Why?*
Mandy:	[*Want*—job of secretary to Managing Director] [*Pessimistic*—get it]
Susie:	*Oh Mandy, work isn't everything!*
Mandy:	*No, I suppose you're right. After all, I have got Rodney. (Phone rings) I'll tell you about him in a second. (She picks up the phone.) Hello ....*
Debbie:	[*Curious*—Rodney?]
Susie:	*Isn't that her dog?*
Mandy:	*Yes ..., right .... Bye. (She puts down the phone). Now, let me tell you about Rodney. He's my new boyfriend.*
Susie:	*Oh.* [*Look forward*—meet him] *You're lucky.* [*Want*—boyfriend] [*Pessimistic*—find one] *I'm much too dynamic for most men.*
Mandy:	[*Hope*—find boyfriend in New York]
Susie:	[*Hope*—will]
Mandy:	*After all, New Yorkers are supposed to be the most dynamic people in the world.*

Now practise the conversation, replacing the parts in square brackets with
proper speech, like this:

 Exercise

or | Susie: | *Oh, Debbie, Mandy, I must tell you! I've been offered another job! (Phone rings) I'll tell you about it in a moment. (She picks up the phone) Hello ....* |
|---|---|
| | Mandy: | *Oh? I'd like to know where!* (Function 20) |

242

● Practise the conversation again as if Susie, Debbie and Mandy are very old
friends.

B6 Functions 28 29 30 31 32 33 34

Look at this circular from a tour operator to a customer. The customer has
written his reactions down the left-hand side of the letter.

Rookman Tours Co

Dear Tour Member,

Here are some more details of our 'London Fun' tour.

Travel

RELIEVED! You will travel to London by air (not by bus and ferry as we said
earlier.)

NOT PLEASED! There will be a £50 fuel surcharge on top of the normal price of
the air ticket.

Accommodation

DISAPPOINTED! You will not stay at the famous Blackstone Hotel after all. Instead
you will stay in a very good boarding house (in London's famous East
NOT PLEASED! End.)

RELIEVED! This means you will now pay only £40 for accommodation instead of £360.

SURPRISED! You will not be given breakfast at the boarding house. (This is an
old East End tradition.)

Entertainment

PLEASED! You will be able to see London's wonderful sights. You will not have
SURPRISED! a guide. (We believe the best way to see a place is to discover it
for oneself.)

PLEASED! You will be also have the chance to visit some of London's famous
theatres and nightspots.

BORED! You will be able to attend our special evening lectures on 'London
Roads in the seventeenth century'.

EXCITED! You may also be able to attend a garden party given by H.M. the Queen.
(We are trying to arrange this at the moment.)

DISAPPOINTED! There will be no daytrips to Oxford or Cambridge. (In the past our
customers have found these places rather dull.) However, there will
BORED! be a weekend trip to Lincolnshire (famous for its flatness.)

EXCITED! And finally, the highlight of the tour: you may be invited to tea with
the British Prime Minister! (We have not succeeded in arranging this
yet, but we are still trying.)

With best wishes,

S. L. Rookman

Tour Manager

Talk or write about the customer's reactions to the letter, like this:

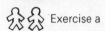 Exercise a

You'll travel to London by air.
*Oh, **that's a relief.*** (Function 31)

Exercise b

As a, but inventing a reason for your reaction, for example:

You'll travel to London by air.
*Oh, **that's a relief.** The journey'll be over quickly.* (Function 31)

 Exercise a

*We'll travel to London by air. **That's a relief!*** (Function 31)

Exercise b

***It's a relief** we're travelling to London by air!* (Function 31)

● Now practise saying the same things:

i to your best friend, who's going with you
ii to the Tour Manager who wrote the letter

B7 Functions 36 37 38

Look at this questionnaire. Put a tick ☑ in the box against the things you like, and a cross ☒ in the box against the things you don't like. For example:

| *People who never stop talking* | ☒ | *Cats* | ☑ |

People who never stop talking	☐	*Cats*	☐
People who always do what you ask	☐	*Big cars*	☐
Your Head of State	☐	*Tobacco*	☐
The opposite sex	☐	*Winter*	☐
Your boss	☐	*Learning English*	☐

Now talk or write about *your* answers to the questionnaire, for example:

 Exercise a

***Do you like** people who never stop talking?* (Function 36)
No, I don't.

***Do you like** cats?* (Function 36)
Yes, I do.

Exercise b

What do you think of people who never stop talking?
***I don't like** them.* (Function 38)

What do you think of cats?
***I like** them.* (Function 37)

Exercise c

As b, but with an invented reason for the like or dislike, using 'because ....', for example:

What do you think of people who never stop talking?
***I don't like** them because they never learn anything from other people.* (Function 38)

What do you think of cats?
***I like** them because they can look after themselves.* (Function 37)

Exercise

I don't like people who never stop talking, (Function 38)
I like cats. (Function 37)

● Practise talking about the same things:

i to an old school friend
ii to an elderly lady you don't know at all at a formal dinner party

B8 Functions 39 40

Look at this list of pairs. Put a tick in the box against the things you prefer in
each pair, for example: tea   ☑
                coffee ☐

tea	☐	large breakfasts	☐
coffee	☐	small breakfasts	☐
people who laugh a lot	☐	rock music	☐
serious people	☐	classical music	☐
colourful clothes	☐	books	☐
dark clothes	☐	television	☐
travelling by boat	☐	using your hands	☐
flying	☐	using your head	☐

Now talk or write about your preferences, for example:

 Exercise

Do you prefer tea or coffee? (Function 39)
I prefer tea (Function 40)

 Exercise

I prefer tea. (Function 40)

● Now imagine you are talking about the same things with:

i a good friend
ii a serious-minded person at a dinner party

B9 Functions 41 42 43

Look at this list of laws (made some time in the future). If you think a law is a
good idea, put a tick in the box against it. If you think it is a bad idea, put a
cross in the box against it, for example:
☒ Education Act
☑ Retirement Act

☐ Education Act: **Young people will go to school until they are 20.**

☐ Retirement Act: **People aged over 65 can go on a free cruise to the
                     Caribbean.**

☐ Travel Act:	No one can travel more than 50 km a week.
☐ Family Act:	No family can have more than 1 child.
☐ TV Act:	No football will be shown on TV.
☐ Labour Act:	The normal working week will be 3 days.
☐ Prisons Act:	The maximum prison sentence will be 2 years.
☐ Marriage Act:	A man can have up to 3 wives; a woman can have up to 3 husbands.

Now talk about your reactions to these laws, for example:

Exercise a

D'you think the new Education Act *is a good idea?* (Function 41)
No, I don't.

D'you think the new Retirement Act *is a good idea?* (Function 41)
Yes, I do.

Exercise b

What d'you think of the new Education Act?
I don't think it's very good. (Function 43)

What d'you think of the new Retirement Act?
*It's **very good.*** (Function 42)

Exercise c

As b, but add reasons for your approval or disapproval.

Exercise

I don't think the new Education Act **is very good.** (Function 43)
*The new Retirement Act **is very good.*** (Function 42)

● Now talk about the same things to:

i a friend you've shared your views with for years
ii an interviewer for an opinion poll

B10 Functions 46 47 48 49 50

Look at the opinion poll below. Fill in the blanks where necessary with an item
of your own choice. For example:

The Great Gatsby

(any book)

Then decide your opinion about all the questions shown.
If you have *no opinion*, put ● against the question. If you have an opinion you
don't want to give (because it may offend somebody, or because it's a very
personal matter), put ○ against the question. Try to put at least two ○'s and
two ●'s. Note down your opinion against the other questions. For example:
alcohol—*a little is all right*
your government—○
supersonic flight—●

246

OPINION POLL

What do you think about:

alcohol

your government

supersonic flight

yourself

marriage

your life at the moment

the question of life after death

_____

(any book)

_____

(any film)

_____

(any famous national figure)

_____

(any recent national event)

_____

(anyone you know well)

Now talk or write about your opinions, for example:

 Exercise a

What do you think about *alcohol?* (Function 46)
I think *a little alcohol is all right.* (Function 47)

What do you think about *your government?* (Function 46)
I'd rather not say anything about *it, actually.* (Function 49)

What do you think about *supersonic flight?* (Function 46)
I really don't have any opinion about *it.* (Function 48)

Exercise b

What do you think about *alcohol?* (Function 46)
I think *a little of it is all right.* (Function 47)
But don't you think *even a little can be harmful?* (Function 50)
No, actually, I don't.

 Exercise

I think *a little alcohol is all right.* (Function 47)
I'd rather not say anything about *my government.* (Function 49)
I really don't have an opinion about *supersonic flight.* (Function 48)

● Then practise talking about your opinions to:

  i a colleague and friend at work
 ii an opinion poll researcher who is being much too persistent

B11 Functions 51 52 53

Look at this timetable of evening classes. Put a circle round at least 6 courses that interest you, and cross out the rest. For example:

 ~~English~~
~~Romantic~~
~~Literature~~

ADULT EDUCATION INSTITUTE

TIMETABLE

Day	Room K13	Room K21	Room L9	Room N10
Mon	Yoga	English Romantic Literature	Poetry	—
Tue	Table Tennis	—	Pottery	Plumbing
Wed	—	—	Car Maintenance	—
Thu	Cookery	Criminology	Karate	—
Fri	Report Writing	—	Becoming Self-employed	Women Today

Now talk or write about which evening classes interest you, for example:

 Exercise a

Are you interested in yoga? (Function 51)
Yes, I am.

Are you interested in English Romantic Literature?
No, I'm not.

Exercise b

What about the Monday course in Room K13?
Yes, I'm interested in yoga. I'll go to that one. (Function 52)
What about the Monday course in Room K21?
No, I'm not interested in English Romantic Literature. (Function 53) *I won't bother with that one.*

 Exercise

I'm interested in yoga. (Function 52)
I'm not interested in English Romantic Literature. (Function 53)

● Now practise talking about the same things with:

i someone you've been going to evening classes with for years and years
ii an official at the Institute where the courses are held

248

Look at these newspaper headlines. Put *yes* beside the ones you agree with, *no* beside the ones you disagree with, and *yes and no* beside the ones you partly agree with. For example:

TV has a bad influence on people—warn sociologists   *yes*

The only school worth anything is the School of Life: Ex-teacher   *no*

Film star: Marriage is more good than bad.   *yes and no*

TV has a bad influence on people — warn sociologists.

The only school worth anything is the School of Life: Ex-teacher.

Film star: Marriage is more good than bad.

Journeys more pleasant by bus than by air or rail: Travel firm.

Housewives should be paid for their labour: Women's leader.

Reform group: Stop all sex on stage and film

We should all become vegetarians, for the animals' sakes' — Animal lovers' group.

World Association of Cooks: **English food is POISON.**

Now talk or write about your opinions on these questions, for example:

Exercise a

I think TV has a bad influence on people. **Don't you agree?** (Function 55)
Yes, I do.

Exercise b

I think TV has a bad influence on people.
Yes, I agree. (Function 56)

I think the only school worth anything is the school of life.
Oh, I don't agree. (Function 57)

I think marriage is more good than bad.
I don't entirely agree with you. (Function 58)

Exercise c

As b, but adding reasons for agreeing or disagreeing or partly agreeing.

I think TV has a bad influence on people.
Yes, I agree.
Mm. Why?
Well, because *people lose the habit of thinking for themselves.* (Function 54)

Exercise a

I agree *that TV has a bad influence on people.* (Function 56)
I don't agree *that the only school worth anything is the school of life.* (Function 57)
I don't entirely agree *that marriage is more good than bad.* (Function 58)

Exercise b

As a but adding an invented justification, for example:

I agree *that TV has a bad influence on people. I think so **because** they lose the habit of thinking for themselves.* (Function 54)

● Say the same things again, but:

i as if you were chatting to a friend over coffee
ii as if you were taking part in a public debate

B13 Functions 61 62 63

Look at this dialogue. It is between a salesman and a temporary secretary. They don't know each other very well. There are five *appropriate* and seven *inappropriate* offers, acceptances and refusals of help (in **bold** type). Decide which ones are appropriate and which ones are inappropriate.

Salesman: *I've just heard I have to fly out to Bahrain in two hours. Could you help me get ready, please?*

Secretary: *Of course.* **I suppose you want me to get your papers together, do you?**

Salesman: **Yes, and hurry up about it.** *Oh dear, I seem to have mislaid my passport.*

Secretary: **Let me look for it.**

Salesman: **No, the plane'll be half-way to Bahrain before you find it, knowing you.** *Here it is.*

Secretary: *Now, what else is there.* **Shall I pack your briefcase for you?**

Salesman: **No, for heaven's sake, I can do it myself.**

Secretary: **If you like I could get your traveller's cheques from the bank.**

Salesman: **Yes, well, that's part of your job, isn't it?**

Secretary: **And shall I collect your tickets from the travel agent?**

Salesman: **Go on then, get on with it, or are you just going to stand around jabbering about it?**

Secretary: **And then I suppose I'll have to phone for a taxi for you, will I?**

Salesman: **That's very kind of you.**

Secretary: *Not at all. Do you know what I like about this office? The pleasant, cooperative atmosphere.*

Now practise the conversation, correcting all the inappropriate speech in it, like this:

Exercise

or

Salesman: *I've just heard, I have to fly out to Bahrain in two hours. Could you help me get ready, please?*

Secretary: *Of course.* **I'll get your papers together.** (Function 61)

● Now practise the conversation again. Imagine that the man and the woman know each other very well indeed.

B14 Functions 64 65 66 67

Look at this dialogue between a director (Mark) and one of his managers
(Roy). Use expressions showing what each person intends, does not intend,
thinks he ought to do, thinks he ought not to do.

Mark: *Well, Roy, what are your plans for the day?*
Roy: *First of all,* [I/intend] *fire John Sharpe. He's not working hard enough.*
Mark: *Right. I think* [we/ought to] *fire Sam Smart, too.*
Roy: *No,* [I/not intend] *fire him yet. Next week, perhaps.*
Mark: *How* [you/intend] *tell Sharpe?*
Roy: [I/not intend] *tell him myself, that's for sure. My secretary can tell him.*
Mark: *I think* [we/ought not to] *do it like that. As managers* [we/ought to] *face
the consequences of our decisions. Even, especially, the unpleasant ones.*
Roy: *Ah well, perhaps* [I/ought not to] *fire Sharpe after all. No, I think I'll give
him another chance.*
Mark: *Right. What else did you plan to do, apart from firing Sharpe?*
Roy: *Nothing.*
Mark: *Good. Let's go down to the club for a game of golf, then.*

 Exercise

or Now practise the conversation, replacing the parts in brackets with proper
speech, like this:

Mark: *Well, Roy, what are your plans for the day?*
Roy: *First of all,* **I'm going to** *fire John Sharpe. He's not working hard enough.*
(Function 66)

● Repeat the dialogue:

i as if Roy is a new, fairly young manager and Mark is a rather pompous senior
director
ii as if Roy and Mark have been close colleagues for years

B15 Functions 68 69 70

Look at this table. It shows (a) the names of candidates for a job where English
is needed; and (b) the language operations the candidates can perform in
English.

	translate business letters	fill out order forms	understand telexes	write business letters
Mr Gosney	✓			✓
Miss Swindells		✓	✓	
Mr Whitfield	✓	✓		✓

Talk about what the candidates can and can't do, like this:

 Exercise a

Mr Gosney, **can you** *translate business letters?* (Function 68)
Yes, **I can.** (Function 69)
Can you *fill out order forms?* (Function 68)
No, **I can't.** (Function 70)

Exercise b

What can you do, *Mr Gosney?* (Function 68)
I can *translate business letters. And* **I can** *write business letters.* (Function 69)
But you **can't** *fill out order forms. And you* **can't** *understand telexes.*
(Function 70)
I'm afraid not.

 Exercise

Mr Gosney : **I can** *translate business letters, and write business letters.*
(Function 69)
But **I can't** *fill out order forms.* (Function 70)

● Practise talking about the same things again, but this time:

i as if it were an important, high-powered interview
ii as if it were a friendly chat

B16 Functions 71 72 73

Look at this dialogue between a group of tourists, and their guide.

Tourist 1 :   *So this is Walton Castle. Is it open to the public?* ✳ ✳ ✳ *visit it?*
Guide :   ✳ ✳ ✳ *The entrance is this way. Let's go in. Now. Let me tell you*
        about the castle. It was built in 1436 . . . er, no, in 1463, by Edward the
        Third, the Fourth I mean, and . . . .
Tourist 1 :   *There's nothing like a reliable source of information, is there? Mr Jones,*
        ✳ ✳ ✳ *borrow your guide book?*
Tourist 2 :   ✳ ✳ ✳
Tourist 1 :   *Thank you.*
Guide :   *Now, this is the king's bedroom.*
Tourist 1 :   ✳ ✳ ✳ *take a photograph?*
Guide :   ✳ ✳ ✳
Tourist 1 :   *Oh dear.*
Guide :   *But don't worry. You can buy postcards in the souvenir shop outside.*
Tourist 1 :   *(to Tourist 2) : Oh look, here's St Martin's Chapel!*
        (to Guide) : Excuse me, ✳ ✳ ✳ *visit the chapel?*
Guide :   ✳ ✳ ✳ *I'm sorry. There's a service in progress.*
Tourist 1 :   *Ah, Walton Castle. What a memorable experience!*

Now practise the conversation, putting in expressions of *asking for, giving* or
refusing permission, like this:

 Exercise

or 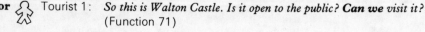 Tourist 1 :   *So this is Walton Castle. Is it open to the public?* **Can we** *visit it?*
        (Function 71)

● Now practise the dialogue as if the guide and the tourists were all on:

i warm, friendly, intimate terms
ii cool, unfriendly, distant terms

Look at these pairs of signs:

Talk or write about each pair of signs in turn. Point at each sign as you talk about it.

 Exercise

Must I keep out? (Function 74)
Yes, I think you have to. (Function 75)
Must I keep out? (Function 74)
No, you needn't. (Function 78) *It's the visitors' entrance.*

 Exercise

I think you have to keep out. (Function 75)
I don't think you should go in. (Function 76)
So keep out, please. (Function 77)
You needn't keep out. (Function 78) *It's the visitor's entrance.*

● Talk about the signs again, this time:

i with a friend you're showing round, who doesn't know what the signs mean
ii with a high-ranking overseas visitor on a tour of England

B18 Functions 80 81 82 84

Look at the items compared below. A businessman, on a week's visit to England, is trying to decide which item in each pair is better.

(hire/car)	Zap 88	Bumble 1
Good looks	yes	no
Excellent acceleration	yes	no
Good petrol consumption	no	yes

(stay at/hotel)	Grand	Royal
Private gardens	no	yes
Colour TV in all rooms	yes	no
Telex facilities	no	yes

(go to/night club)	Belinda's	Amanda's
Sensational floor show	no	yes
Roulette	yes	no
Good rock music	no	yes

(eat at/restaurant)	The Hot Potato	The Red Herring
Continental cookery	yes	no
Polite waiters	no	yes
Lively pianist	yes	no

Talk or write about each pair of items. (The item in each pair with the most *yes's* is better.)

 Exercise a

Do you think I should hire a Zap 88 or a Bumble 1? (Function 80)
A Zap 88.

Exercise b

Which car should I hire?
I think you should hire a Zap 88. (Function 81) *It has good looks and excellent acceleration. But* **I don't think you should** hire a Bumble 1. (Function 82)

Exercise c

Which car should I hire?

254

Why don't you hire a Zap 88? (Function 84) *It hasn't got good petrol consumption, but that probably doesn't matter.*

 Exercise a

I think you should hire a Zap 88. (Function 81) *It has good looks and excellent acceleration.*
I don't think you should hire a Bumble 1. (Function 82) *It has good petrol consumption, but that's all.*

Exercise b

Why don't you hire a Zap 88? (Function 84) *Zaps are better than Bumbles. They always have been.*

● Now talk about the same things again to:

i your host in London, whom you hardly know
ii a teenage member of your host's family, whom you know very well

B19 Functions 85 90 91 92 93

Look at this dialogue, between a manager and his assistant.

Grimshaw: *Michael, as you know I'll be in New York for a week, from the 12th. I'd like you to look after a number of things while I'm away.*
[*Request*—show Mr Jones, DP Components, round factory on 13th]
Lewis: [*Willing*]
Grimshaw: *Good.* [*Request*—draft new contract with Boxer Ltd]
Lewis: [*Willing under condition*—you check it before it's sent off]
Grimshaw: *Of course. Then there's the matter of the sales team's performance. It really hasn't been good enough recently, and they should be told so. Now, if you . . . .*
Lewis: [*Unwilling*] *I really do think it would have more effect if it came from you.*
Grimshaw: *Very well, I'll see to it. Now,* [*Request*—write the quarterly report].
Lewis: [*Willing*] *The usual maximum of 5 pages?*
Grimshaw: *Yes, please. Next, on the 14th, there's a Management Action Committee meeting.* [*Request*—you stand in for me?]
Lewis: [*Refusal*—be away at conference on 14th]
Grimshaw: *Right, I'll ask Jack Stuart to do it. And then* [*Request*—meet chief union representative for initial discussion on their wage claim].
Lewis: [*Unwilling*] *Wage claims are a delicate matter, if I may say so, Charles. I'd really rather you handled them.*
Grimshaw: *I understand. Well, apart from that, there are the interviews for the Marketing post.*
Lewis: [*Willing under condition*—member of Marketing Department help conduct interviews]
Grimshaw: *Yes, that's all arranged. The last thing is the visit of our European representative, on the 20th.* [*Request*—make sure it goes off smoothly]
Lewis: [*Refusal*—away on holiday from 17th] *I'm sorry about that.*
Grimshaw: *That's all right, Michael. I think it'll do us both good to get away for a while. I don't suppose the old place'll fall apart in our absence, do you?*

Now practise the conversation, replacing the parts in brackets with proper speech, like this:

Exercise

or

Grimshaw: *Michael, as you know, I'll be in New York for a week, from the 12th. I'd like you to look after a number of things while I'm away.* **Could you** *show Mr Jones of DP Components round the factory on the 13th?* (Function 85)

● Repeat the dialogue, as if:

i Grimshaw and Lewis are not friends
ii the two men have been good friends for 20 years

B20 Functions 94 95 96 97 98 99 100 101

Look at this dialogue, between three people in the foyer of a conference hall.

Richard King of AA Electronics:	[Starts conversation with a stranger]
Michael Stone of XJ Systems:	[Answers]
Richard King:	[Introduces self]
Michael Stone:	[Answers introduction] [Introduces self]
Richard King:	[Answers introduction] *Goodness, I believe that's Belinda Jones over there, from ST Software Ltd. We worked together for two or three years. I don't think she's seen me.* [Attracts attention] *Belinda Jones, isn't it?*
Belinda Jones:	*Ah, Richard King!* [Greets]
Richard King:	[Greets]
Belinda Jones:	[Asks how he is]
Richard King:	[Says how he is] [Asks how she is] *Er, look,* [Introduces Michael Stone to her]
Belinda Jones:	[Answers introduction]
Michael Stone:	[Answers introduction]
Richard King:	*Well, would you both like to join me for a drink?*
Belinda Jones: Michael Stone: }	*Mmm, thank you.*

Now practise the conversation, replacing the parts in brackets with proper speech, like this:

Exercise

or

| Richard King: | ***Excuse me, ...*** (Function 94) |
| Michael Stone: | *No, I don't think we have.* |

● Practise the dialogue again, but as if:

i the three people were at a party on the last night of the conference, and all very relaxed and happy
ii it was the beginning of the conference, and the atmosphere was still fairly formal

B21 Functions 102 103 104 105 106

Look at this diary. You speak to these people on the days shown.

Talk or write to each person in the diary, as if it was your diary, like this:

 Exercise

All the best *in your new job,* **Mr Robinson**. (Function 102)
Thank you. (Function 103)

 Exercise

All the best *in your new job,* **Mr Robinson**. (Function 102)

● Practise talking about the diary again, but this time speak *informally* to the people with first names only and *formally* to those with surnames.

Look at these invitations. *Yes* on an invitation means you can go. *No* means you can't. Then, opposite the two *yes* invitations, look at the things the host offers the guest in each case. Decide which of these you will have. Put a tick after those you will have, for example: *lemonade✓*; *crisps✓*. Put a cross after those you won't have, for example: *wine* ×; *brandy* ×.

lemonade ☐
wine ☐
crisps ☐
peanuts ☐

salad ☐
coffee ☐
brandy ☐
cigar ☐

Talk or write first about all the invitations, then about the food and drink for the first and second illustrations.

Exercise a

Would you like to *come to our party on Saturday?* (Function 107)
Thank you. **I'd like to very much.** (Function 108)
Would you like to *join us for lunch at the Victoria Arms?* (Function 107)
Thank you, but *I've already made other arrangements.* (Function 109)

Exercise b

Will you have *some lemonade?* (Function 110)
Thank you. (Function 111)

Will you have *some wine?* (Function 110)
No, thank you. (Function 112)

 Exercise a

I'd like to *come to your party on Saturday.* (Function 107)

Exercise b

I'm afraid I can't *join you for lunch at the Victoria Arms.* (Function 108)

● Decide which two invitations are more formal and which two are more informal. Practise invitations and offers again, using the most appropriate language in each case.

B23 Functions 113 114 115 116 117 118 119 120 121 122 123 124

Look at this dialogue between a host and hostess and their guests. It contains 22 examples of *inappropriate* language (in **bold** type). Functions 115, 121, 122, 123 occur *once* each. Functions 113, 114, 116, 117, 119, 120, 124 occur *twice* each. Function 118 occurs *four times*.

Hostess:	*Oh, how nice to see you. Please come in.*
Michael Jennings:	*(Offering flowers)* **Here, get hold of these first.**
Hostess:	**Well, I suppose I'd better say thank you, though quite honestly I'd have preferred chocolates.**
Michael Jennings:	**I'll take them back if you're not careful.**

*   *   *

Jean White:	*We haven't seen each other for quite some time.*
Michael Jennings:	*No, we haven't.* **You look absolutely terrible in that old dress,** *by the way.*
Jean White:	**Thank you for nothing.**
Michael Jennings:	*Well, last time we met, you told me you were hoping to get a part in a local amateur dramatic society production. Were you successful?*
Jean White:	*No, I wasn't actually.*
Michael Jennings:	**I'm not surprised—you can't act to save your life.**
Jean White:	*But I managed to get the part of Cleopatra in another production—with a bigger amateur group this time.*
Michael Jennings:	**Oh, how boring!**
Jean White:	**You're jealous, that's all.**
Hostess:	**Here, get hold of this.** *It's chicken salad.*
Michael Jennings:	**All right, if there's nothing better. Yuk, it's revolting—when will you learn to cook?**
Hostess:	**I hope it chokes you.**

*   *   *

Rodney Burke:	*Jean White! What a pleasant surprise! I thought you might be here. How are you?*
Jean White:	*Very well, thank you. Have you met Michael Jennings?*
Rodney Burke:	*How d'you do! How d'you do! Look, Jean, I must tell you. I've got the most wonderful piece of news. Superfilms International have offered me a top part—starring with Jane Fonda, in a remake of 'Casablanca'!*
Jean White:	**Do you think I care?**

Rodney Burke:	*Better than your feeble amateur dramatic society any day.*
Michael Jennings:	*Oh dear! I've spilt wine down your shirt!* **Not that it matters—it makes the shirt look better, in fact.**
Rodney Burke:	**You clumsy idiot!**
Michael Jennings:	*Oh no! It's happened again! I'm sorry—somebody pushed past.* **Look, frankly, the more wine I spill on you, the smarter you look.**
Rodney Burke:	**I'll murder you.** *You aren't at all to blame. I think I'll try and dry out a little.* **I'm off upstairs.**

*   *   *

Jean White:	*It's twelve o'clock.*
Rodney Burke:	*Goodness, my last train goes at half past.* **Right, I'm going. I don't suppose I'll see you again.**
Jean White:	**I hope not.**

Now practise the conversation, correcting all the inappropriate speech in it, like this:

Exercise

or

| Hostess: | *Oh, how nice to see you. Please come in.* |
| Michael Jennings: | *These are **for you**.* (Function 113) |

● Practise the dialogue again, as if it were:

i   an official reception
ii a relaxed house party

B24 Functions 125 126 127 128 129 130 131 132 133 134 135

Look at this dialogue between two businessmen. They are returning home to the United States from Heathrow Airport after a trip to the UK.

Glen Fisher:	*Now when exactly does our flight go?*
Kurt Wiseman:	*At 2pm British time.*
Glen Fisher:	[Ask him to say that again]
Kurt Wiseman:	[Say it again] *At least, that's the scheduled time. But it may be later. Some of their pilots are on strike.*
Glen Fisher:	[Show you are listening]
Kurt Wiseman:	*And we may not arrive in the States till late morning, our time.*
Glen Fisher.	[Check you have understood—Will not arrive until after 10 o'clock?]
Kurt Wiseman:	*It could be even later.*
Glen Fisher:	*When exactly?*
Kurt Wiseman:	[Give yourself time to think] *Twelve o'clock approximately.*
Glen Fisher:	*That's really very inconvenient. I have an important meeting at 10.30.*
Kurt Wiseman:	*Oh, I shouldn't worry. You know, meetings can be very bad for your health. Sitting watching an in-flight film is much better for you.*
Glen Fisher:	[Change the subject—How did your talks in Manchester go?]
Kurt Wiseman:	*Very well. But I must say, the English style of doing business is unique.*
Glen Fisher:	*How do you mean?*

Kurt Wiseman:	[Say it in another way—No one else in the world has the same approach to work]
Glen Fisher:	*I'm still not sure what you mean.*
Kurt Wiseman:	*Well,* [Give examples—They need several coffee-breaks every day, and lunch time lasts from 12 to 3pm]
Glen Fisher:	[Ask him to say that again]
Kurt Wiseman:	[Say it again] [Sum up what you have said—They spend more time not working than working]
Glen Fisher:	[Take up that point—I had a quite different experience on my Birmingham visit] *They worked hard, and their approach to problems was very inventive.* [Check if he has understood you]
Kurt Wiseman:	*Yes, I'd agree they are inventive. They are extremely inventive, and extremely lazy.*
Glen Fisher:	*Listen—they're calling our flight number.*
Kurt Wiseman:	*The English must have invented a new way of flying an aircraft without using pilots!*
Glen Fisher:	*Come on, let's go.*

Now practise the conversation, replacing the parts in brackets with proper speech, like this:

Exercise

or

Glen Fisher:	*Now when exactly does our flight go?*
Kurt Wiseman:	*At 2pm British time.*
Glen Fisher:	***Pardon?*** (Function 125)

● Practise the dialogue as if:

i they do not know, and are rather wary of, one another
ii they are old colleagues and friends

Structural Code List

What is the Code List for?

The Structural Code List will help you to build correct sentences using the functional expressions in this book. It will help you to make sure that the grammar of your sentences is right. For example, suppose you want to say you like the cinema. You look up the function 'Expressing likes' (p 61) and there you find '*I (really) enjoy ....*'. How do you combine this functional expression with your subject matter—the cinema? Should you add a noun? Or the *-ing* form of the verb? Or something else? You may, of course, already know the answer. But if you are not sure, you should note the numbers next to '*I (really) enjoy ....*' (on the *right* of the page). Look up these numbers in the Code List below where you will find the structures you can use with this expression.

Except for Functions 136–140, all the functional expressions in the book have structural code numbers.

How do I use the code list?

Follow the instructions shown in the diagram opposite.

Are there any special points I should remember?

Yes:

a The functional expression is fixed. Do not try to change it. If you do, you may express something quite different.

    am in
I ~~*do*~~ *love ....*   Don't do this!
But you can put *we* instead of *I*.
We
~~*I*~~ *do love ....* This is all right.

b In some functional sections, the expression (in **bold** type) in the cartoon and the first expression in the neutral, informal and formal sections are shown with example words. When *you* use that expression, you will, of course, use your own words instead of the examples given.

    I like Shakespeare's plays.
Put your own words instead of '*Shakespeare's plays*'.

c The dots in an expression mean 'put in your own words here'. If the dots come at the end, that is where you put your words.

    I'm very keen on ....
Add your own words, using the structure(s) shown in the Code List.

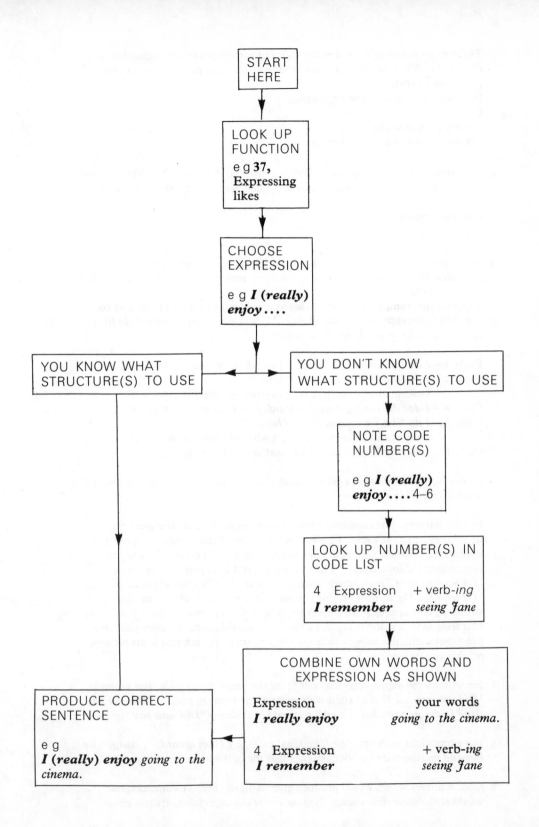

START
HERE

LOOK UP
FUNCTION
e g **37,**
Expressing
likes

CHOOSE
EXPRESSION

e g *I (really)*
enjoy . . . .

YOU KNOW WHAT
STRUCTURE(S) TO USE

YOU DON'T KNOW
WHAT STRUCTURE(S) TO USE

NOTE CODE
NUMBER(S)

e g *I (really)*
enjoy 4–6

LOOK UP NUMBER(S) IN
CODE LIST

4 Expression + verb-*ing*
I remember *seeing Jane*

COMBINE OWN WORDS AND
EXPRESSION AS SHOWN

Expression your words
I really enjoy *going to the cinema.*

4 Expression + verb-*ing*
I remember *seeing Jane*

PRODUCE CORRECT
SENTENCE

e g
I (really) enjoy going to the
cinema.

The dots do not always come at the end, but sometimes at the beginning, or in the middle. Wherever dots are, that is where you must put your own words.

... is wonderful.

Put your own words at the beginning.

Or

I enjoy ... more than ....

Put your own words in both places.

d Sometimes the expression has no dots because you don't need to add your own words. The expression works on its own. Then you will find the code number 0 against it.

Good morning.   0

Add nothing. Leave it as it is.

e If you follow the code numbers in the margin, you will always produce a grammatically correct sentence. But not every sentence will fit the *sense* of what you want to say.

Suppose, for example, you want to say you are fond of English food, and you want to use the expression '*I do like ....*' If you use the codes with '*I do like ....*' (1, 2, 4–6), you will get these results:

Code 1 – *I do like* to eat English food. Just what you want to say.

Code 2 – *I do like* John to eat English food.
          Grammatically correct, but not what you want to say.

Code 4 – *I do like eating English food.* Just what you want to say.

Code 5 – *I do like* John eating English food.
          Grammatically correct, but not what you want to say.

Code 6 – *I do like* English food. Just what you want to say.

So you have to check that a grammatically correct sentence also *fits the sense of what you want to say.*

In a similar way, some sentences you produce from the code numbers will be no good except as answers. This is especially true of the 0 code. Suppose you want to tell someone you would like to travel to Peru. You decide to use the expression '*I'd love to ....*' The codes are 0 and 3. If you use the 3 you get '*I'd love to* go to Peru', which is what you want. But if you use the 0, you get '*I'd love to.*' On its own, in that situation, it is nonsense. But in another situation, for example as an answer to '*Why don't you come for lunch tomorrow?*' '*I'd love to*' is a suitable reply, i e the 0 is a suitable code. So after you have produced a sentence using a code number, be sure to check that it *fits the sense of what you want to say.*

f Sometimes, the expressions may not fit *all* the items in one code. For example, '*Did you say ... ?*' is all right with some of the items in code 6 (*Did you say that? Did you say what he said?*) but not with others (**Did you say him?*).

g For expressions with bracketed, optional parts, e g (*I'm afraid*) ... *might be beyond* me, the code number assumes that the optional part is not used.

h Code numbers which would produce grammatically correct sentences, but would at the same time change the *function* of the expression, are not given.

i Code numbers which would produce grammatically possible but very unusual

264

or very clumsy sentences are not given, e g *I'm not too certain about whether he will come.*

---

1 Expression   + *to* + infinitive

I'd like   *to.*
Can I remind you   *to post my letter.*
I must ask you   *not to.*
I'd advise you   *not to ring before eight o'clock.*

---

2 Expression   + noun/pronoun + *to* + infinitive

I expect   *John to finish the work by tomorrow.*
I recommend   *you to work harder.*
I like   *people to be on time.*
I'd have loved   *him to have come.*

---

3 Expression   + infinitive without *to*

If I were you, I'd   *get my hair cut.*
You must   *leave now.*

---

4 Expression   + verb-*ing*

I remember   *seeing Jane.*
Do you enjoy   *being interviewed on TV?*
Do you remember   *having seen him?*

---

5 Expression   + noun/pronoun/possessive adjective
                   + verb-*ing*

Do you remember   *the Windsor trip being cancelled?*
How do you feel
   about   *him having an accident?*
Remember   *my telling you about my trip to Rome?*

---

6 Expression   + noun/pronoun/noun phrase/noun clause

I'd like   *some fish.*
I don't know   *his name.*
I like   *ice-cream.*
I'm very fond of   *the red car over there.*
I'd like you to meet   *Mr Jones.*
I hate   *it.†*
I get on well with   *him.*
I didn't know   *Mr Jones.*
I don't agree with   *what Mr Smith has said.*
I enjoy   *whatever he writes/that/everything he has written.*

     † not with 'realize'

7	Expression	+ *that* clause

I'm glad to hear	*he's well.*
I think	*that she's resigned.*
Would you rather	*I gave it you now?*
I wish	*their letter would come.*

8	Expression	+ WH-word/WH-phrase/WH-clause (indirect questions)†

I want to know	*who.*
Can you tell me	*which one?*
I don't know	*when I'll see you again.*
Could you explain	*how I should fill in this form?*
I wish I knew	*what.*
Can someone explain	*why the bus is late?*
I'm curious to know	*who you're going out with.*
I've no idea	*where we're going.*

† not 'whether'

9	Expression	+ WH-word† + *to* + infinitive

Please remember	*when to.*
I don't quite know	*what to say.*
Can you remind me	*where to go?*

† not 'why' or 'whether'

10	Expression	+ *whether* + clause

I don't know	*whether the 15.03 has left.*
I wish I knew	*whether he will come or not.*
It's hard to decide	*whether we should keep working, or give up and go home.*

11	Expression	+ *whether* + *to* + infinitive

He can't make up his mind	*whether to or not.*
You must decide	*whether to go by train or by bus.*

12	Expression	+ subordinate clause

It looks as though	*it's going to rain.*
I'd be delighted if	*you could help.*

13 Main clause + subordinate clause with expression included†

If you agree, I'll come tomorrow.
*I did it **in order to** please her.*

†Either of the two clauses can come first.

14 Expression	+ substitute word(s)
I hope	*so.*
	not.†
	†not with negative verb forms
	(e g **I don't hope not*)

15 Noun/pronoun/noun phrase/ verb-*ing*/noun clause	+ expression
The BM reports	***are very interesting.***
A cold drink	***might not be good for me.***
It	***is lovely.***
That	***is a good idea.***
What Paul says	***is nonsense.***
Being cooled by a cold drink	***is a nice sensation.***

16 Expression	+ noun/pronoun/noun phrase/ verb-*ing*/noun clause	+ expression
I don't enjoy	*this*	***very much.***
I find	*your idea*	***rather interesting.***
I like	*her*	***a lot.***
I think	*the Sunset Club*	***is pretty awful.***
Do you think	*getting up at 6 am*	***is a good idea?***
I think	*what you said just then*	***was very sensible.***
Are you a	*chess*	***fan?***
Which	*proposal*	***seems better?***
How does	*Peter*	***come into it?***
D'you reckon	*these shoes*	***are OK?***

17 Expression	+ infinitive without *to*	+ expression
I'll	*do it*	***or bust.***

18 Expression	+ noun/pronoun/ noun phrase/verb-*ing*/ noun clause/ infinitive without *to*	+ expression	+ clause/noun/ pronoun/noun phrase/ verb-*ing*/ noun clause/ infinitive with *to*/ adverb
Do you prefer	*driving slowly*	***or***	*quickly?*
Is	*that pen*	***all right or***	*shall I give you another?*
Don't do	*that*	***or***	*I'll have to report you.*
I generally find	*flying*	***more interesting than***	*going by sea.*
You mentioned	*Ping's restaurant*	***just now. Well,***	*why don't we go there?*

19 Expression	+ infinitive without *to*	+ expression	+ clause/noun/ pronoun/noun phrase/ verb-*ing*/noun clause/adverb
I'll	*do this*	***if***	*you'll do that.*
Would you rather	*go by boat*	***or***	*by plane?*
We can either	*go now*	***or***	*not go at all.*

20	Expression	+ noun/pronoun/ noun phrase/ verb-*ing*/noun clause	+ expression	+ noun/pronoun/ noun phrase/ verb-*ing*/noun clause	+ expression
	Do you find	*poetry*	*or*	*painting*	***more pleasing?***

21	Expression	+ infinitive without *to*	+ expression	+ infinitive without *to*/adverb	+ expression
	We can	*eat here*	*or*	*there.*	***What do you say?***

22	Expression	+ noun/pronoun/noun phrase/verb-*ing*/ noun clause	+ clause
	Compared to ***Talking of***	*Michael,* *catastrophes,*	*he's strong.* *Smith's going to be our new boss.*

23	Expression	+ noun/pronoun/ noun phrase/ verb-*ing*/noun clause	+ expression	+ noun/pronoun/ noun phrase/ verb-*ing*/noun clause	+ clause containing comparison
	If you ***compare***	*Peter*	*and*	*John,*	*Peter is stronger.*

24	Noun/pronoun/noun phrase/ verb-*ing*/noun clause	+ expression	+ noun/noun phrase
	Success *To succeed*	***is one of my great*** ***is less important***	*aims in life.* *than to enjoy life*

25	Noun/pronoun/noun phrase/ verb-*ing*/noun clause	+ expression	+ infinitive without *to*
	That *The committee*	***won't*** ***should***	*happen.* *be informed.*

26	Clause including a comparison	+ expression	+ noun/pronoun/ noun phrase/verb-*ing*/ noun clause
	She works faster *Fishing is more* *enjoyable*	***than*** ***than***	*her friend.* *playing golf.*

The following six codes work without any basic functional expression at all. It is the *sentence type or pattern* that carries the meaning of the function. You can use *any words* suitable to your needs, but make sure you use them in sentence patterns of the type shown.

27	Statement	28	Question (WH- or open)

I'm not going to London tomorrow.
The coin is inserted in the meter.

Where's the station?
Do you want an ice-cream?

29 Statement + question tag/Negative question

You haven't seen John, have you?
He's French, isn't he?
Don't you like lemonade?

30 Imperative

Get up!
Don't shout!

---

31 Noun

Chocolate?   The kettle!

32 Echo question

Is he?   Do they?   Here?   John?

The following six codes are for expressions that *can* be moved around, and others that *can't* be moved around, in the sentence. In the first case, you can put the expression *at the beginning*, or *in the middle* or *at the end*. But check with your teacher, or someone who speaks English well, before moving these expressions around, because they *can change their meaning* when you move them.

33 Statement with expression added or included

*I **certainly** wasn't asked.*
***Let me explain: you see,** he's ambitious.*
***As far as I remember,** he wasn't at the meeting.*

34 Question with expression added or included

*Is he **definitely** arriving at ten?*
***All in all,** do you think he's done a good job?*

35 Statement + question tag/Negative question
with expression added or included

*He's **probably** gone home, hasn't he?*
***As far as I remember,** he was an engineer, wasn't he?*
***Incidentally,** didn't he work for Riley's?*

36 Short answers with expression added or included

*Yes, she **certainly** is.*
***If I recall correctly,** yes he is.*
***If I remember right,** he isn't.*
***As I see it,** they can't.*
***What I'm saying is,** they have to.*

37 Imperative with expression added or included

***Hey,** mind that child!*
***Hey,** don't lean out of the window!*
*Close the window, **would you, please?***
***Go right ahead and** do what you like.*

38 Noun with expression added or included

***Hey,** the toast!*
***Or to put it another way,** a catastrophe.*

Key word index

This index of words and phrases guides you to the expression that is right for what you want to say.
To find the right expression, you need to:
1 think of a word or short phrase that is connected to what you want to say
2 find that word or phrase in the Key Word Index
3 read the section number beside it
4 turn to the section given and find the expression you want

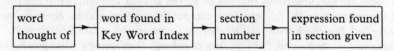

For example, suppose you want to say you *prefer* something. First, think of a work or phrase connected to what you want to say, e g *like better, prefer, rather*. All these words give you section number 40.

Sometimes there is more than one section number. This means the word you have thought of is a key to more than one group of expressions. Check all the sections until you find the group of expressions you want.

Some words or phrases are followed by '?'. They are keys to expressions which show how to ask *questions*. Words or phrases not followed by '?' show how to make *statements*.

For example, *like?, enjoy?, keen on?* are key words for *Asking about likes*; and *like, enjoy, keen on* are key words for *Expressing likes*.

Sometimes the word you think of may be negative. Words like these have either *not* or *no* in front of them, e g *not like, no opinion*, which are key words for *Expressing dislikes* and *Saying you have no opinion*.

	section		*section*
able to	69	angry	30
able to?	68	annoyed	30
about	132	anxious	26
accept	108	apologise	119
acceptable	72	(don't) apologise	120
actually	12	appreciation	114
admit	59	appropriate?	140
advise	81	approve	42
advise?	80	approve?	41
afraid	26	as long as	91
again?	125	ask	1
agree	56	attention	98
agree?	55	aware	3
agree partly	58		
agree(d)	60	back	122
all right	31, 120	because	54
all right?	41	better/worse	44
amazing!	28	birthday!	104